D1506777

# ORGANIZATIONAL COMMUNICATION IMPERATIVES:

## Lessons of the Space Program

Phillip K. Tompkins

*University of Colorado at Boulder*

**ROXBURY PUBLISHING COMPANY**

**Library of Congress Cataloging-in-Publication Data**

Tompkins, Phillip K.
  Organizational communication imperatives: lessons of the space program/Phillip K. Tompkins.
  p. cm
  Includes bibliographical references.
  ISBN 0-935732-40-3
  1. George C. Marshall Space Flight Center
  2. Communication in organizations. I. Title.
TL862.G4T66 1992                                              92-12079
658.4'5--dc20                                                  CIP

ORGANIZATIONAL COMMUNICATION IMPERATIVES:
LESSONS OF THE SPACE PROGRAM

Publisher and Editor: Claude Teweles
Associate Editors: Ingrid Herman Reese and Dawn VanDercreek
Assistant Editor: Michelle N. McEvoy
Cover Design: Allan Miller
Typesetting and Design: Ingrid Herman Reese

Cover Photo: Space Shuttle Flight 51J liftoff. Photo provided courtesy of NASA, The George C. Marshall Space Flight Center, Huntsville, Alabama

Printed on acid-free paper

Printed in the United States of America      10 9 8 7 6

ISBN 0-935732-40-3

**ROXBURY PUBLISHING COMPANY**
P.O. Box 491044
Los Angeles, California 90049

For Elaine:

Without
Whom
Nothing

# ACKNOWLEDGEMENTS

The author wishes to thank Walter Wiesman for the invitation in 1967 to join his team at the George C. Marshall Space Flight Center (we didn't know then that the project he assigned me to would last for 25 years!) and for his unflagging support, sage advice, and warm friendship over the years; may the spirit of his "Confederate Space Patrol" fly high forever. Thanks as well to W. Charles Redding for founding and introducing me to organizational communication, for suggesting my name to Walter Wiesman back in 1967, and for his unfailing support since. Thanks also to Claude Teweles, the publisher at Roxbury Publishing Company, for the lunch at the 1990 Speech Communication Association Convention in Chicago, during which he persuaded me to write this book. He also persuaded Dennis S. Gouran, Susan A. Hellweg, Robert D. McPhee, Michael Papa, and W. Charles Redding, among others unknown to the author, to review the book in manuscript form. I wish to offer thanks for their helpful suggestions.

Additionally, I would like to offer thanks to the managers at the Marshall Space Flight center whom I formally interviewed in 1967, 1968, and 1990. In particular, I wish to convey my deep appreciation to those managers interviewed in 1990 who were willing to have their comments verified by Roxbury Publishing Company.

Thanks also to Lynda Dolan, Judy Mann, and Molly Payne, who helped me in so many ways back in the 1960s at MSFC. Better colleagues I have never experienced.

Deep thanks to two colleagues, George Cheney and Elaine Vanden Bout Tompkins, who read the first draft of the manuscript and made many valuable suggestions. They make me feel like E. B. White's famous pig, Wilbur, only doubly so; hence, the paraphrase: It is not often that someone comes along who is a true friend and a good editor. Elaine and George are both.

iv

# TABLE OF CONTENTS

Preface vi

Chapter 1 The *Challenger* Accident 1

Chapter 2 The Imperative of Studying Organizational Communication 17

Chapter 3 The Marshall Space Center and the Apollo Program 43

Chapter 4 Some Problems of Communication at the Marshall Center 77

Chapter 5 Staff and Board Briefing 97

Chapter 6 Reorganizing the Marshall Center 105

Chapter 7 A Reading of the Rogers Commission Report 121

Chapter 8 Feynman's Two Experiments 141

Chapter 9 Huntsville Revisited 151

Chapter 10 The Lucas Era at MSFC 159

Chapter 11 Organizational Forgetting 171

Chapter 12 Death and Rebirth 179

Chapter 13 J. R. Thompson's Response 189

Chapter 14 The Meaning and Future of the Space Program 197

Appendix A A Summary of the Tompkins-Anderson Study of Kent State University 215

Appendix B Questions and Exercises for Discussion, Essays, and Class Projects 222

References 232

Copyright Acknowledgements 237

# PREFACE

A book about organizations should be of general interest because no one can escape them—organizations, that is. (Plenty of people have escaped *books* about organizations.) Those of us who write books about organizations usually set out to explain all organizations. In order to do this we often write at such a high level of abstraction that readers find our treatises less than gripping.

*Organizational Communication Imperatives: Lessons of the Space Program* concentrates on one organization: The George C. Marshall Space Flight Center (MSFC) in Huntsville, Alabama, the second largest field center of the National Aeronautic and Space Administration (NASA).[1] This book considers MSFC not only at one point in time—an approach that usually leaves the reader wondering what happened before and after the study—but instead over a 25-year period. The methods used for studying MSFC were personal involvement, direct observation, interviews with principals, and close readings of historical documents.

The occasional reader may know about my previous studies of the Marshall Center and, possibly, about my work on the topic of organizational identification. In fact, these two areas of study are closely related. My interest in organizational identification dates back to my first day at the Marshall Space Flight Center in 1967, where I observed thousands of dedicated civil servants who identified with the organization and were committed to the larger space program. My own feelings were a source of insight as the organization and space program "conscripted" my identification and commitment.

I should add that this book does not concentrate on the Marshall Center to the exclusion of social, political, and cultural events surrounding it. Instead, it pauses from time to time to reflect on what was going on outside the organization and inside other organizations. Organizational processes are often affected by seemingly peripheral events in the environment; at the same time, the social environment is often affected by significant organizations.

*Organizational Communication Imperatives* is not dedicated to the rhetorical sport, so popular of late, known as "NASA-bashing." While it questions certain episodes in the organization's history, criticisms are balanced by high praise for other events.

This book attempts to demonstrate the power of an organizational communication perspective in analyzing complex organizations. Organizational communication is a relatively new addition to the larger family of organizational studies, which includes sociology, psychology, economics, management, public administration, and others too numerous to list. The newness of the field almost begs for an unabashed attempt to demonstrate the power of the organizational communication approach.

Tangential to the main focus on MSFC, the book also offers brief profiles of other organizations, including the Nucor Corporation (a rapidly growing and highly successful steel company) and Kent State University (before, during, and after its tragic student crisis in the late 1960s).

If one were to take a survey of Americans who know something about MSFC, Nucor, and Kent State, and then asked them to explain the reasons for their fame or notoriety and the "essence" of each, I predict one would obtain such answers as:

"The Marshall Center? The brainy group of dedicated rocket scientists and engineers that sent us to the moon? That was technology at its best."

"Nucor? The continuous-casting steel company? That's all about efficiency and economics."

"Kent State? That was all about politics, protest, that sort of thing."

My hypothetical survey may not be completely realistic, but I believe that these stereotyped responses are valid in terms of the general public. This book looks beneath them and discovers that how these organizations operate as *communication systems* correlates in a general way with their moments of triumph and tragedy. *Organizational Communication Imperatives* tries to promote *by example* a new and effective way of explaining organizations. The reader, therefore, cannot avoid judging the strength of the case.

This book takes the shape of a first-person narrative. I was a consultant for NASA's Marshall Center in the 1960s, the Apollo era, and returned to interview top management in 1990, four years after the *Challenger* accident. Therefore, I chose to write this book in the narrative mode, employing three points of view: first-person observer, first-person participant, and the objective point of view (the proverbial "fly on the wall"). It is sometimes assumed in the social sciences that objectivity requires the exclusive use of the scientific persona, i.e., the third person. I disagree, concurring with Henry David Thoreau that *it is always the first person speaking*—whether we acknowledge it or not. This book acknowledges it.

"The mode of action of a double plot is the sort of thing critics are liable to neglect," wrote the eminent critic William Empson (1974, p. 27). He might have added, "and other readers miss." Therefore, it is necessary to say a few words about the structure or form of this book.

Empson analyzes examples of works that employ two plots simultaneously, in which the reader finds a "submerged" theme or concept common to both (1974, p. 29). This book alternates between observations about MSFC and the subtheme of contemporaneous race relations both inside and outside the organization. The common concept or submerged theme will be made explicit later in the book.

Organizational success is not self-perpetuating. Even the most successful and confident of organizations are vulnerable to failure. Threats take the form of unperceived changes in the environment, routinized and mechanical complacency, and the *institutional forgetting* of what contributed to the institution's success and confidence in the first place. *Organizational Communication Imperatives* examines collective triumphs and tragedies, achievement and failure, pride and guilt. Changes in leadership, and their effects on the larger organization, are analyzed with some care. Is it necessary to fire the coach when a successful football team begins to lose? What leadership characteristics and strategies contribute to an organization's success? Which ones bring it down? Unexpectedly, the research for this book created an opportunity to analyze what it takes to bring a seriously wounded organization back to good health.

Boulder, Colorado

# NOTES

1. When I consulted to the Marshall Center in the 1960s, it was NASA's largest field center. As of this writing, the Goddard Space Flight Center in Greenbelt, Maryland, is the largest center.

*And [tragedy] particularly concerns the complexities of ethics and psychology because of the close connection between* tragedy *and* purpose. *We might almost lay it down as a rule of thumb: Where someone is straining to do something, look for evidence of the tragic mechanism.*

Kenneth Burke, *Permanence and Change* (1935/1984, p. 195)

## Chapter One

# THE *CHALLENGER* ACCIDENT

The sleek orbiter, vaguely evocative of a killer whale in its white and black tile skin, stood on its tail, waiting. We had seen this expectant profile 24 times before, but this time there was a special sense of anticipation: a *teacher* was on board.

The date was January 28, 1986, the time 11:38 a.m., and millions of people were watching television. The delays had been frustrating, but in a way they deepened the appetite for the launch. Teachers all over the United States were trying to keep their students' attention focused; one of their own was on center stage. At last they heard the disembodied voice intone the final countdown.

*"T-minus 10."*

*"Nine."*

*"Eight."*

*"Seven."*

*"Six. . .we have main engine start. . ."*

*"Five."*

*"Four."*

*"Three."*

*"Two."*

*"One."*

*"And lift-off, lift-off of the twenty-fifth shuttle mission, and it has cleared the tower."* (McConnell, 1987, p. 239)

Roger Boisjoly, an engineer working for Morton Thiokol of Brigham City, Utah, was greatly relieved. Morton Thiokol was the prime contractor for the two solid-fuel boosters blasting the shuttle into space. The night before, Boisjoly had strongly recommended against the launch of the *Challenger* on the grounds that the O-rings—rubber gaskets that prevent the escape of explosive gases—had never been tested under freezing conditions. The ambient temperature at Cape Canaveral, Florida, was 36 degrees Fahrenheit, but icicles still hung from the tower scaffolding due to freezing temperatures the night before. Boisjoly was relieved because he had been advised by his technical team that the greatest risk would be at the moment of lift-off.

### A Major Malfunction

The families of the *Challenger's* crew (Greg Jarvis, Christa McAuliffe, Ron McNair, Ellison Onizuka, Judy Resnik, Dick Scobee, and Mike Smith) watched what appeared to be another routinely successful launch. Then some saw a puff of smoke. Objects appeared to break away from the spacecraft. Then came the shattering message over the loudspeakers:

> "Flight controllers here looking very carefully at the situation. Obviously a major malfunction. We have no downlink. We have a report from the Flight Dynamics Officer that the vehicle has ex-ploded."

> The cries rose to a keening wail. Children sobbed for their fathers and for their mother. The adults were helpless to comfort them. As the escorts led the families from the roof, the cloud spread and softened in the sky. Feathery vapor trails descended, distant, streaming debris. (McConnell, 1987, p. 247)

Boisjoly did not hear the keening wail, but he might have been excused if he had produced one of his own. His worst fear, indeed his implicit prediction, had been realized. Since that day he has never been able to watch a shuttle launch in "real time" (i.e., live); he can only watch it on videotape, with the full knowledge that it was successful.

As for the rest of us, we felt an initial numbness, followed by a yearning for what had been lost. A period of disillusionment ensued, then a diminishing degree of despair. Finally we asked: What happened? What went wrong? Why did it happen?

I certainly felt a personal sense of loss, even anger over the tragedy because of my past experiences with NASA and the Marshall Space Flight Center (MSFC). I had been part of the organization; it was part of me. At the time, I was a professor in the Department of Communication and associate dean of the School of Liberal Arts at Purdue University. Purdue claimed to have produced more astronauts than any other university, excepting one of the military academies. Neil Armstrong, the first man to step on the moon, was a Purdue graduate; so was Gus Grissom. We identified with NASA and the space program, and we agonized over the accident.

### Understanding the Event

The *Challenger* accident was a highly memorable event in many Americans' lives; frequently they can remember exactly when and where they first heard the news. Some researchers in the field of communication reacted quickly to the event and tried to track the diffusion of news about *Challenger*. A team of researchers in the Department of Communication at Arizona State University (Mayer, Gudykunst, Perrill & Merrill, 1990) studied the diffusion of the news among a randomly-selected sample of 538 adults living in a suburb of a large southwestern city and found that the information had spread quickly.

### Diffusion of the Information

Approximately 50 percent of their respondents heard about the *Challenger* accident within 30 minutes, 66 percent within an hour, and almost 100 percent within three hours. About 50 percent learned the news via the mass media, the balance by word of mouth. About 60 percent of the respondents themselves told someone else, with about half of them telling up to three other people.

Because the event took place on a normal working day, more people learned the news from each other than would have been the case had it occurred at night or on a weekend, when, according to previous diffusion studies, the media would have been the first source for a higher percentage of persons. (The data from this study also illustrate how organizational communication networks provide the means for diffusing non-work information.)

Another group of communication researchers at Cleveland State University (Pettey, Perloff, Neuendorf, & Pollick, 1986) also studied the diffusion of the news about *Challenger*, this time with 119 students at their campus. Their data are similar yet different from the Arizona State results. In the Cleveland State study, 79 percent of the respondents heard about the explosion within 30 minutes, 84 percent within 60 minutes, and 88 percent within 90 minutes. The team could find only two cases in diffusion-research literature in which the dissemination of information occurred more rapidly: the death of President Franklin D. Roosevelt and the assassination of President John F. Kennedy.

Measuring a different set of variables from the Arizona State team, the Cleveland group found that some students were more generally reliant on television for news than others. These "TV-reliant" students were also more knowledgeable about the shuttle disaster. For these students, and others who learned of it via television, the *Challenger* accident was essentially a visual message. Such a message is best suited, of course, for quick dissemination by live television and video replay. However, a deeper understanding of the event for most students, no doubt, came from reading and from interpersonal and group discussions of it. The data from these two studies indicate that the *Challenger* accident was a major communicative event to Americans, an event on the order of magnitude of the death of Franklin D. Roosevelt and the assassination of John F. Kennedy.

### Media Accounts of the *Challenger* Disaster

George Cheney, a colleague in the Department of Communication at the University of Colorado, Boulder, made a close study of the mass media accounts and interpretations of the *Challenger* tragedy. In the days and weeks following the event, the accident was the lead story on television, the front-page story in newspapers, and the cover story of many magazines. The Associated Press declared it the top news story of 1986. Every account seemed to label the event a "tragedy." Cheney wrote that few would dispute the use of the word "tragedy" for the *Challenger* accident, showing that it fit two different definitions given by the *Oxford English Dictionary*: a "dreadful calamity or disaster" and the "climax of a human drama 'with a fatal or disastrous conclusion' " (Cheney, 1987, p. 1).

In fact, Cheney saw two tragedies in the case: the first was the dramatic explosion played and replayed over and over on television which "united the nation in grief." The second, discovered only over time, was the disillusionment that came with the realization that a series of flawed decisions had been made by the technocracy of NASA, that "previously untarnished institution" (p. 1).

Cheney found a third response to the *Challenger* episode: a rededication or renewed commitment to the space program—despite NASA's damaged image. Only three days after the accident, President Reagan said, "Sometimes, when we reach for the stars, we fall short. But we must pick ourselves up again and press on despite the pain." Cheney found this theme of rededication showing up in editorials, advertisements, and public opinion polls. One survey of school-age children, according to Cheney, "revealed unswerving desire to support the space program: Many hoped to be astronauts. Mentioned often were personal identification with teacher-astronaut Christa McAuliffe and dedication to the U.S. space program" (p. 2).

Cheney thus found a close connection between *tragedy* and (renewed) *purpose.* Fifty years before, Kenneth Burke, the great American sage, penned some penetrating observations about this connection that Cheney put to good use in his paper. In his brilliant book, *Permanence and Change* (originally entitled *A Treatise on Communication*), Burke wrote of the "close connection between tragedy and purpose. We might almost lay it down as a rule of thumb: where someone is *straining* to do something, look for evidence of the tragic mechanism" (Burke, 1935/1984, p. 195). The Rogers Commission[1] members and journalists alike were finding that NASA had indeed been "straining" to keep to its demanding and unrealistic shuttle-flight schedule. Spare parts were cannibalized from other shuttles in order to meet launch dates. Managers and workers were fatigued by the constant pressure.

In that same book, Burke made the prophetic observation that the "tragic symbol is the device *par excellence* for *recommending* a cause. How could one better picture an issue in an appealing light than by showing that people were willing to be destroyed in behalf of it" (Burke, 1935/1984, p. 196)? Cheney seized upon Burke's general observations about tragedy in the universal drama of communication and human relations as a way of understanding the media's coverage of the *Challenger* tragedy. It allowed him to isolate the theme of *sacrifice* "as a particular type of tragic 'motive'—

motivational in the sense that *the presentation of sacrifice* is highly persuasive in recommending a cause with which it is symbolically linked" (Cheney, 1987, p. 3). Cheney thus presented his thesis:

> In the case of the U.S. space program, the discussion of the *Challenger* disaster has had a far greater effect on reinforcing *purpose* than have recent discussions of potential benefits of long-term space ventures. While this claim is highly speculative and difficult to support, there is a more specific thesis which I will advance in the remainder of this paper: that reports of and commentary on the *Challenger* disaster effectively functioned to equate *sacrifice* with *purpose,* thereby reinforcing a sense of national "mission." The linkage of sacrifice and purpose was dramatized in at least four ways: (1) the visual portrayal of the space shuttle's explosion, (2) the expressions of personal identification with the *Challenger* because of teacher-astronaut Christa McAuliffe, (3) the appeals to America's collective "destiny" in space, and (4) the conveyance of religious significance surrounding the disaster. (Cheney, 1987, p. 3)

The visual portrayal of the explosion was seared into the consciousness of the public, first by the live coverage, then by videotapes replayed again and again. The images were repeated in photos carried by magazines and newspapers. Images of the victims were juxtaposed with photos of their surviving families and shocked observers. Photographs displayed President Reagan and the survivors in a posture of mourning. Tragedy, sacrifice, mourning, and purpose were combined in the images and the words explicating them.

The media expressed serious concerns about the effect of all this imagery on those who saw it, whether in person or on television— particularly the effect on the millions of children in countless classrooms who were already "symbolically unified through identification with the teacher-astronaut" (Cheney, 1987, p. 5). Noteworthy here is that the potentially harmful imagery the media people were concerned about was of their own making. This is an indication that the content of the mass media is increasingly a reflection of and reaction to its own performance and previous output: the mass media as Narcissus.

Tom Wolfe, in his bestselling book *The Right Stuff,* exalted the macho image of the high-flying test pilots of experimental aircraft at the expense of the ape-like passengers of the early space shots. In a *Newsweek* editorial, he explained the symbolic importance of Christa McAuliffe and her mission:

> The presence aboard the *Challenger* of Christa McAuliffe, a woman who taught social studies at a high school in New Hampshire, was meant to symbolize the culmination of. . .endeavors [to develop the space shuttle as coach-and-freight service and to break the political grip of the fighter-pilot, test-pilot astronauts of NASA]. She was the first space coach passenger, not counting a pair of congressional junketeers. Her flight was to be the crossover, at last, from a quarter of a century in which space had been a frontier open only to pioneers who lived and were willing to die by the code of "the right stuff"—the Alan Shepards, John Glenns, and Neil Armstrongs—to an era when space would belong to the entire citizenry, to Everyman.
>
> The last role in the world NASA had in mind for Christa McAuliffe and the rest of the *Challenger* crew was that of pioneer or hero. (Wolfe, 1986, p. 40)

But heroes and heroines the seven crew members did become. Cheney found a letter written by a teacher published in *Time* magazine on March 3, 1986: "I hope many Americans will realize how intensely we in the teaching profession identified with Christa McAuliffe. . . . We are devastated by her death, because, more than we realized, she was our hero." Some teachers still display bumper stickers on their cars that read: " 'I touch the future. I teach' (Christa McAuliffe)." McAuliffe thus became the personification of the *Challenger* tragedy. Increasingly, her memory became linked to the need to "press on" with the space program, as Vice President Bush put it. President Reagan announced renewed dedication for the space program by saying there would be "more teachers in space."

Although McAuliffe became the personification of the tragedy, other important symbols were also rising from the wreckage. Cheney found a symbolic linkage in the press coverage between our "national destiny," an echo of our "manifest destiny" articulated by Thomas Hart Benton and others in the 19th century, and the space frontier. President Reagan's eulogy to the fallen astronauts invoked the frontier metaphor and compared their deaths with grave markers along the Oregon Trail. The sacrifice of those "sturdy souls" and the grief of their survivors "only steeled them to the journey ahead." "Thus," observed Cheney, "the president wasted no time in framing the *Challenger* disaster as a sacrificial motivation to move forward with the space program" (p. 8).

Commentators in the press agreed.   Hugh Sidey, in a *Time* magazine editorial, quoted Frederick Jackson Turner's comments on the closing of the Western frontier in 1893.   The frontier metaphor has been associated with the U.S. space program from the beginning. President John F. Kennedy announced the national goal of landing a man on the moon and returning him safely to the earth within the decade of the 1960s, and the Apollo Program became part of the central slogan of his administration: the "New Frontier."   As we shall later see, this frontier metaphor for the space program was declared and repeated without much thought or reflection and has recently been much criticized.   In 1986, however, the exigence of the tragic aftermath brought this metaphor to its fullest flowering.

Religious overtones to the media accounts were also detected by Cheney.   President Reagan paraphrased a sonnet by John Gillespie Magee, a U.S. pilot shot down during World War II, in saying: "We will never forget them nor the last time we saw them this morning as they prepared for their journey and waved goodbye and 'slipped the surly bonds of earth to touch the face of God.'"   These final 12 words appeared in half-inch letters beside the photo of the fiery explosion in *Time's* cover story.   Cheney found an expression of national *purpose* in those words.   The religious overtones are nothing new in our public discourse, particularly eulogistic rhetoric.   "It is a ritualized part of what has been called American civil religion: that diffuse but powerful admixture of national and religious symbols" (Cheney, 1987, p. 10).   In this case, it worked to revive the sense of purpose for the *Challenger* and future shuttle missions.

## Some Conclusions

We have seen how tragedy, sacrifice, and purpose became linked in media coverage of this sad event.   The visual images, the personification of McAuliffe as "Everyteacher" or "Everyperson," the ritualized recall of our national destiny to push back the frontier, and the religious overtones combined to create, almost immediately after the *Challenger*'s fall, a rededication of our space program.   I reproduce the final paragraph of Cheney's paper:

> The search for meaning, for purpose, in "the tragic" is a basic human tendency, according to Burke—one which recurs quite

forcefully in American history. War losses, economic upheavals, assassinations, scandals, have all been subject to and inspiration for the reinforcement of purpose. This is why the process of interpreting and reinterpreting U.S. involvement in Vietnam has been so long and arduous. The search for purpose in that case was (and is) severely undermined by confused goals, conflicting reports, opposed emotions, and differing overall assessments of the tragic period. The fact that the quest for common understanding continues may be seen readily in recent films and books on Vietnam, each of which offers a somewhat different perspective in a common effort to rescue a clear purpose out of a disturbed collective memory. This case stands in stark contrast to that of the *Challenger* disaster, where the media effectively rescued purpose from the chaos of the event while NASA was still sorting through the debris. (Cheney, 1987, pp. 11-12)

Cheney showed, then, that the space program and the Vietnamese war, although temporally intertwined, were culturally different enterprises because for most Americans the purpose of the one was clear and consistent with our manifest destiny, the other murky and inconsistent.

**The Rogers Commission and the *Challenger* Teleconference**

I followed the reporting of the Rogers Commission's activities and testimony in the press with great attentiveness, trying to compare and contrast aspects of organizational communication in the NASA of the 1980s with the NASA I had worked for as a consultant in the 1960s, during the Apollo era.

I soon noticed that descriptions of certain communicative events leading up to the decision to launch the *Challenger* did not fit with the practices I had observed and learned about in research interviews at the Marshall Center in the 1960s. One example was the highly publicized teleconference held on Monday, January 27, 1986, the night before the launch, between representatives of the Marshall Center, the Kennedy Space Center in Florida, and Morton Thiokol.

Testimony about this telephone conference described Marshall Center representatives as reversing their usual approach in dealing with the personnel of Morton Thiokol. Instead of pressing the contractor to prove that *Challenger* would fly, they insisted that Thiokol prove it would *not* fly. Thiokol could not produce sufficient evidence to show that the shuttle would fail, despite damage to the

now-infamous O-rings during previous flights.[2] One Marshall manager was quoted in the Rogers Commission Report as saying he was
"appalled" by Thiokol's recommendation not to launch (p. 99);
apparently he had not been made aware of the critical nature of
temperature considerations. Another Marshall manager reportedly
asked the Thiokol people whether they wanted to "wait until April"
to launch the *Challenger* (p. 96). This was inconsistent with the
principle of *penetration* as I understood it—as well as the value
premise underlying penetration. It appeared that the Marshall
Center was no longer the organization I had known so well.

## Penetration as a Communication Strategy

Penetration was the practice at the Marshall Center of encouraging engineers to gain access to all levels of a contractor's ranks.
Through penetration, the government hoped to become a "smart
buyer" when the hardware was ready for delivery to NASA. MSFC
engineers were assigned to contractor plants, where they monitored
the work closely and got to know their counterparts in the private
sector very well. As these relationships developed, the contractor's
personnel often found it easier to discuss technical problems with the
NASA engineers and managers than with their own bosses. There
was, for example, an incident (described in more detail in a later
chapter) in which the Marshall Center engineers knew more about
problems with the second stage of the Saturn V (or moon rocket)
than the contractor who built it (Tompkins, 1977). Contractors knew
that they would have to prove to the Marshall Center that their
product would fly.

The *Challenger* teleconference reversed the established "burden
of proof," a concept originally defined by the English rhetorical
theorist, Richard Whately (1787-1863). Burden of proof is a
dialectical term whose meaning is made clear by its opposite, the
presumption. To define by illustration, a person in the U.S. is
presumed to be innocent (the presumption) until proved guilty (the
burden of proof). Presumption refers to the beliefs, attitudes,
institutions, and systems currently accepted—the status quo. The
status quo will continue without defense until sufficient reasons are
adduced against it to produce change. The side or forces which seek
such changes have the burden of proof and must generate sufficient
reasons for change. The presumption at NASA had always been that
manned spaceflight should not be undertaken when there were any

doubts about the safety of the mission. To counter this presumption, the burden of proof demanded that sufficient reason and evidence be cited to prove that the spacecraft will fly safely.

The reversal of this approach in the case of *Challenger* was certainly not an original observation on my part; many researchers in the field of communication came to the same conclusion. Nor was it lost on the Rogers Commission. My concern, however, was somewhat different: I knew that this event also reversed the past practices of the Marshall Center. Wernher von Braun, the director of MSFC from its inception until 1970, was once asked by a congressional committee why contractors performed better for NASA than for other clients. Von Braun's answer was, in a word, penetration.

## Organizational Forgetting?

Apparently the Marshall Center had discontinued use of penetration—at least in this instance. But why? I puzzled over this question, wondering whether it was due to the adoption of new organizational communication practices or some other reason. It then dawned on me that the Marshall Center might have experienced a kind of organizational "forgetting" or institutional memory loss. By forgetting, I mean a gradual process in which successful, proven practices and procedures are not actively promoted or monitored. New people who join the organization may not be actively encouraged to follow these practices, and over time they eventually fall out of use. If the Marshall engineers had forgotten about penetration, could it be possible that they had also forgotten the other principles and practices of organizational communication that had served them so well during earlier periods of success?

There was other circumstantial evidence to consider. Wernher von Braun, who was responsible for defining and promoting the previously successful philosophy of organizational communication at the Marshall Center, had left the MSFC to become NASA's associate deputy administrator for future planning in Washington, D.C., in 1970. Two years later, he retired from government service to accept a position with Fairchild Industries at Germantown, Maryland. Von Braun died of cancer in 1977. Although he had maintained both formal and informal communication with the Marshall Center, it seemed that enough time had passed—16 years since his departure, nine years since his death—to allow a certain amount of organizational forgetting.

After von Braun resigned, Eberhard Rees replaced him as director. Rees had been a long-term subordinate and confidant of von Braun since their days together in Germany. I assumed it was unlikely Rees would simply set aside the philosophy he and von Braun had developed together.

A reservation I had about my "long-distance" hypothesis of institutional amnesia arose from one stubborn fact. The director of the Marshall Center at the time of the disaster was Dr. William R. Lucas, the third successor to von Braun in that position. I remembered Lucas well. He had been director of the Propulsion and Vehicle Engineering Laboratory at the Marshall Center during the Apollo Project, the only American-born engineer to head a design lab at that time. (The rest were Germans.) I had conducted several highly productive interviews with Lucas in both 1967 and 1968; he had given me some useful illustrations of the applications of what were known as the Monday Notes as well as other innovative communicative practices. In my one-on-one sessions with Lucas, I found him to be genial, soft-spoken, open, and helpful. Lucas knew, understood, and practiced von Braun's philosophy of organizational communication. Had he or his predecessors forgotten it—and let the *organization* forget? Or had they simply discarded it, favoring a different approach?

Lucas's predecessor, Rocco Petrone, was the first "outsider" to be appointed director. Transferred from NASA headquarters in Washington, Petrone was believed by some of the Marshall personnel I interviewed in 1990 to have been sent to force out the remaining Germans and carry out a reduction in force—in other words, to fire people. It is not likely that Petrone would set about to learn the von Braun system and promote it vigorously while forcing von Braun's colleagues, who had helped him create it, out of the organization.

The organizational memory loss could thus have begun under Petrone. In fact, his reduction in force could have provided the "blow" or trauma that metaphorically precipitated the forgetting. And although Petrone was only in charge of Marshall for less than two years, that might have been long enough to create new communicative habits and to lead to the forgetting of the old ones. After Petrone came Lucas.

Lucas might have lacked either the inclination or ability, or both, to restore the old proven ways. And there was another possibility: Lucas had one style of communication for his superiors (including me, as a researcher whose work was sponsored and endorsed by his bosses) and another for his subordinates. Had his style of communication affected his promotion or continuation of von Braun's system? Though my collective forgetting hypothesis was admittedly speculative and based on circumstantial evidence, it seemed more likely than the possibility that Petrone and/or Lucas had made a conscious decision to phase out von Braun's organizational communication practices. As the old adage goes, "If it ain't broke, why fix it?" Von Braun's practices had proven consistently successful. Although I couldn't know it at the time, I would later be given the opportunity to test these hypotheses at the Marshall Center. In the meantime, I hoped the Rogers Commission would enlighten me.

As the Commission pursued its own hunches, leads, and hypotheses, I was approached by several news agencies for my own views. CBS News called me one day at Purdue to ask some questions. A local television station in Indiana, aware of my past experiences with NASA, pressed me for an interview. I explained that I had no recent "inside" information, that my ideas were highly speculative at best. They persisted, however, and I granted the interview. I was a bit uncomfortable, however, because the evidence supporting my hypothesis was circumstantial and slender.

### Purposes and Preview of this Book

How can one explain the apparent discrepancies between NASA in the 1960s and in the 1980s? Can a hypothesis of organizational forgetting account for the changes? If so, how can one explain the process of forgetting? Since that time at Purdue, I have pursued these questions with some vigilance. They provided my impetus for writing this book.

There is another reason as well. Having written balanced but mainly favorable descriptions of organizational communication practices at the Marshall Space Flight Center during the Apollo era, I had implicitly recommended these practices to others. If they were still in place at the time of the *Challenger* accident, then it would be necessary for me to revise my evaluation of them.

The bulk of this book, then, is a narrative of my subsequent attempts to answer the questions posed in this chapter. The narrative is interrupted briefly in Chapter Two to consider the question: What is organizational communication? Chapter Three picks up the narrative again, beginning with my experiences as a consultant in organizational communication to the Marshall Center in the 1960s. The narrative thread continues with a reconsideration of the *Challenger* accident as documented by the Rogers Commission Report. Then I report on my return to Huntsville in January of 1990 for interviews with 15 of the top officials at the Center. Some surprises came out of those interviews: accounts of organizational death and rebirth. A theory of organizational rebirth is specified and an attempt made to validate the analysis in an interview with a high-ranking administrator at NASA headquarters. The book concludes with a chapter on the future and the meaning of the space program.

## NOTES

1.   President Reagan charged the Rogers Commission with investigating the causes of the accident and making recommendations for the future of the space program.

2.   I do not mean to imply that the Morton Thiokol managers are without fault in the accident.   They have been widely criticized for caving in to the pressure from NASA, of "putting on their managers' hats instead of their engineers' hats" and not supporting the stand of their engineers led by Roger Boisjoly.

## Chapter Two

# THE IMPERATIVE OF STUDYING ORGANIZATIONAL COMMUNICATION

There are two reasons for interrupting the narrative flow of the book for this rather didactic chapter. First and most important, it contains some ideas that are later applied to my analysis of organizational factors in the *Challenger* accident. This chapter will help prepare the reader for that discussion. Second, I anticipate that many of my readers are unfamiliar with the field of organizational communication. This is an attempt to provide them with a rather brief description. Some readers—space buffs, for example—will be more interested in the inner workings of NASA than in the field of organizational communication. Such readers might be advised to move directly to the narrative. I hope that those who do so will become motivated to return to this chapter.

I will begin by relating four anecdotes that reveal what seems to me to be the essence of organizational communication. Two of the examples were drawn from my experiences with NASA, the other two from different sources. An explication of the anecdotes follows, along with some projections about the future of organizational theory and practice in the United States.

### Four Anecdotes[1]

#### One: 'Five Nines'

This story was related to me during an interview at MSFC in 1967. The interviewee said that it was probably apocryphal but deserved to be true because it so perfectly captured the way organizational communication worked at the Marshall Center. It seems that Wernher von Braun, the director of the Center, was visiting NASA headquarters in Washington, D.C. In a meeting there, someone asked him for the reliability number for a particular rocket stage.

"I don't know," von Braun said, "but when I get back to Marshall I'll find out and call you."

After von Braun returned to Huntsville, he informally called several close colleagues—some several levels beneath him in MSFC's organizational hierarchy. Then he phoned Washington. The NASA official heard von Braun's answer as "five nines," or, he assumed, a reliability figure of 0.99999.

"Fine," said the official. "How did you arrive at that figure?"

"Well," answered von Braun, "I called Walter Haeusserman in the Astrionics Lab and asked him, 'Are we going to have any problems with this stage?' He answered, 'Nein.' Then I posed the same question to Karl Heimburg in the Test Lab and he also said 'Nein.' I kept at it until I got five neins."

**Two: The Mushroom Problem**

I showed up for an interview in Huntsville with a laboratory director early one morning and was shown into his office.

"Ah, Dr. Tompkins," he said in a German accent, "I understand you are here to see me about the mushroom problem."

"There must be some misunderstanding," I replied. "I don't know anything about a mushroom problem."

"Aren't you interested in organizational communication?"

"Yes."

"Do you know how to grow mushrooms?"

"No," I admitted.

"The way mushrooms are grown illustrates a common problem of organizational communication. You put them down in the basement and keep them completely in the dark. Every once in a while you open the door and throw some horseshit on them."

### Three: Ireland in the Middle East

Cynthia Stohl of Purdue University related the following incident during a lecture at the University of Colorado. She described one of the many occasions when officials at the United Nations were preoccupied with the complex problems of the Middle East. They were surprised to learn that one of the best-informed members of the U.N. about that part of the world was the representative from Ireland. Why the Irish delegate? Ireland is geographically distant from the Middle East and removed in race, language, religion, and culture. The answer was found in the alphabetical order in which delegates were seated at the United Nations General Assembly: *I*ran, *I*raq, *I*rish Republic, *I*srael, *J*ordan, and *K*uwait.

### Four: The Collapse of the Soviet Economy

Organizational communication can offer a partial explanation as to why the Soviet economy collapsed in the late 1980s. We will have to wait many years for a more complete analysis, but an "orgcom" explanation for the disaster is beginning to emerge. This story is based on an essay by Robert Heilbroner (September 10, 1990) that appeared in *The New Yorker*, entitled "Reflections: After Communism."

When Heilbroner was an undergraduate studying economics in the 1930s, socialism seemed both desirable and within easy grasp. However, Ludwig von Mises, an Austrian economist of conservative views, concluded that socialism was impossible, "arguing that no central planning board could ever gather the *enormous amount of information* needed to create a workable economic system" (Heilbroner, 1990, p. 92, emphasis added). Heilbroner was skeptical about this "orgcom" analysis because the practice of capitalism didn't seem any less irrational than socialism during the time of the Great Depression.

Two articles by a young Polish economist named Oskar Lange reinforced Heilbroner's skepticism. Lange undercut von Mises' argument by demonstrating that a central board would not need so much information. The board could simply watch warehouses closely. If inventories went up, it could lower prices. If inventories went down, prices could be raised.

As it turned out, von Mises was right and Lange wrong. *Gosplan,* the Soviet Union's Central Board, would issue as many as 2,000 sets of instructions for major sectors of the economy. *Gossnab,* a lower board, divided these into 15,000 categories. Various ministries then subdivided these categories into 50,000 products and their range of sizes. All of this had to be communicated down the line to plant managers, and from them to their workers, who in turn had to send their feedback or responses back up the line. Similar to the "command and control" system of a military operation, this system of organizational communication left little room for independent decisions by the people closest to the problems of production and distribution.

"Moreover, as Lange failed to see, it was one thing to declare that the planning board could adjust prices by watching inventory levels and another thing actually to do it" (Heilbroner, 1990, p. 92). Heilbroner summarized an example originally analyzed by two Soviet economists, Nikolai Shmelev and Vladimir Popov. Shmelev and Popov noticed that moleskins were rotting in warehouses in the Soviet Union and set out to understand why.

It seems that in 1982 the price of these mole pelts was more than doubled in order to encourage increased production of inexpensive gloves. The system over-responded. As the moleskins piled up in warehouses, the appropriate ministry requested *Goskomtsen,* the state committee on pricing, to lower the price. But *Goskomtsen* did not have the time to consider the request: it was too busy with the other 24 million prices its members had to set.

### The Four Anecdotes Unpacked

#### 'Five Nines'

This humorous story illustrates a serious lesson. Effective organizations realize the need for upward-directed communication. As we shall see in greater detail in Chapter Three, von Braun put the highest priority on upward-directed communication from his subordinates, whom he regarded as sensors or highly credible sources. In addition, this example points to the distinction between formal and informal systems of communication. The formal communication system is that rationally devised "tree" of superiors and subordinates represented by the organization chart. It specifies who talks to whom and with what authority. The informal communication system is partly accidental: friends talk to friends and develop networks. In the anecdote, von Braun informally called on his German intimates to check on the rocket's reliability, bypassing several layers of hierarchy, as one might do in arranging a surprise birthday party for a co-worker.

In this case, we see that the informal system of communication coincides with the formal system of communication. We normally think of the formal organization as giving rise to the informal. Chester Barnard[2] recognized that this view of the relationship needs to be reversed: *an informal system of communication gives rise to a formal one* (Barnard, 1938). Consider the task of creating a new business organization. Would it be possible to do so without relying on people one already knows? When the Marshall Center was created in 1960, many of its managers and engineers were transferred to it *as a group* from the U.S. Army.

This anecdote also allows us to comment on another distinction of informal systems of communication. Since the seminal Hawthorne studies, in which researchers from the Harvard Business School discovered the importance of what they called Human Relations, we normally assume that the formal and informal systems are usually at odds, i.e., they have antagonistic goals and "logics." But the informal system at the Marshall Center—the German "family," as I call it—was not at odds with the formal. Von Braun, in his formal capacity as director, consulted directly with members of his informal system two or more layers below him in the organization because he knew their aspirations were congruent with those of the formal system.

**The Mushroom Problem**

This story humorously illustrates an important dimension of organizational communication: downward-directed communication. Too often, top managers keep contributors at a lower level in the organization "in the dark," whether by design or oversight, concerning important matters. And when messages do come down the line to those at the bottom and in the middle of the organization, they often contain bad news. The folk wisdom of organizational communication holds that "good news goes up the line, bad news comes down" (the latter sometimes arriving in the form of so much horseshit).

### Ireland in the Middle East

The lesson of this story concerns the importance of the *network*, a noun important to organizational communication which has recently been turned into the verb *networking*, by business executives who learned the practical significance of the concept. Network analysts in communication question members of organizations about the people they talk to and the frequency of their talks. The answers are entered into a computer for analysis. By comparing who speaks to whom, with what frequency, and about what topics, various communicative roles in these networks emerge. Some individuals invariably talk to more people than their colleagues. (They are termed "centrals" or "liaisons.") People who do not report talking to others are categorized as "isolates." Network analysis in organizational communication has not advanced theoretically much beyond the specification of such roles. No one, however, denies the impact of such networks, which can be used to "map" both formal and informal systems of communication.

The Irish example also teaches another lesson: the importance of *propinquity*, nearness or proximity. Seated among the Iranians, Iraqis, Israelis, Jordanians, and Kuwaitis, the Irish delegate could hardly avoid listening and speaking to them and thus became somewhat of an expert on their regional problems.

Propinquity is extremely important to organizational communication. Some managers overlook its importance, perhaps because advances in electronic communication are assumed to have erased the limiting effect of distance. For example, the invention and implementation of the telegraph allowed a great increase in the size of U.S. corporations during the mid-19th century, because it enabled companies that expanded geographically to maintain rapid communication over long distances. Today, we marvel at the effects of new communications technologies: computer-mediated communication, for example, allows for easy contact between people who may never meet, exchange letters, or even talk on the telephone. However, despite ever-advancing technology, face-to-face access is still terribly important in the view of most managers and employees; it remains the preferred way of communicating for most people. The need for interaction between specific units should be built into organizational design.

## The Collapse of the Soviet Economy

As of this writing, there is much doubt as to how the economies of the republics that once comprised the former Soviet Union will fare in 1993 and beyond. The collapse of the Soviet economy reflected the inability of the country's system of organizational communication to cope with the multitude of messages flowing within it—or should we say messages that were *supposed* to be flowing within it?

The structure of organization, as Chester Barnard showed over 50 years ago, is determined by the limitations of human communication. The span of control—the number of people one can effectively supervise—was set by him at 15 to 20, particularly if those 15 to 20 people need to communicate with each other in dyads, triads, and small groups. If the communicative demands on a manager go beyond those limits, the channels of communication become too numerous for the mind to monitor and manage. Barnard described the "unit organization"—the basic building block of organization—as reflecting those limits. If they grow larger, they must be subdivided. If the larger organization is to grow, it must do so by adding new unit organizations or subdividing existing units (Barnard, 1938). The Soviet system could not process the volume of messages it was forced to generate. The span of control became too broad, which made it impossible to keep track of the many unit organizations within its jurisdiction. Decisions were delayed and deferred so long that the system could not correct itself: it became a deviation-amplifying, rather than a deviation-reducing feedback system, or "vicious circle" (to put the matter in the terms of Weick, 1979).

There is another lesson in the example of the Soviet economy. A perennial issue in organizational communication theory is how to find the proper balance between *centralization* and *decentralization* of decision making. A military campaign needs a "command and control" center because independent and uncoordinated actions at the platoon level could bring about chaos and the loss of the battle, if not the war.

Most organizations function better with a degree of decentralization: Autonomous action by those closest to the problem can lead to innovation and improved efficiency. The modern emphasis on "empowerment" (Kanter, 1983; Pacanowsky, 1988) indicates a trend toward decentralization.[3] However, the historic tension between centralization and decentralization led Alfred P. Sloan, a former executive of General Motors, to promote a policy of "coordinated decentralization" (Sloan, 1964). This apparent oxymoron aptly describes the problems faced by any large organization as it struggles to provide for both unified operations and the relatively autonomous efforts of its many units.

### Definition and Basic Theory of Organizational Communication

Organizational communication is "the study of sending and receiving messages that create and maintain a system of consciously coordinated activities or forces of two or more persons" (Tompkins, 1984, pp. 662-663). Messages placed on bulletin boards and in-house company newsletters would fit this definition, of course, but there are more important examples.

Consider the following mind experiment, which encompasses both the study and the practice of organizational communication: Try to calculate the number of messages that were sent and received during the *creation* of the United Nations. This is a particularly complex example because it involved great distances as well as the translation of messages between and among the many languages of the world. But even a simpler example, the establishment of a pizza parlor by two partners, for instance, requires many messages between the partners, the contractor, bankers or financiers, suppliers, government agencies at all levels, and, not to forget, potential pizza eaters.

*Maintaining* an organization is a similarly complex process. How do messages maintain an organization? Probably the most important way is in the exercise of authority. One person exercises authority over others through messages in one form or another: an order by an army sergeant to her unit, the reading assignment given by a teacher to his class, a request by a chief executive officer for subordinates to come up with a new marketing strategy, an empowered work group reaching consensus about how to solve a production problem. The messages in these examples might be spoken, written, or even conveyed with gestures. The organization is maintained when authoritative messages gain compliance.

And as Barnard (1938) observed, authority resides to a great extent in whether the receiver accepts or rejects the sender's message. In the terms of Steven Lukes (1978), for a message to be authoritative, its content (e.g., "Do this. . .") must be taken seriously, and conflicting messages from another sender (e.g., "Don't do this. . .") must be disregarded. Mary Parker Follett, an American theorist of organizational communication in the early part of this century, largely ignored in her own country but widely appreciated in Japan, argued convincingly that the *mode* or manner of giving orders may be as important as the content of the message. (For a more complete discussion of Follett's contribution, see Tompkins, 1984.)

## Barnard's Three Elements of Organization

Another way of illustrating how messages maintain an organization is to consider the necessary and sufficient conditions for organization itself. Barnard (1938) defined for us the three essential elements of organization. The first is *communication.* There must be a system of communication that reaches every member of or contributor to the organization. Without such a system, no messages could reach the members, eliminating the possibility of influencing their activities. The first responsibility of the executive, therefore, is to provide such a system, an organizational scheme of the right communication lines connecting the right people.

The second element of organization is *common purpose.* An organization in which people work at cross purposes will not be an organization very long. Organizational purpose must be encoded in messages that are transmitted to and received by the members of the organization. Also, organizational purpose may change from time to time. The second responsibility of managers and executives is, therefore, to communicate purpose, values, goals, objectives, a sense of "mission." This is expressed in broadly-worded messages at the top of the organization and then restated in more specific messages at lower levels.

The third of Barnard's elements is the *willingness to serve*, to provide those services the organization requires. People with necessary skills and training must be recruited, which requires messages in both directions. Once recruited, members must be motivated to do the tasks that the organization stipulates. Again, this requires the production and transmission of messages. So the third responsibility of managers and supervisors is to secure essential services by means of messages that offer incentives and motivation to their subordinates.

Although communication is Barnard's first element, it is also the activating agent to his second and third elements as well. In discussing Barnard's three elements of organization, I may have inadvertently given the impression that communication flows primarily in one direction. That is not the case, and most scholars in the area would probably support the assumption that organizations work best when *upward*-directed communication is maximized. (In fact, this theme will be developed at length in this book.) That is, workers who are closer to the problem should themselves decide what should be done about it, rather than be dictated orders from managers who are distant both physically and hierarchically from the problem. The bias for upward communication is often expressed as "participatory decision making," and, although it is much heralded, its practice is not so frequent or as thoroughgoing as observers of organizational communication would hope for.

### Redding's Ideal Managerial Climate

My point can best be expressed by summarizing what W. Charles Redding, who is regarded as the founder of the field of organizational communication, calls the "Ideal Managerial Climate" (1972). Redding did not create the concept out of his own imagination, fertile though it is, but instead inferred its factors from an encyclopedic knowledge of organizational research and theory that had been conducted up to the time of his writing. It is briefly summarized as follows:

*1. Supportiveness.* This word is used in its dictionary definition: furnishing support or aid. A supportive manager communicates with subordinates in a friendly, considerate, and helpful manner, recognizing in the deed of communicating the integrity of the other individual. Hierarchical differences are minimized by not "talking down" to the subordinate. The message received by the subordinate is that he or she has personal worth and importance.

*2. Participative Decision Making.* This concept denotes that people ought to be involved in the decisions that have importance for their work. Hirschman's (1970) concept of "voice" is relevant as well. A person with "voice" in an organization is one who is at least consulted, or listened to, about important decisions. She or he is encouraged to express opinions, even dissenting ones. This obviously implies that conflict is expected and desired. In its extreme manifestation, workers are given the authority to make collective decisions. Thus, organizational communication is not just a downward-directed process.

*3. Trust, Confidence, and Credibility.* Redding treats these concepts as "close cousins" for good reason. Some models consider credibility to be a dimension of interpersonal trust in the communication process; others treat trust as a dimension of credibility. What should be stressed is that these factors are important in both the sending and receiving of messages. The receiver is more likely to be persuaded by a source perceived to be credible than by one who is not. On the other hand, subordinates are more likely to talk about their problems with a boss they trust than with one they don't—one, for example, who might use their problems against them in the future.

*4. Openness and Candor.* Redding means more than self-disclosure by this concept. Certainly it is beneficial to communication when the source is open and candid. It can even increase his or her credibility, as discussed above. It is equally important for receivers, particularly superiors, to be open to dissent and even to criticism. If not, the messengers bringing bad news may be "killed." When this kill-the-messenger attitude is present, "whistle-blowing" is the only alternative for a member of an organization who observes something illicit, illegal, or immoral. Whistle-blowing is a courageous act, because it almost always, even if undeservedly, brings retribution. We shall consider such a case in subsequent chapters and see how openness and candor are crucial, in both their presence and absence, in the history of the space program at the Marshall Center.

*5. Emphasis on High Performance Goals.* At first glance, this factor seems out of place, even irrelevant to the communication process. Upon reflection, however, it does have a place in the ideal organizational communication climate. Redding, by adding this criterion, avoided the trap of describing a "country-club" atmosphere in which people communicate with trust, credibility, candor, openness, equality—and nothing gets done. Some might find such an ideal desirable, but others, concerned with the realities of the new, competitive, international economic order, will accept Redding's final criterion. Redding also suggested that the realization of the first four factors will make the fifth or "bottom-line" criterion more attainable.

It is not possible to summarize the full breadth and depth of the study of organizational communication in this chapter. Instead, I shall identify two recently published handbooks which the reader interested in more specialized topics can track down. Alphabetically by editors they are: *Handbook of Organizational Communication*, edited by Gerald M. Goldhaber and George A. Barnett (1988); and *Handbook of Organizational Communication: An Interdisciplinary Perspective*, edited by Fredric M. Jablin, Linda L. Putnam, Karlene H. Roberts, and Lyman W. Porter (1987). There is something for everyone in these two large collections of readings.

## The Future of Theory and Practice

The remainder of this chapter will address the future of organizational communication in both theory and practice.

### Psychoanalytic Approaches

It appears to me that an informed, coherent, and sophisticated psychoanalytic approach to organizational communication will emerge soon—if it has not already done so. It will certainly not be limited to classical Freudian psychoanalysis. My own work in organizational identification has some of its roots in psychoanalysis. Harold Lasswell adapted Freud's concept to nationalism and world politics. Kenneth Burke further adapted Lasswell's and Freud's ideas to make identification the key term in his new rhetoric, or post-Aristotelian theory of persuasion. Herbert Simon (1976) applied Lasswell's ideas in a chapter on organizational identification in his *Administrative Behavior*. Tompkins and Cheney (1985) drew from all of these writers in developing their ideas on organizational identification.

In 1990 I was invited to give a series of lectures at the University of Helsinki and Helsinki University of Technology in Finland. In preparing, I contemplated discussing the concept of *transference*, which occurs when an individual treats a current relationship as if it were one from the past. An example would be a client who begins to relate to a therapist as a parent. I saw transference as a possible explanation for the development of certain patterns of organizational identification. We speak, for example, of "paternalistic" organizations. We used to speak of "Ma" Bell. However, I decided against speaking on the topic because my audiences were to be psychologists with an interest in organizational communication. It seemed wiser to discuss the idea with them informally before making a public statement about my tentative ideas.

My host in Finland, Antero Kiianmaa of the Helsinki University of Technology, gave me a bundle of papers when I arrived, including several by a scholar named Martti Siirala that, coincidentally, dealt with psychoanalysis. My week's schedule showed that I would be having lunch with Siirala and Kiianmaa on my last day in Helsinki. I quizzed Kiianmaa about Siirala.

"He is one of the founders of psychoanalysis in Finland," was his reply. Kiianmaa also related that he himself was in training to be a psychoanalyst and that Siirala was one of his supervisors.

I read Siirala's papers with great interest, no doubt because they stressed the social as well as the parental effect on neuroses. I even told Kiianmaa that Siirala's work reminded me of Kenneth Burke's writings on Freud. The upcoming luncheon with Siirala seemed like the ideal time to explore my tentative ideas about Freud, transference, and the development of organizational identification.

When we had taken our seats at a table in the Ostrobotnia Restaurant in downtown Helsinki, I asked Siirala if he could accept the notion that a person, in identifying with an organization, could be experiencing a form of transference, acting out a previous relationship with one's parents.

"Yes," was his immediate reply.

I then related to Siirala and Kiianmaa a story told by Roland Barthes. It seems that Guy de Maupassant, the French writer, often ate lunch at one of the restaurants in the Eiffel Tower. He did not particularly like the food there, but it was the only place in Paris from where he could not see the tower. They laughed heartily at Barthes' anecdote. The moral of the story was negation by identification. For de Maupassant to negate the tower, he had to identify with it. I extended Barthes' analysis by explaining that it would not be necessary to slay one's father, according to Freud's master plot, if one could displace or negate him. One could displace the father, I submitted, by *becoming the father.* Or one could identify positively with an organization if one transferred favorable parental attitudes to it. Siirala and Kiianmaa agreed.

"We are using your work on organizational identification in psychoanalysis," Kiianmaa said. He then narrated the case of a young woman (whose name has been changed) who came to him for analysis. Paula Virtanen spoke of the firm where she worked in idealistic terms, idolizing its owner. Kiianmaa was familiar with the firm which was reputed to exploit its workers to some extent. The woman then revealed that her father was an entrepreneur, whom she idolized. In fact, her entire family so adored and respected the man that they never referred to him by anything other than "Mr. Virtanen." "In short, we have here," said Kiianmaa, "a case of overidentification."

I asked what symptoms had led her to seek psychotherapy. Kiianmaa's answer: "She couldn't eat." Siirala leaned toward me. "She couldn't swallow it any longer."[4]

### The Neurotic Organization

I subsequently learned of a book that tentatively explored the application of psychoanalysis to contemporary organizations: Manfred F.R. de Vries and Danny Miller (1984), *The Neurotic Organization: Diagnosing and Revitalizing Unhealthy Companies.* I summarize this book for two reasons, the first of which is to show how institutional psychoanalysis parallels topics in organizational communication and, second, to introduce some concepts that are later used in an analysis of the Marshall Center.

De Vries and Miller briefly sketch five dysfunctional types of organizations from the psychoanalytic perspective: (1) *the paranoid organization* in which "managerial suspicions translate into primary *emphasis on organizational intelligence* and controls. Management information systems are very sophisticated in their methods of scanning the environment and controlling internal processes" (p. 23); (2) *the compulsive organization* that "is wed to ritual. Every last detail of operation is planned out in advance and carried on in a routinized and pre-programmed fashion" (p. 28); (3) *the dramatic firm*: "Dramatic firms live up to their name in many respects: they are hyperactive, impulsive, dramatically venturesome, and danger-ously uninhibited. Their decision makers live in a world of hunches and impressions rather than facts as they address a broad array of widely disparate projects, products, and markets in desultory fashion" (p. 31); (4) *the depressive organization*, which is characterized by "inactivity, lack of confidence, extreme conservatism, and a bureaucratically motivated insularity. . . . There is an atmosphere of extreme passivity and purposelessness" (p. 34); (5) *the schizoid organization*, "like the depressive one, is characterized by a *leadership vacuum*. Its top executive discourages interaction because of a fear of involvement. Schizoid leaders experience the world as an unhappy place, populated by frustrating individuals" (p. 38). We will return to the five categories in an analysis of communication problems at MSFC during the period leading up to the *Challenger* accident.

As is indicated by the terms "intelligence," "control," "information systems," and "interaction," included in these brief definitions, neurotic organizations are defined in large part by the pathologies of organizational communication.

Other concepts and topics advanced in *The Neurotic Organization* show the contribution of psychoanalysis to a communicative approach for organizations. For example, the second chapter, "Shared Fantasies and Group Processes," is amazingly similar to Ernest Bormann's fantasy theme analysis (an approach well known in the field of organizational communication)—but without any reference to Bormann. I do not mean to imply any unacknowledged influence here on the part of de Vries and Miller. They seem to have arrived at their position independently of Bormann. They acknowledge openly their reliance on the chain-reaction process in groups described in the work of Robert Freed Bales (on whom Bormann also relies) and of Wilfred R. Bion (*Experiences in Groups*, 1959) who first discussed the importance of fantasy in group communication. De Vries and Miller put these concepts together to come up with the notion that groups share fantasies which have a chain-reaction; it is described in a way similar to Bormann's fantasy theme analysis.

### Transference

In their chapter "Confused Interpersonal Relationships," de Vries and Miller anticipate the idea I have been exploring by showing how transference helps us understand organizational processes. Although they eschew the concept of identification, which I believe to be crucial, they do come up with a typology that is similar in some respects to the work I have done with Kiianmaa in the development of organizational identification. They chose to revise, on a pragmatic basis, Freud's two categories of positive transference and negative transference into three categories: *idealizing* transference, *mirror* transference, and *persecutory* transference.

The first, idealizing transference, was illustrated by Kiianmaa's case of Paula. We call this "overidentification" by virtue of a powerful positive transference. The second type, mirror transference, is a narcissistic transference in which organizational executives have a "grandiose sense of self-importance and uniqueness and are desperately in search of praise" (de Vries & Miller, 1984, p. 84). The third type, persecutory transference, splits into *hostility* and *moral masochism*, the former associated with destructive attitudes (perhaps illustrated by de Maupassant's desire to negate or displace by identification) and the latter with feelings of persecution coupled with guilt over the desire to become the persecutor.

The greatest congruence of organizational communication and a psychoanalytic orientation to organizations is found in de Vries and Miller's fourth chapter, "Destructive Superior/Subordinate Interactions." Although we cannot fault the authors for not writing a book on organizational communication, which was not their purpose, this chapter would be richer if it had assimilated Jablin's (1979) integrative scholarship on superior-subordinate communication in organizational settings. Nonetheless, it complements Jablin's work by concentrating on the neurotic or negative aspects of superior-subordinate communication.

### Neurotic Superior-Subordinate Communication

De Vries and Miller thus provide new insights into subordinate-superior communication, reversing the typical hierarchical expression. They describe three neurotic modes of communicating through which bosses complicate the lives of their subordinates.

The first is the *binding* mode. A clique of favored underlings is assiduously cultivated. The aim of the superior, conscious or unconscious, is to create a condition of dependence in his or her subordinates; in fact, independence on the part of subordinates is actively discouraged. Control of subordinates is paramount.

The second destructive pattern is the *proxy* mode. The subordinate is, at one level, expected to be independent and autonomous.

At a deeper, more implicit and important level, however, he or she is expected to be an *extension* of the boss, even to support the superior in the continuous political battles in which the superior becomes involved. These contradictory expectations can create confusion and anger among subordinates.

The third neurotic interaction pattern is the *expelling* mode. There is an either/or expectation inherent here. "Expellers either love and bind the loyal employee or ruthlessly reject him forever because of a small slight. Dramatic changes in attitude may terminate earlier binding and proxy interactions as the offending subordinate is castigated and rejected" (de Vries & Miller, 1984, p. 109).

De Vries and Miller also suggest in a tantalizing manner why previous quantitative approaches to job satisfaction have been so inconclusive. Those "variable analytic" approaches have concentrated on correlating one or another variable—for example, decision-making participation or communication satisfaction—with job satisfaction. The results of such studies are disappointingly low correlation coefficients. De Vries and Miller give us a new angle on the problem by showing that job satisfaction may well be related significantly to the stages of life.

As we move, in Shakespeare's words from *As You Like It*, from "mewling and puking" infant to "whining school boy" to "the lover," the "soldier," the "justice," and the sixth stage of "lean and slipper'd pantaloon," we vary in the degree of satisfaction with our job. Although de Vries and Miller's argument is not conclusive, it is too promising not to be pursued further with systematic empirical work.

## Future Organizational Practices: Nucor

This chapter closes with my best "guesstimate" of what organizations in the U.S. and other countries are going to resemble in the future. History teaches that organizational practice outraces theory. Theory is always the tortoise, but unlike the outcome of the fabled race, it never wins. Nonetheless, when the tortoise listens to the hare, it sometimes gains insights that can keep it from lagging too far behind in the race. The interaction of practice and theoretical feedback can produce remarkable results.

Richard Preston's (1991) book, *American Steel*, is the most fascinating organizational narrative I have read recently. It is the success story of a company called Nucor and its CEO, F. Kenneth Iverson. Nucor was the nearly-bankrupt vestige of Reo, a car and truck manufacturer, when Iverson took it over in the 1960s and transformed it into a steel company. It was the ninth largest steel maker in the United States in 1987 when Preston's narrative begins. At that time, Nucor owned 20 plants around the country, all located in rural America, because management believed such areas provide a great untapped source of high quality workers. People who grow up on or around farms know how to *do* things, like fixing machines and welding. Today, Nucor is the seventh largest steel manufacturer, having moved up because of Iverson's gigantic experiment in the cornfields outside of Crawfordsville, Indiana.

Nucor's Crawfordsville project was a big risk that, if successful, would allow the company to "leapfrog" over its competition—including the Japanese—by producing high-quality, low-cost sheet steel. The plan was to melt scrap metal—mainly the hulks of old automobiles—and then pour it into an experimental machine that would send sheet steel out the other end. No one had ever been able to make sheet steel in one step before. The standard process at the time involved two separate operations, pouring the steel and then rolling it.

The machine was designed and built by a factory in what used to be West Germany. No steelmaker was willing to take the risk of buying the machine until Iverson took the plunge, literally "betting the company." Preston's narrative of the start-up of the Crawfordsville Project is a suspenseful tale, fraught with danger and drama, as the workers from the area (most of whom had no experience in making steel) tried to get the machine to work by trial and error. Nucor is now the most efficient steelmaking company in the world.

There are lessons in this story that, I believe, have profound implications for the future of the U.S. economy. These are mainly lessons in organizational communication. I had read Preston's gripping narrative in two installments of *The New Yorker* where it appeared in the spring of 1991. Coincidentally, a few days later a student told me that Kenneth Iverson would be speaking in her management class the next day.

## The Lessons of Nucor

I attended the lecture and introduced myself to Iverson at the end of the class, then asked his opinion of Preston's articles. He said the book, which had just been released, was better.

Much of Iverson's lecture was about the importance of communication. The lessons of Nucor emerged from his description of the company. Nucor's headquarters in Charlotte, North Carolina, occupy a rented office which is comparable in size to a group dental clinic. Currently, there are only 20 corporate staffers at the headquarters including secretaries and the chairman himself, a ratio of one person per factory. Phil's Delicatessen, in the shopping center across the street, serves as the executive dining room. Iverson flies economy class during his heavy schedule of travel and rents a car when he reaches his destination.

**No Union.** Nucor has so far successfully resisted the organizing efforts of the Steelworkers' Union, not because the company wishes to avoid paying the union scale—Nucor's workers' annual wages averaged $34,000 in 1990—but because of union work rules that specify which tasks workers can and cannot perform. Nucor's workers are organized into teams, and everyone is expected to jump in immediately to help fix any equipment that breaks down. (As we shall see, this is remarkably similar to the idea called "automatic responsibility" conceived by Wernher von Braun and also an older cousin to the concept of empowerment.) Nucor's workers are reportedly hostile to the union and its organizers. There are also critics who say the company has a poor safety record. (On July 9, 1991, CBS Evening News ran a story concentrating on Nucor's alleged lack of concern for safety.) Making steel is dangerous work: In his book, Preston relates how one man was killed during the start-up of the Crawfordsville Project. But Iverson hotly denies that there is a lack of concern for safety, citing statistics to support his claim that Nucor is among the safest of the steel-making companies.

Workers receive bonuses as a team and discipline themselves in a kind of "peer management." The rules are rigid. A worker who is absent for one day loses his or her group bonus for the week. As a result, absenteeism is so low that Nucor doesn't keep figures on it. There have been no layoffs. During hard times, workers cut back their hours, but no one loses more than 25 percent of his or her salary. Executives, on the other hand, take a much deeper cut during hard times; they make the decisions, so they pay the penalty. Iverson revealed that his salary dropped from $460,000 in 1981 to $108,000 in 1982. Workers also receive sizable scholarships for children who go to college.

I do not mean to suggest Nucor as a model organization (although others have taken it to be so). I believe that unions often supply a much-needed function of upward-directed communication by means of the formal grievance procedure and collective bargaining. I also believe that the concern for safety must be centralized. In addition, group incentives can create new forms of coercion. To balance these reservations, however, Nucor does seem to have solved some other problems of structure—i.e., vertical communication—and that is the purpose for considering the company at some length in this book.

A number of factors undoubtedly contribute to the success of Nucor, but the main lesson lies in its communicative chain of command, its "flat" hierarchy. There are only four layers of management above the worker: a foreman or team leader, a department head, a general manager, and then Iverson. This is unheard of in the steel industry, in almost *any* industry for that matter. Business organizations have as many as ten or 11 effective levels of management. According to Iverson, even a simple memo, not to mention more complex messages, cannot make its way up or down through so many levels—an important communication lesson.

**Destroying Hierarchical Privilege**. Iverson answers his own phone. This eliminates an insulating layer and diminishes the chances that messages might become garbled. It means that Nucor can act with lightning speed.

Iverson's communicative style is best described as "open," if not dramatic. Preston says that he is given to shouting matches with employees, and, for the most part, they shout back. Iverson claims that about 60 percent of his decisions are correct, and the employees don't hesitate to let him know about the other 40 percent. Every effort is made, Iverson says, to "destroy hierarchical privilege." All employees, including Iverson, wear the same color hard hats in the plants (probably a unique practice in the steel industry, where hats are usually color-coded to represent hierarchical levels). There are no hunting lodges for the executives, no corporate planes or boats, not even a company car.

It is clear that Iverson not only listens to upward communication, he seeks it out. In his lecture, he identified the five elements that make up Nucor's communication philosophy:

1. Every employee must be made aware of exactly what is expected of him and her—and those expectations are "not low" at Nucor. (Women are now entering Nucor's workforce; Iverson claims they make the best crane operators.)

2. Every employee must have an understanding of the rewards, and these are formalized in writing.

3. Every employee has to know where to go to get help.

4. Every employee is encouraged to participate, to offer his or her ideas on all aspects of Nucor, including production.

5. Every employee deserves feedback on "how I, my group, and the company are doing."

There are certain similarities between these points and Redding's five elements in the Ideal Managerial Climate: particularly *participation, high expectations*, and *openness*. Redding might well reevaluate his IMC in light of the Nucor reality.

As word has spread about Nucor's success and unique structure, Iverson increasingly receives calls from executives at other companies asking for advice on how to reduce staff à la the Nucor model. They ask, "How can I fire all these people—some of whom are good friends of mine?" Iverson has no answers for them. He has never faced such a problem because Nucor has kept its corporate profile lean from the beginning.[5]

Iverson referred to a management workshop he had participated in that was conducted by Peter Drucker. Drucker is a legendary management professor, author of a shelf of books, and consultant to major corporations all over the world. This rang a bell because I had read and taught Drucker's (1988) article, "The Coming of the New Organization," in the *Harvard Business Review*. The article begins: "The typical large business 20 years hence will have fewer than half the levels of management of its counterpart today, and no more than a third the managers" (p. 45). Drucker claims that as many as six layers in contemporary organizations (which may have up to 14 layers from top to bottom) serve only as "relays," passing on messages from subordinates to superiors and vice versa. He predicts that traditional departments will disappear and be replaced by task-focused teams. This will require greater individual self-discipline and responsibility in regard to organizational communication.

As an example, Drucker mentioned the former British civil administration in India. The Indian civil service ran the country with an organization that never exceeded 1,000 employees. For most of its 200-year existence, the service's communication technology consisted of the quill pen and a system of barefoot runners. Organizational communication consisted mainly of a monthly report (which required a full day to write) from the district officer to the political secretary in the provincial capital, who, in turn wrote back a full response to the district officer. Although Drucker's example is unfortunate in that it involves the military control and discipline of an entire people by a colonial power, it does make the point that most of our present-day organizations are greatly overstaffed.

**No 'Relays.'** Drucker might well have used Nucor as a paradigm case, a model of the future organization. With its flat hierarchy, Nucor contains few if any "relay" managers. Its lean staff and minimal paperwork allow it to move more quickly than its competitors. For example, the construction of the plant in Crawfordsville was begun before the blueprints were completed, in contrast to the years of planning that Big Steel puts into opening a new facility.

As a negative example, Drucker might have selected IBM. Until recently, "Big Blue" was the very model of what was good about business in the United States. For much longer than Nucor, IBM has proudly maintained a policy of not laying off workers. But unlike Nucor, IBM grew, particularly around the waist, by creating layers and large staffs. During the waning years of the 1980s and the beginning of the 1990s, IBM realized that it was becoming fat and slow. On November 27, 1991, *The New York Times* reported that IBM had announced a sweeping overhaul of its organization. The goal was to create a federation of smaller, quicker organizations in place of the huge centralized bureaucracy. At least 20,000 employees had to be induced to leave the company in this "restructuring," so the company implemented an aggressive policy of encouraging employees to "retire." I know IBM retirees and transferees who say they had little choice in their reclassification. Thousands of people have retired or been forced out.

If IBM does recover, it will have to learn a new management art, one that Nucor has not had to learn: the art of "delayering" a bureaucracy, the elimination of hierarchical levels and the cadre of relays. If it does, IBM will perhaps join Nucor among the ranks of the organizations of the future.

Completing these thoughts about the future makes it possible and necessary to turn to the past. Our narrative begins in 1967.

## NOTES

1.   These anecdotes are based on a lecture I gave at the Helsinki University of Technology in 1990.

2.   Barnard, formerly chief executive of New Jersey Bell, wrote a seminal book that helped found the field of organizational communication entitled *The Functions of the Executive* (1938).

3.   Empowerment has recently become something of a buzzword in the U.S.   Everyone claims to promote if not practice it.   David K. Noller, a graduate student in the Department of Communication at the University of Colorado at Boulder, recently looked beyond the label in an effort to specify the four components of a Weberian Ideal Type of empowerment.   His tentative definition is summarized in the following paragraph:

> I would propose the following definition of "empowerment" in the spirit of a Weberian "ideal type."   We may speak of empowerment for an individual or a group of individuals in a   given situation or set of situations when the individual(s) has (have): 1) Full decision-making ability. 2) Complete responsibility for implementation of any decisions. 3) Complete access to relevant tools for both making decisions and implementing them.   4) The complete right/ responsibility to accept the consequences of any decisions made. This formulation may be remembered by the handy acronym of "DIT-C" (pronounced "ditzy").   The four components (decisions, implementation, tools, consequences) may even be thought of as the necessary and sufficient conditions for empowerment—although, because empowerment is offered here as an ideal type, it is not expected that the fullness of these conditions could normally be met in reality.   (Noller, 1991, p. 12)

Noller's playfulness about the "ditzy" acronym should not be taken as an excuse to dismiss the potential of his formulation.   His definition has some promise.   It also has the virtue of making empowerment difficult for the exploitative to commandeer and easy to detect when misused.   I note that responsibility is a key term in his model, supporting the notion that automatic responsibility (the practice and the ideal type) is at least a relative of empowerment.

4.   Kiianamaa later wrote up the case, under Siirala's continuing supervision, and then translated it from Finnish into English (Kiianmaa, 1991).   He and I subsequently wrote a paper about the role of transference in the development of organizational identification (Tompkins & Kiianmaa, 1991); I return to the topic later in this book.

5. The September 17, 1992, issue of *Rolling Stone* magazine carried an interview with the Democratic candidate for president, entitled "Bill Clinton: The Rolling Stone Interview" by William Greider, P.J. O'Rourke, Hunter S. Thompson, and Jann S. Wenner (pp. 40, 42, 43-44, 47, 51, 53, 55-56). A question was posed implying that the U.S. government is too responsive to "the biggest corporations." Clinton answered in the following way:

> That's right. . . . You also have to make clear distinctions between corporations. We've got a company in my state—Nucor—that's nonunion but has two steel mills, pays their workers an average of $42,000 a year. They get weekly bonuses, and no one has ever been laid off. When profits go down, bonuses go down. If Nucor loses money, the boss takes a bigger cut than the workers do.
>
> You don't want to generalize about [sic]—but this is not so much business versus labor; it is dumb versus smart. The really smart businesses today empower their workers, reward them for being productive, take care of their interests. I'm not going to ever be antibusiness, 'cause that's where the jobs are. But do we need more power concentrated in the hands of people who are going to take care of workers? You bet we do. (p. 53)

It is not obvious to me whether it is more unusual to hear a presidential candidate argue about organizational communication theory and practice or to see the topic discussed in *Rolling Stone*. Perhaps this illustrates that its time has arrived.

## Chapter Three

# THE MARSHALL SPACE CENTER AND THE APOLLO PROJECT

### The Ambiance in 1967

Civil rights and the war in Vietnam were the two most talked about concerns of the day. President Lyndon B. Johnson had been able to push Kennedy's civil rights bills through Congress. But despite his antiwar campaign rhetoric in the 1964 election campaign against Barry Goldwater, Johnson believed he could produce both "guns and butter," and after his election he stepped up the U.S. effort in Vietnam. An ardent promoter of the space program, he continued a high level of support for NASA.

As the U.S. casualties mounted in Vietnam, so did opposition to the war. Martin Luther King, Jr., who had become the most visible and effective leader of the civil rights movement, began speaking out against the war in February of 1967. In April, King proposed a merger of the civil-rights and anti-war movements and encouraged draft evasion. Later that summer, he called for a national campaign of disobedience to bring pressure on the government. King would be assassinated the following spring in Memphis, Tennessee.

Students at the University of Wisconsin forced the withdrawal of Dow Chemical Company recruiters from the campus. Demonstrations on April 15th drew 100,000 protestors in New York, 50,000 in San Francisco. The war, and conflicting responses to it, became a national obsession. Muhammed Ali was stripped of his heavyweight boxing title for evading the draft; later, he would go to prison for his crime.

The Six-Day War broke out on June 5th in the Middle East. Israel turned back an Arab invasion, wiped out the Soviet-supplied air forces of Egypt and Syria, and took the Golan Heights in Syria and the West Bank of the Jordan. The United Nations demanded that all actions be rescinded, but Israel ignored the order. The Soviet Union broke diplomatic relations with Israel.

### A Research Opportunity at MSFC

In 1967, I was an associate professor of communication at Wayne State University in Detroit, Michigan, having left Purdue University in 1965. Detroit had its own civil rights and anti-war movements, and its own counter-culture as well. I had been active as a volunteer in Johnson's War Against Poverty, which was based on the premise that poor people should be allowed to participate in how money allocated for programs should be spent so as to benefit most effectively their neighborhoods. I soon began to understand why we were losing the War Against Poverty. As indicated in Chapter Two, organizations that encourage and allow participation by those at the bottom are often more effective than those that do not. I found that professional social workers, still in power, were parental in dealing with their clients and found it difficult to delegate decision-making authority to them.

I received a phone call in January of 1967 from a total stranger who spoke with a German accent and said he was calling from Alabama. He identified himself as Walter Wiesman, then coordinator of internal communication at NASA's Marshall Space Flight Center in Huntsville. He had obtained my name from my Ph.D. adviser and former colleague at Purdue University, W. Charles Redding, and asked whether or not I would be interested in spending the summer as a consultant in organizational communication at the Marshall Center.

The summer faculty consultant was expected to review Wiesman's internal communication program and five-year plan and supervise research conducted by doctoral students in organizational communication. Wiesman had organized a conference on organizational communication for interested parties in government, business, and academic organizations, to take place in August of 1967. The consultant would deliver a lecture to the conference and help coordinate it. More importantly, the consultant would conduct a research inquiry into some aspect of organizational communication at the Marshall Center. The exact nature of the project would be decided after an orientation period. The consultant would be free to publish the results of his or her research.

Despite my concern about spending a summer in Alabama because of its race relations problems, I eagerly accepted the assignment. I was to begin in late June of 1967 but had to start on obtaining a security clearance immediately. My role was to be that of a participant observer, and I was treated as a salaried civil servant (GS-13) in almost every way.

As I drove from Detroit to Huntsville, I was alternately depressed by the radio news of the war and elated by the prospect of joining the Apollo Project, of becoming a participant in the Space Age. President John F. Kennedy had stirred me, as well as most Americans, with his special message to Congress on May 25, 1961: "I believe that this nation should commit itself to achieving the goal, before this decade is out, of landing a man on the moon and returning him safely to Earth." Heading south, I reflected on the fact that there were only three and a half years left in which to fulfill this commitment.

I had very little idea about what I was getting into at Marshall, which was NASA's largest field center. I knew that the director of MSFC was the legendary Wernher von Braun and that the mission of the Marshall Center was rockets. In 1967 its main concern was the Saturn V, the mighty moon rocket which, if successful, would enable the U.S. to overtake the Soviet Union in the Space Race. Ever since the Soviet Union had demonstrated its apparent superiority in space by launching Sputnik, the first artificial satellite, in 1957, the United States had suffered from a technological inferiority complex, intensified by the fervent anti-communist sentiments of the period.

### The Ambiance in Huntsville

I arrived in Huntsville at night, too late to move into the furnished apartment Walter Wiesman had arranged for me, so I checked into a cheap motel on Huntsville's "strip," picked up some hamburgers and beer, and repaired to my rather seedy accommodations. What I had seen so far of Huntsville had not made a favorable first impression: A sleazy strip of neon-lit honky tonks and country music were the salient sights and sounds I experienced that first night. I moved into my apartment the following day, June 23, 1967, three days before I was scheduled to begin work at the Marshall Center. I was fairly faithful in keeping a journal during this period. As a single man who knew no one in Huntsville, I had plenty of time for my "Alabama Journal."

I began to explore my surroundings and the culture of the Deep South. I had visited the South only once before and had been disturbed by the blatant racial inequality I had observed there. Selma, Alabama, after all, had been the focus of civil rights activities only two years earlier and a white northerner of liberal racial views, Viola Liuzzo, had been fatally shot in Alabama during that same period. As I explored my apartment complex, no blacks were to be seen. I saw only white people at the two swimming pools; some of them spoke German. The morning newspaper was an incredible—my journal used the word "uncredible"—rag. It railed against federal spending on the editorial page and assailed Congressional cuts in the NASA budget on the front page. Numerous accounts of violence, shootings, and knifings were chronicled, most committed in the honky-tonks surrounding Huntsville.

Music was an important companion. In Huntsville, country and western music was inescapable, and it was something of a surprise to discover an FM classical music radio station. I noted hearing Richard Strauss' *Ein Heldenleben*, Yehudi Menuhin playing Mozart's *Fifth Violin Concerto,* and Richard Strauss' *Thus Sprach Zarathrusta*. It was clear that the station seemed to favor Germanic music. There was even a "German Hour" with news from the Federal Republic—in German, of course. Later, I would learn that some of the Marshall Center's German engineers had been invited to join a chamber music group, which grew into the Huntsville Symphony Orchestra. (A brief history of the German involvement in the U.S. space program appears later in this chapter.)

The German question was thus much on my mind, which led me, somewhat uncomfortably, to consider the Nazi question. Had not von Braun done Hitler's bidding by building the formidable V-2 rockets that had wreaked so much death and destruction on England and the Low Countries? Was it wise for the U.S. to turn its missile and rocket programs over to an ex-Nazi? Had Walter Wiesman been a Nazi? Had I been conscripted by a gang of closet fascists?

On Sunday night, June 25th, I met Walter and Erica Wiesman. They took me to the U.S. Army Officers' Club for dinner, and I found them to be charming people with broad interests. "Huntsville is not part of Alabama," they assured me. Since 1950, the population had increased from 25,000 people to 150,000 and so had its level of sophistication. Huntsville had experienced relatively little racial strife compared to other Alabama cities such as Selma and Montgomery. I asked the Wiesmans how Huntsville had weathered McCarthyism. This was my oblique way of probing their political attitudes.

"I was one of the first to give speeches against McCarthy," Wiesman replied. "I used to begin by saying: 'I burned books for Hitler—but I was 12 years old and didn't know what I was doing.' " Erica referred to "our short life under the dictator" and the horrors of war. My curiosity was somewhat satisfied, my fears quelled.

## The Space Center

June 26th was my first day at the Space Center. I was a part of what was called the Manpower Office, working under Wiesman. He was the youngest—"the kid," as they called him—of the German Rocket Team, the 120 experts that von Braun had brought with him to Texas during "Operation Paperclip" (the code name for the U.S. Army's interrogation and recruitment of the team after the war). Wiesman was one of the few non-technical members of the team. From his reading and observations he had concluded that communication was the essence of organization and management. Earlier, he had been responsible for innovations in organizational communication at the Redstone Arsenal. Because of his interest in the field, he had joined several professional and academic communication organizations, met W. Charles Redding, and was in turn referred to me.

## Wiesman's Program

Wiesman had developed a highly organized network of internal communication at Marshall to deal with its 7,000 employees. He had systematized the layout and use of the Center's bulletin boards. Specialized newsletters were published regularly, directed from management to various "audiences" he had identified among the Center's employees. Wiesman gave illustrated lectures on communication and supervision to every office and laboratory that would hear him. He developed a five-year plan for improving internal communication within the Center, one step of which was to bring in an academic summer consultant in organizational communication. My journal entry for that first day at the Center read: "Exciting. Walt *believes* the textbooks." This was no academic exercise, however, for Wiesman had tentatively decided that I would interview von Braun and other top managers.

*Walter Wiesman and the author, Phillip K. Tompkins, in the summer of 1967*

On my second day of work, I attended a meeting of the Advanced Systems Operations, a "think tank" within the Center devoted to planning for space flight as far into the future as 1992. (Some members of the group, I was told, served as consultants to Stanley Kubrick during the filming of *2001: A Space Odyssey.*) Wiesman was scheduled to speak to the group, and I went along as part of my orientation. Before Wiesman spoke, the deputy director of the unit reported on a recent Staff and Board meeting, which included the top 50 or 60 officials at the Center. Coincidentally, the subject of organizational communication came up in the report. James Webb, the top official of NASA in Washington, was report edly upset that he had been ignorant of certain problems within the agency that had emerged during investigations of the Apollo 204 accident. A fire in the Saturn V command module had claimed the lives of three astronauts, Virgil "Gus" Grissom, Edward White, and Roger Chaffee. They were killed in the capsule while running routine tests on the ground. The Marshall Center had only been responsible for the Saturn V rocket, not the module, I was told. The chief blame lay with the Manned Space Center (now the Johnson Space Center in Houston) and with the contractors they had supervised. The accident, and its subsequent investigations, had delayed the moon program.[1] I was impressed by the substance of this discussion. It was a demonstration of how MSFC worked both *at* and *on* organizational communication.

Walter Wiesman then gave his speech. He emphasized the importance of organizational communication, stressing that technical people often forget the *human* side of work when they accept supervisory responsibilities. His pitch was masterful and very well received.

### A Brief History of the German Rocket Team

That afternoon, I asked Wiesman about the background of the rocket program in Germany, as I needed to learn the history of the organization. The program had been centered in Peenemünde on the Baltic. Von Braun had received his Ph.D. in physics at the age of 22 from the University of Berlin and became the top civilian manager of the program. Wiesman joined the group as a young Luftwaffe corporal in mufti and served as a non-technical staff assistant to the center. The rigidity and regulations at Peenemünde made him realize early on the importance of open lines of communication.

I asked about von Braun's relationship with Hitler. Wiesman related an incident in which Hitler asked von Braun to make a presentation about the V-2 rocket program. The Führer was impressed and promptly pronounced von Braun a "Professor" (a titular state honor that did not carry any academic weight). Heinrich Himmler, the head of the SS, tried to take over the Peenemünde Works and, when frustrated by a lack of success, had von Braun thrown in jail. The crime was "defeatism." Von Braun was accused of the crime of being more interested in space travel than in military rocketry. *To be thrown in jail by Himmler is not a bad character reference,* I thought. Furthermore, none of the Paperclip 120 was found to have any use for Nazi ideology. My appetite was satisfied, and my conscience was clear.[2]

Wiesman also explained how the Huntsville Germans had come to work for the U.S. Army. Toward the end of the war, with the Russians approaching from the East, von Braun and the others were ordered to defend the Peenemünde Works to the last man. Von Braun called a meeting of his top people and let them debate whether to stay and be captured by the Russians or flee to the West and surrender to the Americans.

The group chose the latter course. Wiesman somehow commandeered a train, loaded up the team and important documents, and headed toward Berlin, where they transferred to an anti-aircraft railroad car. Their destination was a mountain hideout in Bavaria where they waited for the American advance to reach them. Von Braun's younger brother, Magnus, was sent to offer their surrender.

*Original Peenemünde team in Fort Bliss before moving to Huntsville (U.S. Space & Rocket Center archives photo)*

After lengthy interrogations, only those Germans deemed not to be fervent believers in Nazi ideology were recruited to work for the U.S. Army. Then they were transported to Fort Bliss, Texas, where they spent five years testing and refining the V-2 rocket. In 1950 they were transferred to the Army's Redstone Arsenal and during the next ten years developed most of America's Cold War missile arsenal: the Hermes A-1, Redstone, Jupiter, Jupiter C, Juno II, and

the Pershing missiles. The team also built and launched the West's first satellite. There is evidence that they could have accomplished this feat before Sputnik had not the Eisenhower administration forbidden them to do so until the Navy's Vanguard Project succeeded. Only when Vanguard failed was the Redstone group allowed to place the first U.S. satellite into orbit.

NASA was established in 1958. The von Braun team chose, despite the Army's protests, to leave the Army for the space agency. The George C. Marshall Space Flight Center was officially activated on July 1, 1960, with von Braun as director. It would be NASA's main field center for the development of rockets and propulsion systems.

**Orientation at Marshall**

As part of my orientation, Walt Wiesman arranged several tours of the huge campus-like space center for me. I visited the design and manufacturing labs and "clean" rooms, and watched astronauts simulate neutral gravity with scuba gear and weights in a tank of water. Rockets and boosters were tested in ingenious ways to imitate the tortures of space flight. Giant shake tables, like huge backyard swings with locomotive drive rods, mimicked the stresses of launch. Most exciting was the test of the mighty F-1 engine (five of which were clustered at the base of the Saturn V moon rocket). I was shown into a concrete bunker from where we watched the test through a slit. Outside, on a patch of red Alabama dirt, sat the mighty engine, held in place by a towering test stand. The rocket blast would roll off a special metal deflector at a 35-degree angle. Cold water began to run down the shields and deflector during the ignition countdown. My guide, an engineer, explained that this would prevent the test stand from melting. "Think of a rocket engine as a kind of controlled and continuous explosion," he told me.

The explosion was the loudest sound I have ever heard: 1,500,000 pounds of thrust from one rocket engine. As the flames hit the water, a vast cloud of steam engulfed the test stand; enormous clouds of smoke roiled skyward. Trees several hundred yards away bent over backwards from the shock waves. Then the roar abruptly ceased.

"Why didn't the engine launch the test stand?" I asked in the uncanny silence.

My guide answered, "It's the difference between starting to tow a car with a chain that's either slack or taut. We do not allow the engines to lunge at the test stand."

As my orientation period progressed, I could not help but notice the relative absence of blacks in important jobs at the Marshall Center and made a point of spending some time with a personnel specialist whose job today might be called director of affirmative action. He convinced me that Marshall was making a sincere effort to bring more blacks into the workforce. There was a dilemma, however: It was virtually impossible to persuade black engineers educated at MIT or Cal Tech to move to Alabama. Further, he explained, applicants from what were then called "negro colleges" often majored in such subjects as "electricity"; their technical training was simply inadequate for space research and development.

Therefore, Marshall was stymied in its attempt to recruit qualified blacks. Its short-range policy was to hire them for non-technical but highly visible positions, such as tour-guides for the Space Center's throngs of curious visitors. This public relations strategy, it was hoped, would help persuade the world that blacks were welcome to work at Marshall. (I reflected on this conversation years later when a black mission specialist, Ronald Erwin McNair, perished in the *Challenger* explosion.)

The problem of race relations nonetheless penetrated even the predominantly lily-white Marshall Center. Since the Watts riots of 1965 in Los Angeles, two years earlier, the prospect of a "long, hot summer" in U.S. cities was a matter of concern, if not fear, for many Americans. Members of the Executive Staff at Marshall, a large group of experts who gave support of a technical and political nature to the director (in relations with Congress and the administrative branch), thought they could ameliorate the problems of the cities. I was surprised to learn they were conducting some brainstorming about and preliminary analyses of the problem. A tentative idea they mentioned to me was to provide air conditioning for black ghettoes. Their confidence and "can-do" attitude led them to believe they could solve any problem. (I was not surprised to learn a year later that when NASA headquarters got wind of these plans, it brought them to an abrupt halt.)

## Mean Cuisine

If I arrived at the Space Center early enough, I would stop at the cafeteria for breakfast. After trying grits (coarsely ground corn cooked to the consistency of porridge) twice, I gave up forever. But I did become fond of—almost addicted to—those Southern breakfast biscuits enclosing a spicy, pepper-ridden sausage patty. For lunch, I usually stopped at one of the Center's several cafeterias, except on an occasional Friday when Walt Wiesman and I would treat ourselves to the Officer's Club at the Redstone Arsenal. If things had gone well during the week, we allowed ourselves a vodka martini.

At the end of the workday, I would usually race back to my apartment for a dip in the pool, a respite from those humid summer afternoons. I seldom cooked at home, preferring the fare of Boots', the Black Angus, the Steak Barn, El Palacio, and the Piccadilly Cafeteria. Nothing fancy, but consistently good eating. I learned about the Carriage Inn, the best restaurant in town, from Walt Wiesman. It was located in an unassuming cinder-block motel, but the dining room served continental cuisine and fine wines. The first time I dropped by, I was amused by the cosmopolitan crowd at the bar: a white professor, a German engineer, an Austrian maitre d', and a black army officer. A mustachioed gentleman in tweeds, with hair long enough to qualify him as a hippy, approached the Chinese bartender to place his order.

"Haig and Haig," he said in an impeccable Oxbridge accent.

"Mix?"

"None."

"Ice?"

"I should *hope* not!"

This incident illustrates the schizophrenic culture of Huntsville in 1967. The Army and NASA were dramatically changing the culture of the region. It was at once the most provincial and the most sophisticated of locales.

## The Arsenal Concept

As I developed a better grasp of how the organization functioned, I learned about the history of NASA's methods for dealing with its contractors. Early on, NASA had to decide whether to follow the U.S. Army approach or the Air Force approach. At that time the Army and Air Force had radically different modes of generating their weapon systems. Under its "arsenal" concept of developing weapons, the Army had maintained an in-house technical capability which permitted it to conduct its own research and development (R&D), including the capability of manufacturing weapons prototypes. Thus, the Army had a yardstick by which to measure the efforts and costs of its contractors.

The Air Force, by contrast, maintained very little technical expertise, relying instead on private contractors to propose new weapon systems, conduct R&D, and manufacture the weapons. As a consequence, the Air Force lacked the means to assure quality control of what it was buying and to monitor costs. However, this approach proved to be rhetorically (which in this case is to say politically) effective with Congress. The larger the corps of contractors, the larger the lobby for the Air Force. According to Nieburg (1966) and information provided by MSFC personnel, such a system generated a large, geographically diffuse team of senators and representatives to vote for higher military appropriations, which, in turn, were translated by the contractors into jobs and payrolls in their legislative districts back home.

When James E. Webb became administrator of NASA in 1961, he wanted to eschew the arsenal concept in favor of the Air Force's contract system. According to Nieburg (1966), NASA officials sought to dismantle the Marshall Center's in-house capability. MSFC, fearing the consequences of breaking its yardstick, resisted this attempt mightily, and the ensuing struggle produced long-term tension between MSFC and NASA headquarters. Von Braun and his colleagues wanted not only to do the R&D for the Saturn V, they wanted to build the rockets at the Marshall Center. NASA reportedly overruled them.

### Organizational Structure of MSFC: A Mitosis

In Germany, in the U.S. Army, and initially at NASA, von Braun had acted as a kind of chief engineer, supervising the efforts of ten or more laboratories during the R&D and initial manufacturing stages. But as the tasks multiplied with the creation of the Apollo Program and the goal of sending men to the moon, the team had to change its methods and organizational structure. The Mercury and Gemini programs had used upgraded Redstone missiles, but Apollo required the creation of new rocket technologies. This led to the development of the Saturn series, culminating in the Saturn V. The organization had to grow, and it did so by *mitosis* (a form of metamorphosis by which a living cell divides into two separate organizations), the two divisions bound together at the top by the director's office. This growth period for MSFC followed the pattern described by Barnard (1938) of all complex organizations: "[All] organizations of complex character grow out of small, simple organizations. It is impossible for formal organizations to grow except by the process of combining unit organizations already existing, or the creation of new units of organization" (p. 104).

**RDO and IO**

The muscle of the MSFC organization was supplied by its laboratories. They were retained in much the same form they had taken in the Peenemünde days under the organizational title of Research and Development Operations (RDO). RDO was organized along the lines of various science and engineering disciplines. There were 12 laboratories in 1967: the Advanced Systems Office (futurists); Systems Engineering (integrators); the Aero-Astrodynamics Lab (trajectories); the Astrionics Lab (electrical engineering); the Computational Lab (computer science and service); the Manufacturing Engineering Lab (prototype builders); Propulsion & Vehicle Engineering (rocket motors); the Test Lab; the Space Sciences Lab (astrophysics); the Quality & Reliability Assurance Lab; and two small units, Experiments and Operations Management. Personnel in RDO continued to "keep their hands dirty," a high engineering value, with R&D and some fabrication, but now they were working alongside thousands of the contractors' engineers and managers.

In the mitosis of MSFC, the new division of the organization, created for the Apollo Program and to accommodate NASA headquarters, was called Industrial Operations (IO). The chief responsibility of IO was to direct and monitor the efforts of prime contractors. (Over 100,000 people in the public and private sectors were involved in the Apollo Project). IO was also organized into offices relating to the various programs or projects for which the Center was responsible. The Saturn V Program Office, for example, monitored R&D and manufacturing for the huge rocket. It was further divided into project offices, each specializing in the various stages and engines of the Saturn V.

## NATIONAL AERONAUTICS AND SPACE ADMINISTRATION
# GEORGE C. MARSHALL SPACE FLIGHT CENTER

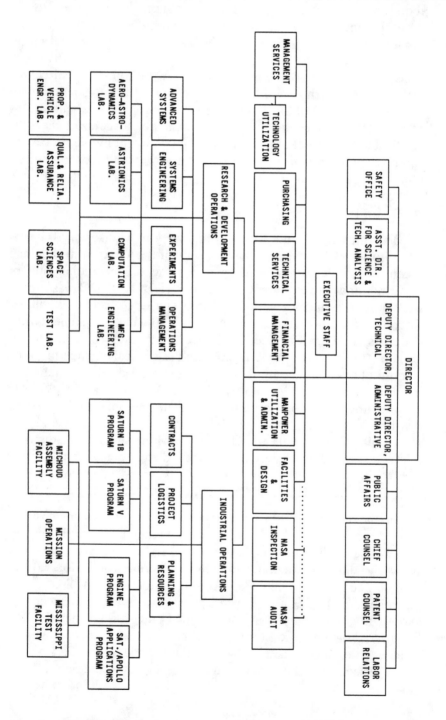

**Project Management**

The theory of project management, new at the time, was that personnel could shift from office to office as projects and programs came and went. Each rocket was managed by a matrix[3] of offices, one concentrating on the whole, others on individual stages and engines. This created a part-whole relationship and a certain degree of redundancy. The program and project managers in IO could ask for help from RDO as well as from the contractors they were monitoring. Von Braun described the changes during my first interview with him: "We went through a metamorphosis into a management organization—monitoring and detecting. We went from a do-it organization to see-that-it-is-done job. We had to hire many new people and new occupations, such as accountants."

Both RDO and IO reported to their respective directors, who, in turn, reported to the director of the Center, von Braun. For the first time in his experience, there was a level of management between von Braun and the laboratory directors. He was assisted by two deputy directors, one for technical matters, the other for administrative affairs. Various staff offices were also connected to the director's office.

After mastering the organization chart and visiting most of the offices and labs, I had a good grasp of the structure of the Center. I would soon come to understand the dynamics of the organization by sitting in on briefings for von Braun and from formal interviews with the top managers.

**The First Interview with Von Braun**

My initial meeting with von Braun was scheduled for July 24. Walt Wiesman had arranged the appointment and walked me over to the tall, gray cement-and-glass building housing the management group. When we exited the elevator, we were guided to our destination by a black woman who served very conspicuously as the floor receptionist.

We ran into von Braun outside his office. He was a handsome man with a large smile. I noticed a scar above his lip, suffered, I was later told, as the result of an automobile accident during the race to flee Peenemünde and surrender to the Americans.

He invited me in. As Wiesman started to leave, von Braun called out for him to stay and listen to the interview. "Don't be so goddamn lazy," he joked. Von Braun sat at the head of the table; his assistant Jim Shepherd and I sat on the left side, with Walt Wiesman opposite us on the right.

To my opening question about the importance of organizational communication at Marshall, he responded in the following way:

> In such a dynamic organization you have to keep up, keep the organization informed from top to bottom. People with problems and suggestions must be able to get the attention of top management. Communication up must be free, not tied to channels, if management is to be kept informed. However, there must be a clear action and command channel. Closed and open loops. For example, there are weekly reports from lab directors and project engineers in RDO and from project managers in IO which bypass intermediate layers of management, but directives go back down through Mr. Weidner [Director of RDO] and General O'Connor [Director of IO].

It would take weeks for me to completely understand what von Braun meant in practical terms by "bypassing," "action and command channel," and "open and closed loops." He spoke rapidly, with a slight accent, praising Walt Wiesman's five-year organizational communication plan. It was clear that for von Braun, upward-directed communication was crucial.

> This [MSFC] is like being in the earthquake prediction business. You put out your sensors. You want them to be sensitive enough, but you don't want to get drowned in noise. We have enough sensors, even in industry. There are a lot of inputs about trouble. Some are too sensitive; they overreact. Someone else might underestimate. You want to know the name of the guy. Is he one of the perennial panic-makers? Some guys always cry for help. You need balance in the system—to react to the critical things. Exposure teaches you how to react. Some create problems and then proudly announce they have solved them. Others make a lot of noise just to get the mule's attention.

As I typed up my copious notes after the interview, I thought to myself, *he must have heard the story about the farmer who hits the mule in the head with a two-by-four.* I also realized that he had a keen understanding of what my field calls "source credibility," that he appreciated the need to read his "sensors," or sources, carefully.

## Riots in Detroit

On July 24, after a pleasant dinner with the Wiesmans, I received a phone call from friends back home. Detroit was in flames. My friends had the impression that the whole city was burning as a result of a race riot. I had no television set, and the radio news was sketchy.

Detroit had experienced a major race riot in 1943. Since then the city had achieved considerable progress in integration. There was no single ghetto; blacks lived in nearly all parts of the city. The suburbs of Detroit were another matter, and one Detroit politician called them a "white noose" around the neck of the city.

Later in the week it appeared that the rioting had not abated. The National Guard was called in, and Federal Troops followed. *Somebody should have established an "earthquake prediction system" in Detroit,* I thought to myself. Von Braun's metaphor for stimulating and listening to upward-directed communication from those at the bottom worked to avert technological disasters. Why wouldn't the same philosophy and techniques of communication work to avert such *social* disasters?

### An Expanded Study

Soon after my first interview with von Braun, it was decided that I should enlarge my sampling from nine or ten to 45 to 50 engineers and scientists. However, I was warned that a recent questionnaire survey of morale had irritated employees. They did not like the reductionist forced-choice options.

We decided that from now on the interviews were to be anonymous so as to guarantee a candid discussion of problems. My interview guide was simple and flexible. I would ask: What is working well, and what isn't? Answers to these questions, as well as the occasional non-answers, would be subjected to probes. If a particular topic did not surface, I would bring it up and ask in a neutral way what the interviewee knew and thought about it. This would help to indicate that I already understood the organization fairly well. It also helped that the interviewees knew that the results were going to be reported to the director and the entire organization. (In other words, the possibility of organizational change made them open up.) Von Braun sent a memorandum to all of the prospective interviewees, summarizing my credentials and asking them to cooperate.

### Shepherd's Three Problems

Before the interviews got started, Jim Shepherd, von Braun's assistant who had sat in on my initial interview with von Braun, called me over to his office. He wanted me to help him solve three particular problems while working concurrently on the larger study.

The first problem had to do with the Saturn V Control Center. I had been given a standard tour of the facility during my orientation and was impressed. It was a huge room with an oversized conference table in the center. The walls were covered with floor-to-ceiling charts. These graphic displays tracked every vehicle of the Saturn V rocket series as well as the time intervals between events, using PERT (Program Evaluation and Review Technique), a technique widely used by the Defense Department, NASA, and industry. A crew of attendants posted milestone stickers on the charts as each step was completed. The charts indicated what tasks had moved into the "critical path" and who was responsible for completing them. These displays also showed the remaining steps and their completion deadlines in order to meet the schedule for the project.

Shepherd explained the problem: "Administrator [James E.] Webb believes in the Control Center so much that he brought 75 university people to see it. He wants them to create a curriculum around it and have students come in and critique us. But we aren't all that sold on the Control Center. Mr. Webb wants to establish a total management concept for government. So the first question for you, Phil, is how valid and timely are the data in that room?"

I said I would work on it.

The second problem was about briefings and reviews. "You get a briefing and it's canned," Shepherd complained. "The briefers use alphabet soup: acronyms like ICN and ICD and so on. I don't believe half the guys hearing a briefing understand it. Even von Braun doesn't understand some of this stuff. We need a set of guidelines for briefings."

Again, I said I would work on it.

The third problem had been created by the success of what were known as the "Monday Notes."[4] After the elaborate investigation of the fire in which Grissom, White, and Chaffee were killed, everyone had realized that von Braun was the best informed person in NASA. People asked how that was possible, and they found out about the Monday Notes. As a result, James Webb decided that NASA headquarters should receive a similar weekly report. "We're supposed to send it to Mueller," Shepherd said, "and he'll excerpt from it for Webb. But the problem is what should we send them? What should we take from the notes to von Braun? If material is misunderstood or taken out of context, what problems will that cause us the next week?"

I was glad that Shepherd had given me these problems to work on. Now I would have some specific, directive questions to ask if my general questions drew blank stares. It also meant that I would have to get back to him with a preliminary report before making my more general report to von Braun.

As I began the interviews, moving from office to office and from lab to lab, I began to understand the dynamics of the organizational communication system, the nervous system that connected the brain to the muscles at Marshall. I conducted interviews with top management, the directors of RDO and IO, the director of each laboratory and RDO office, the chiefs and managers of the IO offices (with the exception of Arthur Rudolph, the Saturn V Program Manager because his frequent trips did not fit my busy schedule of interviews), and the chiefs of all the staff offices. The reader will note the preponderance of German surnames in the following partial list of interviewees. This conveys a flavor of the culture and structure of the organization in 1967.

Director: Wernher von Braun
Deputy Director, Technical: E.F.M. Rees
Deputy Director, Administrative: H.H. Gorman
Director, Research and Development Operations: H.K. Weidner
Director, Industrial Operations: E.F. O'Connor
Director, Aero-Astrodynamics Laboratory: E.D. Geissler
Director, Astrionics Laboratory: W. Haeussermann
Director, Computation Laboratory: H. Hoelzer
Director, Manufacturing Engineering Laboratory: W.R. Kuers
Director, Propulsion & Vehicle Engineering Laboratory: W.R. Lucas
Manager, Mission Operations Office: F.A. Speer

Manager, Michoud Assembly Facility: G.N. Constan
Manager, Mississippi Test Facility: J.M. Balch

The last two interviews necessitated trips to New Orleans and Hancock County, Mississippi. At the Michoud Assembly Facility in New Orleans, I watched Boeing workers assemble stages of the giant moon rocket under the supervision of Marshall Center managers and engineers, and I learned that the distance—the lack of propinquity—between New Orleans and Huntsville created some communication problems. Also, the Mississippi Test Facility (MTF) had been built in what had been thought to be an isolated region so that the testing of the rocket engines would be neither a danger nor a nuisance to local residents. During construction, however, it was discovered that the area was riddled with moonshine stills. Further, at MTF I learned first-hand about communication problems that can occur when a complex organization works around the clock. A day shift had begun fueling a rocket for a static test; later, the night shift somehow failed to receive the message that the fueling had already been started and the tanks were inadvertently filled beyond capacity. The result was an explosion.

I opened each interview with the question, What works well? Invariably, the answer was "The Monday Notes."

## The Monday Notes

The Monday Notes came into being during the growth stage of the organization. Kurt Debus, one of the Paperclip 120, had always been in charge of launch operations for the organization. During a period when Debus was away at Cape Canaveral supervising a launch, von Braun felt his lack of propinquity diminished vital communication between the two of them. He asked Debus to send him a weekly one-page note every week from the Cape, describing the week's progress and problems.

Finding that he looked forward to reading the weekly note, von Braun decided that a similar note from other key managers would help keep him informed. He asked almost two dozen managers (all of whom I interviewed), lab directors in RDO, and project managers in IO who were removed from him by *at least one layer of management* to send him a weekly, one-page note summarizing the week's progress and problems. Simplicity was the key. There was no form to be filled out. The requirements: no more than one page, headed by the date and the name of the contributor. They were due in von Braun's office each Monday morning. In this way, a layer of management was bypassed on the way up, inasmuch as the RDO and IO directors did not edit these notes.

As von Braun read each note, he initialed it and wrote the date in the upper right-hand corner. (The first time I saw a set of the notes, the teacher in me automatically flipped through them looking for an "A" paper.) He also added a considerable amount of marginalia in his own handwriting, asking questions, making suggestions, and dishing out praise. The notes of July 10, 1967, for example, include a hand-written question directed to a manager about some vehicle cost figures he had included in his note: "Have we passed this on to Mueller [a NASA headquarters official]? B." There is the suggestion to another manager that a new computer mentioned in his note "could be immensely useful for earth resources surveys from orbit. B." To a lab director, whose earlier recommendations about the superiority of one kind of weld over another had been rejected and who had conducted additional tests which supported his original position, von Braun wrote, "Looks like you won after all! Congrats. B."

These collected and annotated notes, arranged in alphabetical order by the authors' surnames, were reproduced and returned as a package to all of the contributors. What was the organizational effect of this simple, yet innovative communicative activity? I put that question to each of the contributors. The answer came back as almost totally unqualified praise for the device. The reasons offered to me in support for this praise are worth examining.

The first advantage should be obvious. The notes served as another method, in addition to briefings and memoranda, for the director to be kept informed of problems and progress.

There were other advantages. For example, the managers pointed out the crucial horizontal or *lateral function.* Each lab director learned what all the other laboratories had been up to during the previous week; in addition, units in IO knew about the activities in RDO and vice versa, which often stimulated the horizontal communication needed to maintain coordination of the 'projects. A good illustration of this occurred during the interviewing period. A lab director mentioned to me that the recently arrived Monday Notes revealed a need for him to telephone a project manager in IO about a mutual problem.  By chance, my next interview happened to be with that very project manager in IO. Coincidentally, while talking about the Monday Notes, he volunteered that he had discovered a suggestion in the notes that made him realize that he needed to telephone the lab director whose office I had just left.

The marginalia supplied by von Braun made the notes "the most diligently read document" at MSFC, according to a lab director. This crucial *feedback function* was mentioned by nearly every contributor.  Employees saw how the boss reacted to the week's work in their own units, as well as his response to other contributors' notes.

Another desirable effect mentioned by most of the interviewees was closely related to this feedback function.  Because von Braun found it increasingly necessary to travel to California, the Cape, Washington, D.C., and other locations, the Monday Notes "kept the channels open" during the times of decreased or limited face-to-face communication.

The notes also served as an antidote to the sterile, formalized procedures that dominated much of the Marshall Center's activities. The contributors derived considerable satisfaction from the *personalized* nature of the notes, a break from the code-numbered, U.S. Government-NASA-MSFC format designating the lab or office from which it emanated.  Just the name and the date were all that was required.  The contributors also derived satisfaction from the *informality, quickness,* and *frankness* of the notes.  In regard to frankness, some rather fierce arguments were carried out in the notes.  One unit's notes of the previous week might be challenged by the following week's notes from another unit.  This controversy, said one lab director, gave the notes their particular "charm."  Another lab director said with a smile, "We sometimes misuse them—to get attention."  In other words, the notes provided a public forum and, in some cases, a kind of court of last resort.

During my interviews, I discovered something that von Braun and most of the others did not realize.  Curious about how the 24 contributors generated the content of their weekly notes, I systematically asked about their procedures.  In most cases the lab director would ask his subordinates, the division chiefs, to provide him with a Friday Note about their activities. (During the summer of 1968, I had the opportunity to interview 14 division chiefs; most of them reported that they requested a similar note from their subordinates, branch chiefs, and so on.)

Moreover, some of the directors and managers organized meetings to determine what should be put in next week's notes and to discuss von Braun's responses to the most recent packet of notes. Relevant portions of the notes were reproduced for distribution down the line. In short, von Braun's simple request for a weekly note had generated a *rigorous and regularly recurring discipline of communication* within the organization. Once a week, almost every supervisor in the organization paused to reflect on what needed to be communicated up the line. Lab directors and project managers stopped to read what their peers had communicated to the director and how he had responded.

"Excellent," "best thing we do," and "remarkable innovation" were some of the evaluations made to me by the interviewees. One former military officer said that such a practice, the conscious bypassing of levels, could not have been tolerated in a military organization. Indeed, it is difficult to imagine such a practice in other civil service organizations. One comment, prompted by a discussion of the Monday Notes, made a comparison between von Braun's atypical emphasis on upward-directed communication and the downward-directed communication at the Center. Said one manager in IO, "If we only had something coming *down* the line as powerful as the Monday Notes."

The Monday Notes illustrate two general principles in von Braun's philosophy of organizational communication—*conflict* and *redundancy*—that were manifested in other ways as well. As indicated above, some rather heated conflicts surfaced in the notes from time to time, as well as in briefings and memoranda. My interviewees sometimes tried to draw me into the conflicts in hopes that I would advocate their side to von Braun. Occasionally I did. Usually I intervened when von Braun asked me to look into this or that controversy. Conflict was natural to such a large organization, and much of it was petty. Von Braun had a positive attitude toward conflict and sought to encourage it; perhaps he had even engineered the means to impress it into the very structure of the organization.

The principle of redundancy was also built into the system, not only in the normal sense of syntactic or semantic redundancy, as a property of messages, but in the sense of redundant *channels* as well. To assure that no problems "fell through the cracks," more channels than were logically or ideally necessary had been built into the system. Whether it was a conscious decision or not, this was a case of life imitating technology. To achieve the high degree of reliability needed for manned space flight, the design philosophy of the Apollo Project was to engineer every component to be as reliable as possible and also build in a backup system in case the original failed. This technological redundancy saved more than one of the Apollo flights. In the practice of the Monday Notes, for example, one might read the reports of the static firing of F-1 engines in the note supplied by IO's Engine Program Office, in the note supplied by RDO's Test Laboratory, and perhaps in others. In addition, the director might hear about the test results while visiting a lab or office, or perhaps in a briefing or telephone conversation.

**Automatic Responsibility**

One of the most remarkable concepts in von Braun's philosophy and practice of organizational communication came up during these interviews. I had come across a paper he had given at a conference in French Lick, Indiana, entitled "Building a Research Team." He said that at the Marshall Center the laboratories "have full cognizance and *responsibility* for all efforts that fall within the purview of their respective disciplines, including active projects, further project studies, and supporting research work. . . . [The lab director] is expected *automatically* to participate in all projects that involve his discipline and to carry his work through to its conclusion [emphasis added]."

My interviewees called this concept "automatic responsibility" and explained that it had long been part of the organization's method of operation. In practice, it meant, for instance, that an electrical engineer working in the Astrionics Lab, assumed automatic responsibility for any problem he perceived to fall within his area of competence, regardless of whether or not the task had been assigned to his lab. He was expected to stay with the problem until it was solved. I heard a story about the case of an American-born engineer who assumed responsibility for a problem and wound up recommending a solution opposed both by his superior and much of the technical talent at the Center. However, in the end he was found to be correct and was subsequently rewarded with a top management post.

If the person who perceived a problem lacked the technical ability to see it through to its conclusion, he or she then assumed the responsibility for communicating his or her perceptions of the problem up the line so that top management, thus alerted, could direct the appropriate specialists to it. Automatic responsibility sometimes ruffled the feathers of certain managers who felt other people should tend to their own affairs, but such irritations were thought to be worth the price because the system guaranteed that problems would receive the attention they deserved.

A question arose during the metamorphosis from a "do-it" organization to a "see-that-it-is-done" organization. Should automatic responsibility be continued under new arrangements in which contractors were to be given much of the responsibility for engineering and fabrication? The answer came from von Braun on August 16, 1962, in what he called "MSFC Management Policy Statement #1." "In the past," wrote the director, "such a paper was needless . . . . As in the past, the [lab] director is expected to participate *automatically* in all projects that involve his discipline and to carry his work through to conclusion." Automatic responsibility was definitely to continue in effect.

I made two observations about automatic responsibility in an article about my research at the Marshall Center (Tompkins, 1977). The first: This was a radical departure from typical bureaucratic practice. It was such a radical innovation that since 1967 I have found few executives who felt they could administer such a principle. They feared it would foster anarchy. How could you run an assembly line with such a principle? they asked. Perhaps, I often answered, it would help turn out a better product. Then I discovered Nucor (the innovative steel-making company discussed in Chapter Two). According to Kenneth Iverson, CEO of Nucor, the company practices something quite close to automatic responsibility. The reader will recall Iverson's opposition to unionization due to his reluctance to implement standardized union work rules. Work rules, though usually well intentioned, tend to *restrict* what a worker can do; Nucor has *expanded* the responsibilities of steel workers. They hire people with skills for fixing things, and if a piece of equipment fails, everyone is expected to jump in and repair it. Automatic responsibility is radical, but it also seems to work for those willing to give it a chance.

The second observation: Automatic responsibility seems to be consistent with Douglas McGregor's (1960) Theory Y. In an over-simplification that is nonetheless interesting for analytical purposes, McGregor bifurcated management styles into Theory X and Theory Y. The former, said McGregor, was derived from classical management theories such as Taylor's Scientific Management and from the actual practices of most managers. Theory X rested on several assumptions, one of which is that *"the average human being prefers to be directed, wishes to avoid responsibility, has relatively little ambition, wants security above all"* (McGregor, 1960, p. 34). Theory Y, by contrast, derives from what McGregor thought social science teaches us about human behavior. One of its relevant assumptions is that *"the average human being learns, under proper conditions, not only to accept but to seek responsibility"* (McGregor, 1960, p. 48).

These assumptions of Theory X and Theory Y are clearly relevant to the concept of automatic responsibility. My argument is not that everyone is eager to seek and accept responsibility. There are people who clearly do not wish to do so. Nonetheless, many, if not most, organizations seem to be designed as if none of us can. The examples of the Marshall Center and the steelworkers at Nucor indicate that large numbers of people will seek and accept responsibility for organizational problems. If rocket scientists in the 1960s and steelworkers in the 1990s can accept responsibility, then perhaps more of our organizations should be designed to give more opportunities to those who want to assume responsibility. This would be an important way to counteract the tendency of bureaucracies to centralize authority and responsibility.

**Penetration**

Shortly after first hearing about penetration from my interviewees, I found documentation for it in a book by H.L. Nieburg (1966), *In the Name of Science*. This book provides, among other things, a catalogue of atrocities committed by the Contract State. The book reviews systematic waste, profiteering, technical failures, cost overruns, and plain ineptitude in the work of corporate contractors, mainly in the defense industry and the government agencies that were supposed to be monitoring them. Nieburg describes a congressional sub-committee inquiry into how a specific contractor, General Dynamics Astronautics, could have made some fundamental mistakes in its development of the Centaur rocket for the Air Force. The project was transferred to NASA, and von Braun was called to testify. According to Nieburg, von Braun's testimony "euphemized the situation yet succeeded in conveying a sharp indictment of the Air Force management" (p. 275). Von Braun's words were: "I think what we felt was a lack of depth of *penetration* of the program on the part of government personnel, in very general terms. We believed that this staff of eight people. . .[was] just an inadequate coverage on the part of the government, no matter whether it is NASA or the Air Force" (Nieburg, 1966, p. 275, emphasis added). When NASA assumed the management of the project, von Braun assigned 140 technical employees to supervise and penetrate the contractor (in contrast to the Air Force's eight).

An even more dramatic illustration of the practice of penetration emerged in 1967 in an interview with a top-ranking manager at MSFC. He explained that a contractor's first experience with the Marshall Center was usually "traumatic" because the Marshall engineers and managers were so aggressive in assuring that they were going to get exactly what they had ordered. One such contractor delivered a rocket stage to Huntsville. This stage had rigorous "heat leak" specifications that virtually required a vacuum seal; the requirements were so exacting that an ice cube placed inside it at a temperature of 70 degrees Fahrenheit would take eight and a half years to melt and another four years for the water temperature of the resulting puddle to rise to 70 degrees Fahrenheit. The Marshall personnel quizzed the contractor on the possibility of cracks in the stage. The contractor's people finally admitted there might be some cracks in it. How many cracks?

"Twenty-one," was the answer.

"No, there are 26 cracks," asserted an MSFC official.

The rocket stage was submitted to an examination and X-rayed. The stage contained twenty-six cracks—along with a few workers' tools and lunch boxes and other debris that shouldn't have been there. How could the customer know more than the manufacturer about the product at the moment of its delivery? Because the buyer in this case had *penetrated* the manufacturing organization, observed the production process in the contractor's plants, monitored workbenches at times, and quizzed the contractor's employees who were willing to talk about any problems. The contractor's management, by the way, was reportedly well known for discouraging the upward flow of bad news, and earlier its top managers had apparently been forced out after the Apollo 204 fire.

I found a document, "MSFC Personnel Assigned to Contractor Plants and Other Areas," which revealed that in the summer of 1967, 716 persons—10 percent of the Center's work force—were assigned to Milwaukee, Wichita, Seal Beach, Tulsa, Birmingham, Cambridge, Massachusetts, and many other locations. Contractor personnel, sometimes fearful of communicating bad news up the corporate line, readily reported what they knew to MSFC personnel. That, I realized, was the meaning of von Braun's remark in my first interview (quoted above) about the necessity of positioning earthquake detection "sensors" in industry.

The primary application of the penetration concept was this interorganizational process of intelligence and supervision. There were *intra*organizational applications as well. A thoughtful lab director who had read widely in the management literature explained his personal adaptation of the principle. Just to get the job done, he suggested, every person has to penetrate two layers up and two layers down. He qualified his principle by explaining that in penetrating two layers down, to his subordinates' subordinates, his purpose was not to direct them. Instead, he listened and talked in order to keep up with them. Another lab director told me that his group was falling behind the pace of the Center because he had not been given sufficient lead time to erect a large test stand for the RDO people. The lab director solved this problem by means of intra-organizational penetration. He persuaded a German engineer to come to work for him and then dispatched the man to attend all reviews and briefings so that he could anticipate future needs. This practice enabled the unit to keep ahead of the rest of the organization.

### Layers and the Span of Control

Studying the Marshall Center also provided insight into some central problems of organizational communication: the relationship between the number of hierarchical layers and the span of control. I discussed the problem of hierarchical layers in Chapter Two while explaining Nucor's four levels and what Peter Drucker considers to be the rule in most organizations—10 or 11, and sometimes more. The span of control is closely associated with a management theorist by the name of Lyndall F. Urwick. He expressed the principle in this way: No superior can directly supervise the work of five or six subordinates *whose work interlocks.* Urwick cited the writings of A.V. Graicunas for providing "mathematical proof" for this principle. Graicunas reasoned that as people are added to a group, cross relationships increase at a much faster rate, arithmetically speaking. When a sixth person is added, the number of these relationships jumps to 200; a seventh subordinate increases the number to between 450 and 500, and so on, until the ability of a superior to keep track of these relationships is surpassed.

The question is crucial to the theory of communication for two reasons. First, the span of control is based on the network of relationships among subordinates that must be understood and managed by the superior; this is relevant to the design of an organization. Second, it is important to consider the inverse relationship between the size of an organization's span of control and the number of levels or layers of supervision from the top to the bottom of the organization. In other words, a narrower span of control requires more layers of supervision and vice versa. A wider span of control reduces the number of serial transmissions of a message going through the scalar chain from the top to the bottom. Reducing that number theoretically improves vertical communication, which again increases the desirability of a broader span of control.

The more "humanistic" theories of organization and management tended to reject Urwick's and Graicunas' mathematical proof which limited the span to five or six. They urged a wider span of control, since in this case the superior cannot maintain the close supervision that is possible with a smaller span. The desired effect of "looser" supervision is to allow greater initiative, responsibility, and personal growth on the part of the subordinate. An important case in the argument was the attempt on the part of the Sears Roebuck management after World War II to "flatten" the vertical lines of communication by radically extending the span of control. (As many as 100 buyers were said to report to *one* manager.)

The Sears example was thought by some to refute Urwick's "law." But Urwick refused to give up. He examined the functions of Sears' personnel and found that they presented an exception that proved the rule. He argued that the work of Sears' employees failed to meet the qualifying phrase, "whose work interlocks." The departments of each store, Urwick argued, are isolated and independent units with little or no need for interdepartmental relationships.

The German Rocket Team is an interesting historic example. Until its metamorphosis in the early 1960s, von Braun directly supervised the work of 10 to 12 R&D organizational units, exactly double the number expressed in Urwick's rule. After the change, the director of RDO alone supervised 10 to 12 units. Moreover, Urwick's qualifying phrase—"whose work interlocks"—aptly describes the situation at the Marshall Center. Unlike Sears, the Marshall Center was highly interdependent and the work of the various organizational units interlocked. This interdependence was part of the organizational consciousness at the Marshall Center because of the shared knowledge that the mistakes of one office or lab could bring failure for all.

These facts seem to refute Urwick's principle. They also tend to support a competing theory of the span of control. Of the model of organizational communication I employed while conducting my studies of the Marshall Center, Barnard (1938) says:

> But a leader likewise is limited in time (and capacity) in communicating with many persons contemporaneously, especially if they are widely separated so that he must move about. In practice a limit of usually less than *fifteen* persons obtains, and for many types of cooperation five or six persons is the practicable limit. (p. 106, emphasis added)

Thus, the number of R&D lab directors at Marshall was within Barnard's limit of 15 and outside Urwick's limit of five or six. It appears to me that another distinction should be added to discussions of the span of control, that between subordinates who in turn supervise their own subordinates and those who do not. I do not know of any theorist who has made this distinction, but no doubt someone has. It does make intuitive sense that there is a difference between (a) supervising 12 engineers who have no subordinates and (b) supervising 12 lab directors who in turn are supervising supervisors of engineers, and so on. If so, it makes the case stronger for Barnard's larger limit of 15, as compared to Urwick's five or six, to know that the 10 or 12 lab directors in RDO were supervising others.

The relationship between span of control and hierarchical levels at the Marshall Center is also interesting in both theoretical and practical ways; it seems to have important implications for contemporary organizations as well. There was a wide span of control at the Marshall Center, as established, but in retrospect there also appears to have been a relatively "flat" structure. There were only five layers of management above an engineer in a lab: branch chief, division chief, lab director, the RDO director, and center director. It is true that there was another level above the director—NASA headquarters—but even adding that level and allowing for a level I may have forgotten, this is a rather flat organization, closer to Nucor's four levels than the norm of 10 or 11 found by Drucker. In short, Drucker's organization of the future is also the organization of the past: the Marshall Center of the Apollo era.

Joseph J. Trento (1987) would much later make the same point in explaining the success of NASA as an agency in those days:

> . . .what really made NASA different was that it was also a flat organization. A mid-level employee at NASA could get an answer from the deputy administrator faster than a three-star general at the Pentagon could from one of his clerks. A middle manager at NASA could speak for the administrator of the agency when the Pentagon could not get the head of one of the armed services to speak with authority. (p. 17)

In addition, von Braun's priority on facilitating upward-directed communication made the organization seem flatter than it was. In bypassing a layer of management, the Monday Notes had a flattening effect (and created—at least on Mondays—a span of control of two dozen). So did automatic responsibility and the intraorganizational application of penetrating two levels up and down. These practices brought the top and the bottom together, regardless of the layers formally existing between them. These are a few of the elements of MSFC's organizational communication that I believe made it work so effectively in getting us to the moon two years later. But there were some problems that needed to be addressed and a conference to help coordinate.

### Conference on Organizational Communication

Walt Wiesman had conceived of a need to spread the word about the importance of organizational communication and decided that a conference would be the best way to satisfy it. Part of my responsibility, while pressing on with my interviews and participant observation at the Center, was to serve as conference coordinator and give a major address. Wiesman, as conference chair, had sent out invitations to government agencies, colleges and universities, prime and support contractors. The response was gratifying, even though the phrase *organizational communication* was not yet in popular usage. Representatives from NASA headquarters, the Kennedy Space Center, the Marshall Center, and the Lewis Research Center, as well as the U.S. Army Missile Command and the U.S. Civil Service Commission, attended. Three prime contractors—Boeing, Chrysler, and Douglas Aircraft—participated, along with support contractors General Electric and RCA. Least encouraging was the academic turnout: Only six colleges and universities sent participants, probably because the field was so new.

W. Charles Redding, the founder and historian of the field of organizational communication, much later reflected on the significance of the conference:

> Under the direction of Walter Wiesman, internal communication coordinator for the Marshall Center (NASA), the four-day conference brought together management representatives from government agencies and MSFC contractors, as well as academics from four universities. The major address, delivered by Phillip K. Tompkins (then of Wayne State University and a consultant to the Center) consisted of a comprehensive review of *empirical research* that had been completed in the field up to that time. It was a pioneering "state-of-the-art" effort, and the earliest (to my knowledge) to be published explicitly under the title "organizational communication" (Tompkins, 1967). This 1967 conference at Huntsville was also, so far as can be determined, the first conference specifically devoted to theory and research (along with implications for practice) ever held under the label "organizational communication." (Redding, 1985, p. 22)

This statement, I believe, says volumes about the leadership of Walter Wiesman in the development of the field, as well as about the general concern for organizational communication at the Marshall Center.

At about this time my other big concern—the situation in Detroit—was somewhat clarified. It was estimated that more than 40 people had been killed, but the picture of the Detroit I would go home to at the end of the summer was still unclear to me. I had realized, as indicated above, that von Braun's philosophy and techniques of communication brought the top and bottom together, regardless of the layers formally existing between them. I was becoming curious as to why our political leaders could not do the same to reduce the huge gaps between themselves and their poorest constituents.

Before I could head north, however, I had to pull together my interview data on the problems of communication I had uncovered in preparation for my briefings for Shepherd and von Braun.

## NOTES

1. Von Braun later told me in conversation that one of the problems, aside from shoddy work by one of the contractors, was that no one realized that a fire was more dangerous on the earth than in space. In space, astronauts had only to open a hatch; the vacuum would snuff out the fire. On the ground, however, a fire would continue to burn.

2. However, I was to learn later that, based on recently opened FBI files, there is still controversy about the extent to which certain members of the German Rocket Team may have been culpable of war crimes.

3. "Matrix" was a new term as applied to organizations in 1967. NASA's use of matrix management during the Apollo Project was a pioneering effort. The Industrial Operations (IO) segment of MSFC was made up of program and project offices. IO had a line of authority separate from Research and Development Operations (RDO), but the lines converged in von Braun's office. IO's various program and project offices directed and monitored the efforts of contractors, and in addition, called on the labs in RDO to assist their management with technical advice and engineering studies. In their dealings with RDO, IO did not have the traditional kind of vertical authority to give directives. Instead, it had a kind of horizontal authority, ultimately backed by the Center director. IO's project and program directors preferred to cajole and argue rather than fall back on von Braun's authority to compel RDO to comply with its wishes. The term matrix is appropriate for the arrangement because of the intersecting vertical and horizontal lines of communication.

The inherent ambiguity of authority in a matrix organization made horizontal communication the most serious problem I dealt with at the Marshall Center. Its virtue, however, was that the management offices existed only for the life of the project. In theory, they came and went, and had a certain single-mindedness during their short existence.

As the Marshall Center shrank in size after the Apollo Program, Lucas's strategy of diversification increased the number of project offices, making the "matrix" denser, more complex. For all its problems, the matrix organization at MSFC proved to be superior to the lead lab alternative, tried briefly in 1968, in which units in RDO simultaneously played the roles of both a line organization "doing" the work and a project office "managing" the effort. The problems of the lead lab concept are detailed in Chapter Six of this book.

4. The "Monday Notes" were one of von Braun's innovative techniques for facilitating upward and horizontal communication (described in detail later in this chapter).

## Chapter Four

# SOME PROBLEMS OF COMMUNICATION AT THE MARSHALL CENTER

While finding out what worked well from my distinguished interviewees, I was also learning about their problems and the problems of the system. Their openness and candor about such problems gave me a satisfying and slightly surprised feeling. Here they were, some of the best rocket scientists in the world, opening up to a 33-year-old associate professor of communication.

In addition to pressing my interviewees about the strengths and weaknesses in the system, I also inquired about the three specific problems Jim Shepherd (von Braun's assistant) had assigned me to investigate: the Saturn V Control Center, how to send a weekly note to NASA headquarters, and the endless briefings that moved so much information up the line to the Center's management. While I was still completing my interviews and sorting the problems into categories, there was enough information to answer Shepherd's questions.

### A Briefing for Shepherd

I met with Jim Shepherd on September 5, 1967, in his office adjacent to von Braun's and briefed him on the three issues. We started with the Saturn V Control Center, and I gave him an outline to use in following my briefing. My evidence came from inter-viewees' perceptions of the Control Center plus most of an afternoon spent in the Control Center, interviewing other middle- and upper-level personnel who served there. I had found the personnel remarkably candid about its limitations.   After explaining my methods to Shepherd, I opened the argument with my conclusion: "The   Saturn V Control Center is more for show than utility."

## The Saturn V Control Center Problem

PERT (Program Evaluation and Review Technique) had been abandoned, I explained, apparently because Arthur Rudolph, the program director of the Saturn V, did not understand it.   (I was not able to interview Rudolph himself, as he was out of town.)[1]   The staff had replaced the PERT chart on the wall with cartoon cutouts and a system called the "waterfall" that Rudolph had used in Germany.  I was told he visited the room about three times a week. I asked Rudolph's assistants where Rudolph normally spent his working day.  They led me across the hall to a room about a tenth of the size of the Control Center.  In contrast to the quiet and empty Control Center, the room was alive with activity: people were on the telephone, talking to contractors and NASA personnel all over the country, making notes and then translating them onto the grease-pencil charts that almost filled the room.  Here I had found the beehive, the real control center for Saturn V.  Rudolph visited this room daily, I was told, and he kept another chart in his own office.

I informed Shepherd that the information on the walls of the official Control Center was outdated by as much as three months. The reason for this was that in some cases information had to flow from the contractor to the resident civil service employee to the rocket stage manager to the Control Center and then to the people who plugged the data into the PERT chart.  PERT then also had to be translated into Rudolph's "waterfall" system.   Staff members admitted that Rudolph frequently discovered discrepancies between what he knew and what was visibly displayed in the Control Center. For the up-to-the-minute status of a problem, one had to call as many as three Saturn V stage managers.

Further, the information in the Control Center was in some cases invalid, I explained.  If someone in a critical path did not meet a deadline or "milestone," it was called a "slip" in the schedule.  The staff in the Control Center would not be likely to admit a "slip" because they would not want the subsequent units in the critical path to relax.  Rather than acknowledge a slip of a week's time, they would parcel it out day by day.  Consequently, opportunities for improving quality and reliability were lost. (In one of my interviews, a lab director was concerned about a swing arm on the tower that held the Saturn V in place until the moment of launch. He knew it could be rebuilt and improved in just a few days but could not obtain permission to do it because the "slip" was being meted out day by day.)

Milestones were not posted, I continued, until all the formalistic documentation had been completed, even though the work was finished and had been adequately evaluated. A lot of paperwork was required to certify the completion of a task, and postings of milestones reached was delayed until the necessary paperwork reached the Control Center, which took time. Hence, work that was done might not be formally displayed as such. Also, everyone I talked to admitted that the contractors played games with their inputs, i.e., they manipulated the time frames by denying they were behind when in fact they were.

I presented Shepherd with evidence from the formal interviews that Marshall managers usually knew the information on display was inaccurate when they went to the Control Center for a review. But their most acrimonious complaint was that the Center's intimidating atmosphere prevented open discussion. "You can't argue or compromise with PERT or 'waterfall,'" they told me repeatedly. The result was a classic case of goal-displacement. Methods that were devised to serve as management tools, as means to organizational ends, had become ends in themselves. There was grave concern among the interviewees that *things* rather than *people* were threatening to gain control of decisions and events.

Shepherd seemed delighted by the exposé. He was also convinced by the arguments and the evidence. He then explained that the NASA administrator, James E. Webb, had a background in public administration, not in the technical side of the enterprise. Webb was apparently fond of bringing Congressmen and other VIPs to Huntsville to show them the Saturn V Control Center as NASA's contribution to new management-communication developments.

### The Briefing Problem

We then turned to the general problem of briefings. My objective was to improve the overall organization of the briefings, which often became lost in an incredible amount of detail. I reminded Shepherd that I had attended several briefings for von Braun in the staff and board room with its three massive screens for visuals. Particularly vivid was a briefing for von Braun dealing with projected trajectories for a Voyager launching. The launch windows and possible trajectories displayed were so complicated that an engineer sitting next to me leaned over and whispered, "You can't hardly get there from here."

The briefers from the Astrionics and Aero-Astronautics labs seemed to be doing a competent job. Von Braun interrupted the proceedings to explain the U.S. Congressional funding system to his American briefers, particularly the distinction between authorizations and appropriations. While we were looking at pictures of Mars on the huge screens, he cracked up the large audience with a remark about the canals: "Looks like there may be good trout fishing on Mars." He did it again with the observation that two thirds of Voyager's film would be used in mapping Mars and the other "one third would go to *Life* magazine." It appeared that von Braun liked to show off a bit, to demonstrate his vast knowledge and quick wit, and the briefers played to him. They established eye contact with the rest of the audience only when others asked questions. He described the "overdone contingencies on Apollo" and explained that NASA had discovered earlier that the "astronauts were confused" until the contingencies were simplified. He stopped one briefer to ask, "What is a yag?" When a briefer started to take down a visual display, von Braun asked him to leave it up. "I have to work my way through your alphabet soup."

The briefing also seemed rather disorganized, I told Shepherd. There was no overall outline for the presentation and the briefers ran out of time, which forced von Braun to say, "let's go as far as we can—till 5:45, and we'll try to squeeze in an hour tomorrow." And the room erupted with laughter again when he said, "I'll ask Bonnie for permission," a reference to Bonnie Holmes, his long-time secretary who patiently tried to keep him on schedule.

In another briefing, a senior manager was describing a difficult technical problem when a young man sitting across from me made a suggestion. After questioning him, von Braun nodded and asked a senior briefer to look into the idea. The director appeared to have little respect for hierarchy and was open to ideas from everyone, whatever what the person's age or status. Now I was seeing first-hand how his approach made the organization work.

I gave Jim Shepherd a set of suggested guidelines I had developed for solving the problems in these briefing sessions. The ideas included identifying young and inexperienced employees who would be expected to make formal presentations to Center management in the future. These individuals would be encouraged to begin practicing making presentations at lower levels and to obtain constructive criticism from their peers. This approach might help make their later presentations to Center management a less traumatic experience. I advised that these rehearsals be timed, which would allow for questions and answers within the limits assigned. My guidelines recommended that an overall outline of the entire presentation be projected on one of the three briefing room screens with the other two reserved for more detailed information. My final suggestions for the briefings were, "Beware of the alphabet soup. Spell out all acronyms and abbreviations at least twice. Also, try to remember that you are communicating with more than one person."

My final remark was based on numerous complaints during my interviews, plus my own observations, about briefers who maintained eye contact with von Braun alone, acting as if he were the only person in the audience who counted. (My experience was that von Braun did not demand such attention; rather, this behavior was a function of his truly commanding presence. Norman Mailer also observed that phenomenon in press conferences with all the NASA brass assembled. The reporters asked von Braun most of the questions.)

Shepherd said that he would write a cover letter for the guidelines and send them out to every office at the Marshall Center.

### The Problem of Weekly Notes for Headquarters

I told Shepherd that I couldn't offer much help about how to prepare the weekly notes for Washington. The contributors to the Monday Notes were alarmed by the possibility that their notes might be excerpted and relayed to headquarters out of context. They said that if they thought they were writing for an audience beyond the Marshall Center, their notes would become sterile. They indicated that they would be willing to consider putting an asterisk or "bullet" next to items that might be culled for transmission to Washington. The concern was that Washington might well misinterpret some of their "behind the scenes" intra-Center quarrels and statements of alarm—the very qualities that gave the Monday notes their "local charm" and much of their usefulness.

⌈Shepherd told me that since giving me the assignment regarding the preparation of weekly notes for Washington, NASA headquarters had lost interest and the plan had been abandoned.  Headquarters did, however, direct other field centers to emulate the Marshall Center and establish their own system of weekly notes.  True to bureaucratic form, they produced a full volume of directions, including numbered forms, about how to initiate them.  The bureaucrats seemed to miss the point of the advantages of informality and simplicity.⌋ Shepherd was appreciative of our briefing and added that I had already earned my GS-13 salary for the summer.  He planned to sit in on my briefing for von Braun later that week and looked forward to learning what else I had discovered.  He urged me to emphasize all the problems I had uncovered in my interviews to von Braun.

### A Briefing for von Braun

I began then to put my briefing together.  As I polished the presentation and the time approached, my nervousness and anxiety increased.  I spent much time contemplating my "audience."

### A Portrait of the Director

During my orientation, I had begun to sense the profound *organizational presence* of Wernher von Braun, something I had never experienced before nor have since.  He was a legend before I arrived, but it was the way his colleagues talked about him that heightened my perception of this presence.  Years later, I tried to describe it in an article.  The people at the Marshall Center had conferred on him, I wrote, a status "which seemed to fall somewhere in that unexplored territory between Aristotle's concept of *ethos* and Weber's concept of charisma" (Tompkins, 1977, p. 6).

Aristotle believed that *ethos* was probably the most effective means of persuasion, and his analysis of it held that if a person was regarded as possessing good sense, good character, and good will, he or she would by that very fact be more persuasive than others.  Von Braun, with his brilliance and vast learning, was so regarded.  Germans and Americans alike said that he inspired trust. Employees repeated stories to me about acts of kindness, such as his concern for an engineer in one of the labs who had lost her son in Vietnam. By these stories they sought to convince me that von Braun was a man of good will. For the "audience" of the Marshall Center at least, von Braun had *ethos*.

Weber's charisma is a similar but more powerful kind of authority, the kind that brings revolutionary changes. In Weber's "Ideal Type" of charisma, the leader is perceived to have produced miracles. Von Braun's followers, themselves intelligent and skeptical people by nature and training, did not fall much short of such faith in him. He had brought about a technological revolution, and the Apollo moon project, which fulfilled a lifelong dream for von Braun, was seen by many as almost miraculous. Hence, von Braun's people conferred on him a status of both expertise and sheer personal power.

Others sensed this presence and even applied Weber's term to it. John N. Wilford, a science reporter for *The New York Times* would later write that "von Braun had charisma" (1969, p. 135). Norman Mailer, in the curious persona of Aquarius adopted in his book *Of a Fire on the Moon* (1971), would spend several pages trying to capture von Braun's presence on the eve of the Apollo 11 flight. He wrote that von Braun "is of course a legend" (p. 62) and that "he had obvious funds of charisma" (p. 69). Malcolm McConnell much later (1987) wrote that "von Braun had been a charismatic visionary who instilled loyalty through personal magnetism" (p. 107). He was, in a word, the *star* of the space program, even bigger than the astronauts, who enjoyed great popularity. To the insiders, the people at NASA and the contractors, von Braun was the central figure.

During my orientation program I had visited the space museum at the Center, where I had viewed the tiny, cramped capsules from the Mercury and Gemini programs and other impressive memorabilia. Walt Wiesman tipped me off about a separate room in the museum devoted to von Braun's personal awards and artifacts. The director was embarrassed by the pretentiousness of it all and insisted that it be closed to the public that passed through the larger museum, but Walt had access to the key and made it available to me.

The medals and awards *were* somewhat pretentious and after a while even became boring, so I understood why von Braun kept the door locked. On display, however, was some correspondence that I found fascinating. The letters were in German but had been translated, probably by Wiesman, into English. The first letter was from von Braun and addressed to Albert Schweitzer. Von Braun wrote to the old man expressing, as I recall, his admiration for Schweitzer's life and careers in music, theology, and medicine. He then politely invited Schweitzer to visit Huntsville, mentioning the availability of an airport.

Schweitzer wrote back that he was very much aware of von Braun and his work. He thanked him for the invitation to Huntsville but indicated he had no plans to come to the United States. Von Braun was also welcome to visit him, and Schweitzer explained that there was also an airstrip near his compound in Africa.

One of my favorite stories about von Braun was told to me by Walt Wiesman. Knowing of my interest in classical music, Walt told about the time Arthur Fiedler and the Boston Pops Orchestra came to Huntsville to give a concert. Walt was assigned to show Fiedler around the Space Center and indicated that they had scheduled an interview with von Braun. Fiedler protested, saying that he didn't know which end of a rocket to light and that he wouldn't know what else to talk to von Braun about. Walt told him not to worry, that the boss had a wide range of interests.

Fiedler was warmly greeted by von Braun, and they immediately began to talk about Fiedler's interests. The director indicated that he played the piano and cello, and that while working on his Ph.D. in physics, he had taken a course in the theory of composition with Paul Hindemith at the University of Berlin. He then showed Fiedler some of his own compositions.

History has not to my knowledge recorded Arthur Fiedler's critical judgment of von Braun's compositions, but I was not unimpressed by this anecdote. It would have been interesting to learn Hindemith's opinion of von Braun's ability and performance as a student of music theory.

My interviewees had also informed me that von Braun was a jet pilot and an avid mountain climber. All of this was on my mind, and more than once I asked myself, *What am I doing briefing this guy?* [2]

## The Briefing

The briefing was scheduled for 3:30 p.m. on September 8, 1967, in von Braun's office. I arrived early in order to put my outline on the blackboard. Von Braun came in at 3:25, and we chatted about a new piece of metal sculpture given to him by a Greek artist named Ikarus. The sculpture, entitled *The Fire*, an abstract piece suggestive of a rocket in flames, was dedicated to the three astronauts who had died in the 204 fire. Holes had been burned through the metal with a welding torch. Von Braun remarked, "I don't think this would pass our quality control." I responded with nervous laughter.

*Wernher von Braun (right) and Eberhard F.M. Rees, deputy director, technical, (left) examine a ruby crystal used in laser experiments in MSFC's Space Sciences Laboratory, 1967 (NASA photo archives)*

The other attendees began to arrive. They were Jim Shepherd, assistant to the director; Hans Neubert, associate deputy director, technical (sitting in for the deputy director, technical, E.F.M. Rees, who was out of town); Harry Gorman, deputy director of administration; General O'Connor, director of industrial operations; and Hans Hueter, deputy director of industrial operations. They were a formidable group. How were they going to respond to my criticisms of their respective domains? The notes I made immediately after the briefing were so detailed that I was able to reconstruct the proceedings almost word for word.

I began my presentation, standing in front of the blackboard. After a moment or two, von Braun interrupted. "Wouldn't you be more comfortable sitting down?" he asked. I took my chair and continued, saying that while I had found much that worked well at Marshall, I wanted to concentrate on the problems I had found. At this point I was on my feet again, and von Braun was trying to get me to sit down again. After a while he gave up.

During the briefing I referred to my outline on the blackboard.

MANAGEMENT COMMUNICATION WITHIN MSFC

    I. Methods and Limitations of the Study

    II. Findings

        A. What We Do Well[3]

        B. Problems and Challenges

        C. Recommendations

    III. Conclusion

Under the point "What We Do Well," I limited myself to the Monday Notes, explaining the advantages to them as discussed above, along with a description of how the contributors to the Notes were now asking their subordinates to generate their own sets of Friday Notes. Von Braun was delighted by this unexpected communicative discipline of note writing taking place within the organization.

*1. The Formalism-Impersonality Syndrome.* Under "Problems and Challenges," ten items were listed on the board. The first was what I called the "formalism-impersonality syndrome." I told the group that in my interviews it had been refreshing to hear people who had made important contributions to the development of computers and information-management technology sternly denounce the sterility, formalism, and impersonality of many of the management tools they used, some of which had been imposed on them by NASA headquarters. Then I moved on to the specifics: overuse of computers, control centers, and "canned" reviews. Following this, I made the same presentation I had given Shepherd about the Saturn V Control Center. Shepherd smiled. Now I had their attention.

Von Braun immediately challenged me about the Control Center. Using an analogy to newspapers, he pointed out that a certain degree of obsolescence was necessary. I replied, "But that's my point. If it is obsolescent, it must be more for show than utility." We argued back and forth, and several others began to take my side. Later I learned that von Braun had been convinced by my arguments early on; this dialectical devil's advocate approach was his way of testing the strength of my evidence and arguments. (I also subsequently learned that von Braun stopped attending briefings at the Saturn V Control Center. It became Administrator Webb's white elephant, a place where he brought VIPs for show-and-tell to keep them out of the hair of the busy teams getting ready for the moon launch.)

As I started to move on to the next problem, von Braun interrupted again, saying, "Wait, isn't there something we can do about this?" I reminded him that I wanted to identify all the problems before moving on to recommendations.

*2. It's a Family Affair.* The second problem I referred to as "It's a family affair." It was the most sensitive issue I presented to this audience. However, it seemed to enhance my credibility by convincing von Braun and the others that I would hold nothing back. The "family" was the remaining members of the original Paperclip 120—the Germans. Several American-born managers had told me that they felt shut out and related a story about how a key technical decision had been made by the Germans in "Papa" Eberhard Rees' living room. One of these outsiders said, "We've been invited to the table, but we haven't been accepted into the family." Von Braun was incredulous and said, "I can't recall any recent decision made by an inner circle." He turned to the American-born managers in the room and asked them if they thought the "Peenemünde gang" still operated that way. They doubted it, but said they believed I had pointed out an important perception that was circulating at the Center and had never been openly discussed.

Nine years later, in 1976, this was brought out into the open by a reporter for *The Huntsville Times.* According to the article, there was a long standing resentment at NASA toward the Germans. They were characterized as arrogant, wont to fill key posts with their own, and insistent on complete control of the operations. The definitive history of the German Rocket Team was published in 1979. The

authors, Frederick I. Ordway and Mitchell Sharpe (1979), responded to the *Times* article as follows:

> A few of the indictments were true. The Germans did tend to be somewhat clannish and did occupy the top positions. However, at von Braun's urging, some of his top lieutenants adopted young American protégés and brought them up through the ranks. In a few cases, these younger men developed into competent managers who would serve the center capably during the next decade or so. (p. 398)

I told the group that there was an ironic dimension to this problem. While the outsiders were describing the "family" as an informal but cohesive and monolithic organization, so-called members had made clear to me that it had its share of illegitimate children and undesirable in-laws. This line evoked a hearty laugh from the three Germans in the room. To add to the irony, my earlier German interviewees had expressed deep regret at what they regarded as the disintegration of the old "family" ties.

As I started to move to the next problem, von Braun interrupted to ask, "Phil, do you have any ideas about how to deal with this?" Once more I reiterated the structure of my outline.

*3.  The Invisibility of the Boss.*  The third problem, like the presence of an informal system inside every formal organization, was also characteristic of most organizations I have studied. In the field of organizational communication, we called it the "invisibility of the boss." In this case, however, it evoked more nostalgia than criticism. The interviewees realized the director's absences from the Center were necessary and that the recent growth of the organization made it impossible to maintain the frequency of interaction with von Braun that had been enjoyed in the past. There was a certain amount of nostalgia in conversations about this problem that referred to the "good old days" when one could walk across the hall and speak to von Braun, and everyone knew the names of his or her colleagues' children. My journal indicates that, in response, von Braun asked for certain clarifications and showed no defensiveness whatsoever.

*4.  Lack of Lateral Openness.*  The fourth problem was the most serious. I called it the "lack of lateral openness": insufficient lateral or horizontal communication between the laboratories in RDO and the project offices in IO. Another manifestation of the problem existed between the laboratories within RDO. The problems

between IO and RDO had a variety of causes. Part of it was what the RDO people called the "IO odor." A deeply-held value premise among the engineers in RDO was that engineers had to "keep their hands dirty" to be productive. People in RDO were prejudiced against the "paper shufflers" in IO, even if they were former engineers. RDO believed that there was an inverse relationship between paper work and productivity.

When IO was created, a number of engineers and managers were transferred from RDO to the new project offices. Some of these transfers were more difficult than others. After a "hard" move (e.g., losing a respected or key colleague), some lab people were bitter about what they regarded as defections to the enemy. Some of the moves were upward as well as horizontal, putting the new IO managers into positions where they now communicated as equals with their former RDO bosses. Some of these lab directors admitted to me that they created problems for themselves by "praising away" inferior talent to IO and then later having to cooperate with them. The cleavage between RDO and IO was serious.

Compounding the problem was the fact that each group misunderstood the purpose and authority of the other. In the "MSFC Management Policy Statement #1" of August 16, 1962, von Braun had given IO clear authority for "directing, coordinating, programming, and budgeting all effort that relates to individual projects. This total effort includes all that which is expended by the technical division (RDO laboratories), as well as that performed by the contractors" (p. 2). RDO laboratories, on the other hand, were to function as they had in the past and "through instruments such as working groups, technical committees, or task assignments" were to "directly assist the director of the project office to make the technical decisions required for effective project management" (p. 2). Contrams interpretations of these charges were given by RDO and IO. IO tended to assume much more authority than RDO was willing to grant.

The lack of openness between the two major segments had reached dysfunctional proportions, I reported. It affected the way in which the labs interacted with each other. Lab directors in RDO admitted that competitiveness and jealousy were widespread, and lack of trust, even secrecy, characterized their lateral communication. "We have our little empires," a lab director told me, "and we don't tell others what they need to know unless asked." Some interviewees

admitted playing a mischievous zero-sum game with other labs by recommending technical solutions that would make their own lab look good and also "make the other guy look bad." In other words, certain technical decisions were made because they would make work more difficult for another lab. Obviously, I said, this was a dangerous game. Von Braun expressed disbelief that the problem could be that serious. Neubert, the associate deputy director, technical, came to my defense by citing a case well known to everyone at the table and diagnosing it as an example of this kind of gamesmanship. Von Braun was visibly concerned.

5. *The Science-Technology Barrier.* The fifth problem had been a surprise to me. I was aware that some professors in the natural sciences look down on their engineering counterparts, but I did not realize the extent of the gulf between the two groups.

Rocketry is chiefly an engineering activity, and the R&D engineer lives in a world concerned with *time, cost,* and *reliability.* He or she often rediscovers Newtonian Physics while working on a problem. The success of an engineering project, such as the moon rocket, often depends on the artistry of a welder. The technologist keeps up to date by reading "state-of-the-art" papers circulated among fellow workers rather than by writing for academic journals. Very often the engineer's work is classified, which limits communication about technical matters.

The scientist, on the other hand, worries much less about time, cost, and reliability. He or she may be thinking in terms of a lifetime, a career in pursuit of a Nobel Prize. The mode of communication in science is the academic journal article. Scientists sometimes denigrate the "applied" science of the engineer.

The problem experienced at the Marshall Center, this "science-technology barrier," manifested itself in several ways. Some scientists felt left out, unappreciated, and neglected. Engineers, on the other hand, had to work with academic scientists called "principal investigators" to develop the rocket experiments. These scientists maintained a communication loop with NASA headquarters, unavailable to the engineers, which produced directives inconsistent with ones received from the lab directors. Also, the different orientations and technical languages made it difficult for the two parties to understand one another, even in face-to-face interaction. In a 1977 article about MSFC, I wrote:

It was obvious that because scientists were to play an increasingly important role in post-Apollo projects. . .this problem could only grow in seriousness with time. (Tompkins, 1977, p. 18)

*6. The Future of MFSC.* The future of MSFC was a perennial human problem of uncertainty and anxiety made more salient at Marshall because the R&D and manufacturing stages of the Saturn V were nearing completion. The organization had never worked on anything other than missiles and rockets. Moreover, NASA headquarters was opposed to the arsenal concept (i.e., maintaining a significant in-house capability). All organizations seek to perpetuate themselves, and this organization had always prided itself on accepting new and bigger challenges. There were rumors of RIFs (Reductions in Force), and the absence of any official word coming down the line increased the uncertainty and anxiety.

*7. Below the Branch Level?* The seventh problem was posed with a question mark, but I had a hunch behind it. My interviews in 1967 took me no deeper than the level of lab directors, two levels below the director's. There were nonetheless indicators of difficulties below the branch level, at the first or bottom level of supervision. For example, a federal employees' union had recently experienced a rapid growth of membership below the branch level. My inquiry in the personnel office revealed that 60 percent of the employee complaints from below that level required corrective action. The evidence indicated a potential morale problem at that level.

Informal conversations with new friends and acquaintances at the Marshal Center had brought to my attention that there was an apparent discrepancy between lab directors and workers in the perceived need for support contractors. The workers perceived the contractor's employees working beside them (at much higher salaries) as unwanted and overpaid interlopers who were doing work that should have been done "in-house." The lab directors felt the contractor's employees were necessary to some extent, but it seemed to me that their presence was perceived as a status symbol by the lab directors: the larger the number, the bigger the symbol.

My inference and the discrepant perception were not inconsistent with another of Nieburg's (1966) observations, the contention that NASA headquarters' biases forced von Braun into "arranging with contractors to recruit technical people who were placed on inflated,

government-reimbursable company payrolls while assigned to work at Huntsville side by side with civil servants" (p. 232).

*8. Bottleneck at RDO.* The eighth problem was rather superficial in itself but gained in importance because it had an impact on other problems. The bottleneck was at the office of the director of RDO, a busy man with 12 organizational units reporting to him. Exacerbating this problem was the fact that the position of technical deputy director of RDO had been vacant for some time, throwing even more communicative responsibility onto Herman Weidner, the director, and his staff. Lab directors complained that his staff often garbled and distorted technical messages and that the absence of the deputy made it difficult to iron out the labs' collective problems within the RDO structure. It was thought that the bottleneck was aggravated by the increasing invisibility of von Braun and the lack of lateral openness within RDO.

*9. External Interfaces.* Although *interface* has become a word in the active vocabulary of many Americans in recent years, I first heard it in 1967 listening to the people at the Marshall Center. When a rocket was assembled stage-by-stage for a launch at the Cape, it would have been embarrassing, to say the least, if the plumbing and wiring had not matched. This was the original sense of the word "interface," the physical point of contact between technological sub-systems. Gradually, this technical term was applied to problems of human communication and organization, providing another instance of life imitating technology, or what might be called *technomorphism.*

Thus, interface came to refer to the point of contact between two organizational units. External interfaces, then, would be the point of contact with all organizations other than MSFC. The problem with these external interfaces, from MSFC's perspective, was twofold. The first was that the complexity of the work simply required too many interfaces with NASA headquarters, other NASA field centers, universities, and of course the ubiquitous contractors, prime and support. In retrospect, MSFC was involved in what is now called an organizational "set," or network of organizations which some (e.g., Perrow, 1979) say should become the unit of analysis for organizational studies. The Marshall Center was the nexus of a complicated organizational set.

The second dimension of the interface problem was poor quality and reliability of the "bonds." The Marshall Center was then seen as a confident group, some even said arrogant, and MSFC personnel detected fear and insecurity in people from other organizations. They found it perplexing that the Manned Space Center (now the Johnson Center) did not enjoy the same depth of technical ability as enjoyed at the Marshall Center, which made joint problem-solving ventures difficult and one-sided. Marshall personnel also felt the same problem with NASA headquarters, and NASA headquarters personnel were said to regard the Marshall Center as too autonomous (a problem that would later surface in the Rogers Commission hearings and report). Contractors, as indicated above, often found their first dealings with the Marshall Center to be "traumatic."

*10. The Problem with the Staff Offices.* The staff offices were those groups not dedicated to the mission of the Center—designing, building, testing rockets—but to providing support services necessary to the engineers and scientists in the "line" organization who were pursuing the organization's mission. These offices were the Manpower Utilization & Administration Office (which included the Personnel Office and Wiesman's Internal Communication Program to which I was attached), Financial Management (the accountants), the Purchasing Office, and several others. The problem here, according to my interviewees, was a rash of two different kinds of complaints: those *about* the staff offices from the other segments of the organization and those *by* the staff offices.

The complaints about the staff offices were the same ones heard in almost any organization as a result of the inevitable and almost universal "line-staff" cleavage, another form of controversy over means and ends. Staff offices are often accused of adhering to bureaucratic rules even when they interfere with meeting the organization's objectives. At the Marshall Center, however, these criticisms, which arose in IO as well as RDO, were especially trenchant. Part of the reason was that many of the line managers had worked for the U.S. Army before transferring to NASA, and the MSFC staff offices suffered by comparison with those in the Army. They were said to be slower and less responsive than their Army counterparts, mired in bureaucracy. For example, a lab director said in connection with the civil service regulations interpreted by the personnel people, "We don't need them to read the Bible to us, we need them to show us how to get around it in order to get the job

done." The lab directors also felt that people in the staff offices knew too little about technical work, were defensive about their lack of knowledge, and spent little time in the labs. Minutia about these matters had to be forced all the way up to the deputy director for administration for decisions. The man holding that position, Harry Gorman, was sitting at my right during the briefing.

I then summarized the complaints voiced by the managers of the staff offices. Each office chief was aware that decisions in his area often had an impact on other staff offices. For example, a decision in the Manpower Office could have a serious impact on the Financial Management Office and vice versa. The managers said that such decision making was not being coordinated. At the time of the interviews, months had passed since a meeting of staff representatives had been held. The deputy director for administration, responsible for the coordination of these meetings, was said to be spending an increasing amount of time as an "interface" with NASA headquarters. This responsibility, along with administering individual cases funneled up to his office by the lab directors, left him too little time for coordinating the staff offices.

A lively discussion of this problem ensued. Von Braun again commented that he had been hearing variants of the problem throughout his career and doubted the complaints were any worse than during the Redstone days. But I suspected von Braun was trying to be supportive of Harry Gorman, who was conspicuously silent during this discussion of his domain.

We then marched through my ten recommendations (which will be presented in the next chapter), and von Braun was full of suggestions. We had a serious debate over his spontaneous recommendation for the suspected problem below the branch level of management. Von Braun instantly diagnosed this as a problem of supervision by the branch chiefs. He proposed a weekly meeting between supervisors and employees in which they would talk about their problems. I replied that he could not simply write a memo and, as if by magic, make such meetings effective, that "it won't work if the supervisor was not inclined to *listen* in the first place." We finally found a compromise. Such an edict might be effective if coupled with an attempt to educate the supervisors about their communicative responsibilities to their subordinates. I had in mind the speech Walt Wiesman had given to the Advanced Systems Operations office during my first week of orientation.

The briefing had lasted two hours. As it came to a close, von Braun shook my hand, congratulated me, and moved to his desk. He leafed through his calendar and asked when I would be going back to Detroit. When I answered that it would be in just a few days, he said that he hoped I would be willing to come back to make the same presentation to his next Staff and Board Meeting on October 6th. I agreed to do so. He made it clear that he did not want to edit my presentation in any way, although NASA headquarters would not be happy to hear about the "family" problem. (This was one of the first indications to me how sensitive this issue was in Washington.) He did, however, want to talk about the order in which I would present the problems and recommendations to the Staff and Board meeting. The others in the briefing had ideas about this as well. In the end, we agreed that because of its importance, the lateral or horizontal communication problem would be the first presented.

After leaving von Braun's office, I drove to Boots's for several drinks and made notes on the briefing, even making a diagram indicating where each person had sat at the table. I also contemplated what work I had left to do in my remaining week at Marshall. Keith Wible, chief of the Manpower Office, had asked me for the same briefing I had given von Braun's group, and I obliged him. Several of my interviewees wanted to know what I told von Braun, so I gave them an abbreviated briefing.

Two nights before my departure, a group of my new friends took me to dinner at the Officer's Club and then five of us celebrated until 2:30 in the morning. I was both happy and sad to see the summer come to an end, but as I drove back to Wayne State University to begin the fall term I knew, with both a sense of pride and a little apprehension, that I would be back in three weeks to present my report to von Braun's Staff and Board. And I was curious about what I would find back in Detroit.

## NOTES

1. I was never to meet Arthur Rudolph. A few years before this writing, the U.S. government deported him to Germany. He remains a shadowy and controversial figure.

2. On March 26, 1992, the Space Programs and Technologies Awards Banquet of the American Institute of Aeronautics and Astronautics was held in Huntsville, Alabama, on what would have been Wernher von Braun's 80th birthday. Walter Wiesman rose to give a tribute to the late leader.

Wiesman told the audience several stories to make the point that von Braun was more than a visionary in the exploration of space. He was a "driving force," Wiesman said, at the local and state level in "creating an understanding that the educational and cultural climate of a community is the key to attracting citizens of high caliber."

Turning to von Braun's talents as a leader, Wiesman said "he was the consummate communicator. . . . Some academic colleagues who worked with us for two summers were amazed by Wernher's grasp of organizational dynamics and communication principles. His concept of 'automatic responsibility' is now, a quarter-century later, applied under some other labels to let people at all levels be part of the decision-making process. . . . To be a bit poetic, for a while there we may have had a 'managerial Camelot!' "

In his concluding remarks, Wiesman noted that we read and hear a lot these days about the ideal managers and leaders we need to face the challenges of the 21st century. The best leadership profiles, he said, "show a composite of some of the traits and characteristics that made Wernher von Braun a man ahead of his time. Terms such as 'Man for all Seasons' and 'Renaissance Man' are now used frequently and may have lost some of their luster. I found recently," said Wiesman, "what I consider to be a most appropriate designation: the specialist with a universal mind."

3. An observant reviewer of the manuscript for this book found it interesting that I used the word "we" in point II.A. Was some transference involved in this blossoming identification? No doubt.

## Chapter Five

## STAFF AND BOARD BRIEFING

During the long drive north to Detroit, I contemplated my experiences at MSFC and realized that I had entered a state of *identification* with the organization. I felt a part of it, a sense of belonging, and had persuaded myself that we had common interests: What was good for the space program was good for me. There was an inherent emotional component, positive in nature, a symbolic satisfaction in my relationship with the organization (similar to what I had observed about NASA personnel). I also experienced a change of identity as a result. The organization became part of me; I mentioned my involvement in the space program in conversations with friends and acquaintances and in my lectures to students. It was not just an involvement with an organizational abstraction, although that was true to some extent, but was also implicated by my personal bond with Wiesman, von Braun, and the many others I had come to like and respect during my research residency. Nonetheless, it was not a blind loyalty. I felt an automatic responsibility to identify problems and try to solve them. Thus began my theoretical interest in the concept of organizational identification (see Tompkins and Cheney, 1985).

When my thoughts alternated to my destination, I tried to envision Detroit in ashes but was not creative enough to come up with a realistic and meaningful picture of the whole. Once I got home, friends filled me in on the details. The rioters had set over 1,000 fires and because they were scattered throughout the metropolitan area, reporters had become confused and reported the whole city ablaze. The human consequences were significant: 43 killed, 36 of whom were black. Many had been killed by National Guardsmen.

The situation was still tense. H. "Rap" Brown, a black militant in the Student National Coordinating Committee (SNCC), had been arrested in Cambridge, Maryland, for urging his followers to "burn this town down" on July 25, two days after the Detroit riots started. In August SNCC leader Stokely Carmichael had urged blacks to arm for revolution. Martin Luther King, Jr., however, rejected Carmichael's black power movement and clung to his campaign for nonviolence and civil disobedience. And I had been more concerned about race relations in Alabama than in the North!

I tried to make sense of the riots from the perspective of my own field. Could the behavior of the rioters be, at least in part, communicative acts? I concluded that the behaviors constituted a *message*, upward-directed communication to those at the top of the social and political hierarchy. Those at the bottom were expressing a rage born of frustrated ambitions and inattention. I began to see a concept common to both the structure of the Marshall Center and the structure of society. The one system was functioning effectively because of the high priority given to the problems and needs of those at the bottom; the other had erupted from an absence of such a priority.

At least one other person got the message: Henry Ford II, grandson of the founder of the firm he headed, the Ford Motor Company. After the Detroit riots of 1967, Ford made hiring the hard-core unemployed a corporate goal, the first such occurrence in U.S. history. Ford's Department of Urban and Community Affairs came up with a comprehensive program called "How Industry Can Help Detroit" and sent company interviewers into the ghettoes to hire the chronically unemployed.

As a result of Henry Ford's commitment, the company hired 14,000 jobless people. Two years later, 40 percent of these people were no longer with the company, while 60 percent were still employed. (For a discussion of this program, see Collier and Horowitz, 1987, p. 334.)

Two days after I returned to Detroit, I received an envelope from Huntsville. It contained a copy of a letter on NASA-MSFC letterhead sent by Wernher von Braun to William R. Keast, president of Wayne State University. He spoke highly of the work

I had done and mentioned the Staff and Board presentation I had been asked to give. It was a nice touch, another indication of the considerateness von Braun's colleagues had talked about. As I reflected back on the summer, it occurred to me that bringing summer faculty consultants into the organization and asking them to search for problems was an indication of organizational strength, a sign of good health. Von Braun's request for me to report to the entire Staff and Board was a further indication of that healthy openness and candor that characterized the Center.

I flew back to Huntsville and stayed with Gary Richetto and his wife Suzanne. (Gary was a Ph.D. candidate in organizational communication at Purdue University, who had also joined the group as an intern and become a good friend.) Walt Wiesman had arranged for the preparation of my visual aids: an outline for one screen and the list of problems and recommendations for the other two screens. Since most of the people I had interviewed would be present, the presentation would be a powerful check on the validity of my analysis.

As I rode the elevator to the ninth floor, my apprehension mounted. In a few minutes I would be addressing 50 or 60 of the brightest rocket people in the country. Heightening my anxiety was the fact that my remarks would be critical of some very powerful individuals present.

### The Briefing

Von Braun played on that theme as he introduced me. After mentioning my credentials, he explained that he had received a briefing from me and had asked me to present it to the Staff and Board. He described my report as so "hard hitting" that he felt it necessary to ask that no one leave the room. The tension in the room grew tighter. Then von Braun deadpanned that because an important phone call was coming in from NASA headquarters, he would have to leave the meeting for a few minutes. The audience exploded with laughter, releasing the tension.

I began the briefing by explaining that when I had first arrived at the Marshall Center I didn't know which end of a rocket to light (a bit of hyperbole I had borrowed from Arthur Fiedler). I added that after my extensive interviews and participant observation, I felt I now knew quite a bit about the organization. I began with what worked well, limiting myself to a discussion of the Monday Notes. As I finished, I was interrupted by a sharply spoken question in a German accent: "Is that the only thing we do well?" I realized that we were going to be playing hardball.

"No," I snapped back, "you do other things well too. But I don't want you to feel too good about yourselves at this point." In the laughter that followed, I began to relax. We marched through the problems one by one. As I made my case, some participants raised objections while others came to my defense, supplying evidence to support the analysis, all in a medley of German and American regional accents, including the unmistakably high-pitched voice of von Braun who had slipped back into the meeting without my having noticed. It was good give-and-take, typical of a Marshall briefing. (The entire two-hour briefing was audiotaped by NASA, which allowed me to reconstruct the dialogue verbatim.)

**Recommendations**

The discussion became even more intense as I moved through the recommendations, which I had reordered as suggested by von Braun. Recognizing that some of the problems were universal and probably insoluble, I felt the need to make some suggestions that would stimulate discussion.

*1. Cooperation and Dialogue.* My recommendation for the lack of lateral openness was cooperation and dialogue. Given the fact that top management often rewarded the aggressive competition of the laboratories (for example, von Braun's note: "Looks like you won after all! Congrats. B."), I thought it was the right time to reward *aggressive cooperation* among the labs and offices of RDO. Several lab directors had told me they were willing to give such a policy a chance—that is, to cooperate, give recognition and praise to other units for their cooperation, and praise their own subordinates for reciprocating cooperation.

My recommendation for the larger problem—the cleavage between the engineers of RDO and the project managers of IO—was to bring the key managers of the two units together, along with the Center management, for a candid discussion of matrix management and to resolve the different interpretations of each group's authority.

2. *Confrontation*. Moving to the "family affair" problem, I acknowledged the sensitivity of the topic and the existence of informal organizations within every organization. No recommendation came to mind, I said, other than facing the problem head-on. It seemed wise to bring it out into the open, forcing members and non-members alike to face the facts and acknowledge that at least a *perceived* problem existed. (I believe the strategy worked. A meeting held immediately following the briefing was devoted to the selection of MSFC personnel to be dispatched to the Cape for the preparation of the first launch of the Saturn V. I was told later that day that Eberhard Rees, the senior member of the "family" and von Braun's deputy director, broke up the meeting in both senses of the phrase by saying, "Well, that makes two from the 'family' and three who aren't.")

3. *Visits and Presentations*. Two recommendations were made for the problem of the "invisible boss." Lab directors had described to me the great results when von Braun had made visits to their labs. He listened to presentations, moved from group to group, and was able to communicate to each individual how his or her work contributed to the whole. The visits had a deep and positive impact on morale. The first recommendation, was, of course, to increase the visibility of the boss by increasing the number of visits he made to the labs and offices, despite the time this would take from his busy schedule.

I also recommended that von Braun give a speech on the future of the Marshall Center in the Morris auditorium and on closed-circuit television to the entire workforce. This recommendation was intended not only to increase his visibility, but also to allay anxieties and fears about the future of the organization. I suggested that the director candidly communicate his best estimates of what the future would bring in the way of new projects, budget cuts, and reductions in force.

4. *Perspective and 'Reality Reviews'*. After I described the fourth problem, the "formalism-impersonality syndrome," one of the German laboratory directors broke in to say, "But you forget that's only the IO way." This humorous allusion to the cooperation and dialogue problem illustrated the fact that although these problems and recommendations were analytically separable, they were in fact intertwined in practice. The wisecrack had the place going crazy with shouts and laughter, and I was delighted by the fact that the

participants were now joking about the most serious problem we had uncovered, the tension between RDO and IO.

I had three recommendations. First, management should take a more balanced perspective on such management tools as PERT, control centers, computers, and so on, which had become ends in themselves.

Second, I suggested that the Center extend the principle of the so-called "reality reviews" that had been introduced earlier that summer, in which MSFC had launched the first Saturn V rocket by simulation. Acting as if the rocket were to be launched from Huntsville (which was a not-so-secret wish for some), each person was forced to evaluate his or her participation in the event. Naturally, the "launch" was scrubbed at the last second, but the simulation was found to be highly successful, and the reality review proved a useful alternative to the endless succession of rehearsed lecture-presentations in control centers and conference rooms.

Third, I made a general plea for simplicity. By this time I was leading a problem-solving group discussion of 60 people or so as we tried to find ways of implementing Thoreau's advice to simplify, simplify, simplify. Soon a consensus emerged: R&D for Skylab, then still in the planning stage, should not be "over-managed." Smaller future projects should be managed without a control center and with a minimal use of PERT-style tools. IO would be allowed to shrink, to "wither away" as the larger projects came to conclusion.

*5.   Learn to Live with It.* The fifth problem, the science-technology barrier, was addressed by reminding these managers that as R&D for the Saturn V was completed, the future would call for an increasing number of scientific experiments. That would involve constant communication between the technologists of NASA and principal investigators in the academic community. I recommended that Marshall's Space Sciences Laboratory (and its scholarly director, Dr. Ernst Stuhlinger) be given a more prominent role in the interface with scientists. My reasoning was that the personnel of this lab were the "purest" of the scientists at the Marshall Center; its members worked in the world of science as well as technology. They could play an important translation role between the engineers and academic scientists.

*6. Presentations and Training.* The sixth problem, anxiety about the changing future, had already been addressed in Recommendation

Three above. I also challenged the Center to identify new skills and bodies of knowledge that would be needed in the future so that the Training Branch could begin to develop new courses and workshops for workers whose specialties would become obsolete.

*7. Research, Meetings, and Training.* The seventh problem was my hunch that there were morale problems below the branch level. Gary Richetto, as noted above, had recently joined Wiesman's team as an intern. I recommended that Richetto look closely below the branch level in two of the larger laboratories: the Manufacturing Engineering lab and the Propulsion and Vehicle Engineering lab. If Richetto found serious problems there, some training programs in communication would be in order for the supervisors. I also did a bit of "log-rolling" with von Braun by recommending his pet solution, periodic meetings between supervisors and subordinates, *if* and only if they were coupled with the training.

*8. Deputy Needed.* Regarding the bottleneck in the office of the director of RDO, I recommended that the deputy director vacancy be filled as soon as possible. The criteria for selection, I suggested, should be a person of technical competence, the younger generation of space scientists, American birth, and proven effectiveness in communication. These criteria would deal with the "family" problem as well as the bottleneck.

*9. Maintain/Enhance Penetration.* We saw the problem of the external interfaces as a permanent and insoluble one, and my recommendation—"Punt!"—facetiously reflected that. More seriously, I did praise their practice of penetration and recommended they continue it. Until the *Challenger* accident, it never occurred to me that the practice might one day be forgotten or abandoned.

*10. Move in with Them—And an AO.* My recommendations for the complaints both of and about the staff offices were, first, that the personnel providing staff services should move in with their clients in the labs and offices. Personnel officers were spending 75 percent of their time at their desks, only 25 percent in the labs they were servicing. I recommended that these percentages be reversed. We hoped that this recommendation would force the personnel officers to be more available for consultation and become more knowledge-able about the work in the labs.

The second recommendation was the most controversial. I recommended that a new office be established, a director of administrative operations, whose chief responsibility would be to coordinate the activities of the staff offices. The position would be parallel to the directors of RDO and IO. An AO office performing the necessary coordination would permit his or her boss, the deputy director of administration, to concentrate on center-wide problems and the interface with NASA headquarters. I admitted that the tradeoff was a costly one in that it created an additional layer in the hierarchy, which would, no doubt, create new communication problems. The staff offices had an inferiority complex in regard to IO and RDO, and I thought it might give them a new sense of confidence to see a box with an AO in it at the same level as their counterparts on Marshall's organizational chart. I had drawn up such a chart and displayed it with RDO on the left, AO in the middle, and IO on the right. A very sincere man near the front was alarmed that such an arrangement would add to the barrier between RDO and IO. I was momentarily speechless, then explained to this man, said to be a very smart engineer, that this was only a *symbolic* representation, that the office would not physically be placed between the other two units in such a way as to block communication between them.

My presentation was finished. We had been at it for a gruelling two hours, and the group gave me a nice hand.

We had a big party that night at the Richettos' place. Before retiring for the night, Gary Richetto turned to me and said, "Do you realize that today with von Braun you shook the hand of a man who's shaken hands with Eisenhower, Kennedy, and Johnson—plus Himmler, Goering, and Hitler?"

## Chapter Six

# REORGANIZING THE MARSHALL CENTER

As I settled into the routine of the academic year of 1967-1968, my thoughts were often with my new friends in Huntsville. I wondered whether my research and recommendations had made any difference. Walt Wiesman had already invited me to return to the Marshall Center in the same capacity for the summer of 1968, and I had tentatively accepted.

### Reductions in Force

A few weeks later two copies of the November 29th edition of the *Marshall Star*, MSFC's house organ, arrived in my mailbox, one sent by Wiesman, the other by Lynda Dolan, a secretary in the Manpower office to which I had been attached. The front page was devoted to the text of a speech given by von Braun after NASA had received some bad news. Congress had passed, and the President had signed, a budget-cutting appropriations bill. The Marshall Center had been requested to reduce personnel by 700 (effective January 13, 1968), travel by 10 percent, and all other administrative costs by 15 percent.

"Seldom have I faced a more painful job than to announce these decisions during the holiday season," von Braun said. "Let me assure you, it is no hasty action. During the past weeks we have painstakingly explored every avenue in search of an alternative, but found none."

He had followed through on my recommendation, delivering his speech in the Morris Auditorium and broadcasting it on the Center's closed-circuit television system. Rather than have the personnel office mail out termination notices, he wanted to make the unhappy announcement himself. This humane concern for his employees was characteristic of von Braun's management style.

He went on to discuss the changing role of the Center. The ground test facilities vital to the Saturn Program were no longer needed. "Only a very few of the more versatile facilities in our Test Laboratory can be used in the job of developing payloads for the Saturn vehicles," he said. The Test Lab was the hardest hit of all MSFC organizations. I thought of Karl Heimburg, its director, with whom I had spent a stimulating two hours during the summer. *How would he follow up on the bad news?* I wondered.

Von Braun then discussed the RIF (reductions in force) numbers by personnel categories and revealed a detailed plan to help place the unlucky ones in new jobs at other NASA Centers. In addition, more than 100 government and industrial organizations would be asked to help by filling their vacancies with those affected. A special placement office was to be established for this purpose.

A proportionate reduction in support contractor personnel would also be made. "As in the case of the Civil Service personnel," von Braun said, "I deeply regret we have to convey this type of information to our friends and colleagues in local industries, particularly at this time of year."

Then came his peroration:

> Our job with the Saturn vehicles is by no means completed. We still must ride herd over the hardware that is coming up. Quality and reliability standards, both for flight and ground equipment, will continue to require our attention. Our success in the future will come only if we continue to operate as conscientiously as we have in the past.
>
> NASA has announced there will be 11 Apollo flights, involving either uprated Saturn Is or Saturn Vs, in the next two years. We must make every one of them as perfect as possible. In the future we also must continue fulfilling our tasks in the new, vital, and interesting projects that we have: the Orbital Workshop, the Apollo Telescope Mount, and the Multiple Docking Adapter. And, of course, our primary mission of space research technology must continue unabated. If there is less money, then we simply must roll up our sleeves and make do with the funds available.

I am personally urging each of you—I am challenging each of you—to work even harder in the future than we have in the past toward building for America the technological base to explore and exploit space.

We must continue to do this job well.

I was impressed. The only words I would have changed were "exploit space," but the rest of the speech was just what was called for.

Lynda Dolan had also attached a note directing me to an article in the *Marshall Star* announcing that Gary Richetto had embarked on a study of internal communication at the Marshall Center. "The idea may be a first within NASA," the article read. "The actual study will begin early next month with assistance of some 200-250 interviewees from the Manufacturing Engineering and Propulsion and Vehicle Engineering Labs." Richetto was quoted as saying he was interested in problems of communication at the "laboratory branch levels." Needless to say, I was pleased to see that three of my recommendations had already been tackled: more visibility for the boss, a candid presentation about the future of MSFC, and Richetto's investigation beneath the branch level in two of the largest and most important laboratories.

### Saturn V Flies

On November 9, 1967, I got up early to watch the first unmanned launch of the Moon Rocket, the Saturn V, on television. It was a tense situation because of the "all-up" gamble in this first unmanned flight. With previous multi-stage rockets, each stage was successively tested in flight with "dummy" stages above it. With the first flight of the Saturn V, all three stages were being tested "live." If everything went well, NASA would be on schedule to keep Kennedy's promise to land a man on the moon, and return him to earth, within the decade. If not, the program was in trouble. I sat down in front of the television set and listened to Walter Cronkite count down the launch. Even the speaker on my tiny set conveyed the thunderous thrust of the five F-1 engines firing simultaneously, so powerful that Cronkite announced that vibrations were bringing the ceiling of his control booth down on top of him. The Saturn V soared into space, each stage functioning as designed. We were on schedule.

In 1968 the country seemed to be falling into disarray, which made success for the Apollo Project particularly important, or so it seemed to me. The great Tet offensive had begun on January 30 of 1968, and although it did not succeed militarily, the war was henceforth rhetorically and psychologically doomed for the United States. North Korea had seized the U.S.S. *Pueblo* one week earlier. The massacre of My Lai village by U.S. troops took place six weeks later: hundreds of men, women, and children were rounded up and "wasted" by the American forces. Communism seemed on the rise on all fronts. Martin Luther King, Jr. and Robert Kennedy had both been assassinated. President Johnson was unable to leave the White House because of the demonstrations and protests against the war in Vietnam. These events no doubt contributed to the public's willingness to pay the tax bill for the moon shots. To many people, the moon shots represented the country's hope; they were a sign that the United States had finally caught up with the Soviet Union in the "Space Race."

### Return to Huntsville

My trip to Huntsville for the summer of 1968 was going to be somewhat circuitous. I had accepted a position as full professor at Kent State University for the following year, but would first teach an early summer school course at the University of Kansas. So, I moved my furniture into storage in Kent, Ohio, and headed west for Lawrence, Kansas (where I had begun my teaching career in 1957). At the end of the summer session, I again packed my convertible and headed to Huntsville.

The Marshall Center was ready for me this time. Our work for Walt Wiesman was now well known at the Center. One of the RDO labs had even mentioned my work and Gary Richetto's follow-up research below the branch level in the Monday notes. My first appointment was with von Braun. He brought me up to date and gave me a new set of problems to investigate. Because the Saturn V had proved itself the previous November, it was time to think about new projects and how to communicate about them. NASA had given the Marshall Center a new mission: the Apollo Applications Program (AAP), the chief components of which were the Orbital Workshop, the Apollo Telescope Mount, and the Multiple Docking Adaptor (as noted earlier), a configuration we now know as Skylab. Historically speaking, MSFC had been devoted to the research and development of missiles and rockets, but now that what some called the "ultimate rocket" was operational, the organization was undertaking a different task and again faced the need for a metamorphosis.

## The 24 Questions

As a result, there was a change in my role as a summer faculty consultant. My assignment the previous summer had been to conduct a diagnostic study of MSFC as a communication system, to search for systemic problems by means of anonymous, in-depth interviews with the top and middle managers of the organization. Von Braun handed me a document entitled "Questions Related to the Organization and Implementation of the Systems Engineering Effort and Related AAP Management Areas at MSFC." The three-page paper consisted of what became known as "The 24 Questions." Several of these questions will convey the flavor of the document:

1. Assuming that the primary technical resources (manpower) available to do the Systems Engineering "job" include (a) the design laboratories, (b) the R&D Systems Engineering Office (formerly the Technical Systems Office), (c) the Program Systems Office, (d) a System Integration Contractor (Martin), and (e) certain hardware contractors (e.g., McDonnell Douglas); how do you organize the total job around these resources?

3. What are the roles of the RDO Systems Engineering Office and the Program Systems Engineering Office in the AAP Cluster Systems Engineering area? What are their relationships to each other? What is the status of these two organizations?

16. What are the lead lab functions and responsibilities of the OWS [Orbital Workshop]? What is the relationship of the lead lab functions and responsibilities to those of the Program Office?

Several key issues were imbedded in the 24 questions:

1. Given a finite number of resources (e.g., MSFC's engineering labs, project management offices, and contractors), how should they be reorganized so as to optimize the systems engineering effort?

2. Should the experiment with the lead lab concept (in which engineering labs assumed managerial responsibility for subsystems) be continued, or should there be a build-up of new project offices as had been done in the case of the Saturn V?

3. Should the build-up in systems engineering (by an increase in both authority and personnel) be placed primarily in the small RDO-based Systems Engineering Office, in the IO-based project management offices, or in contractor organizations?

Von Braun had requested answers from several offices and asked me to come up with a set of my own. The basic question echoed Barnard's (1938) theory of authority and organizational communication (discussed in Chapter Two): Who should communicate with whom and with what authority? Von Braun stressed to me that he most wanted to avoid what he called a "foul compromise." He wanted a *theoretical* solution to the questions, not a political one. He explained that the three-component cluster—the workshop, telescope, and docking adaptor—required somewhat different methods of R&D than those used by the Marshall Center in the past. There had been some criticism that the Saturn V had been developed with subsystems engineering rather than with true systems engineering. That is, the Marshall Center's discipline-oriented laboratories had optimized subsystems of the huge rocket at the expense of the total system. "Brute force" was then required to integrate the various subsystems into a whole. For example, if you set four different crews to work building four walls (subsystems) for a cabin (the total system), and the crews "optimized" each wall without regard for the other, you would have problems putting the four walls together to form the cabin. Von Braun's superior in Washington, George Mueller, wanted the Skylab cluster to be designed with an emphasis on systems engineering.

## Systems Engineering

Von Braun explained the basics of systems engineering with his characteristic analogies. A rocket, he said, is like an airplane or car, a piece of machinery that moves. A telephone, however, is an entirely different game. To design telephones, it is necessary to think in terms of a larger system; the receiver itself is just a gadget. To make it useful the engineer must think of it as a small part (or subsystem) of larger system which also includes other elements or subsystems such as trunk lines and central switchboards. Another analogy he used was the nervous system. One must not think of parts such as the fingers, he said, but rather of the whole system. For example, the United States had never taken a systems view of the air transportation system as it had developed. Instead, the country had optimized subsystems without sufficient regard to the air traffic system as a whole. As a result, he said, today it takes almost as much time to get to and from airports and to board and deplane as it does to fly across the continent. George Mueller had been trained in electrical engineering and automatically thought in terms of the nervous system, von Braun explained. He, on the other hand, had come into space-flight engineering thinking in terms of the airplane as a machine and had moved more slowly toward thinking in terms of systems engineering.

To avoid such problems, the Marshall Center was determined to optimize systems engineering in its R&D of Skylab, and this was likely to require radical reorganization. Von Braun understood more than most managers that organization consists of patterns and lines of communication. The way these were structured could either *limit* or *enhance* the likelihood of integrating a systems engineering orientation. The answers to von Braun's 24 questions would determine how the reorganization would be effected.

Von Braun also explained an ad hoc solution which had been adopted during the interim. The program management for Skylab was located in IO. Rather than build up project offices for its three main subsystems, as had been done with each stage of the Saturn V, laboratories in RDO were given management responsibility for the components. Astrionics, for example, was the lead lab for the Apollo Telescope Mount. Von Braun wanted me to find out how well this concept was working in practice. The lead lab concept was covered in several of the questions, but von Braun emphasized that he wanted my opinion on the concept itself. He also outlined some additional "action items," as he put it: administrative questions he had to decide on immediately, such as which of two competing labs should do the design work for future on-board computers.

So it was back to work. Another 50 in-depth interviews were conducted, this time including 14 division chiefs (one scalar level below the lab director). My main objectives were to discover new schemes of organizational communication that would give systems engineering a central role in future R&D work and, of course, to find out how well the lead lab concept was working. It was a highly educational period for me. I read textbooks on systems engineering and asked for explanations and definitions from every interviewee possessing technical expertise. I also asked them to sketch their "pet schemes" for me and critique ones I had developed on my own.

The wide range of responses about systems engineering was bewildering; it was not a stable and widely-understood concept. Some admitted that they did not understand what it meant. Others argued that systems engineering was more a matter of genius than of training or discipline. Everyone admitted that von Braun had such a genius; so did Ludie Richard, the director of the small Systems Engineering Office. At the division level, it was repeatedly asserted that "any *good* engineer is a systems engineer." Consider, for example, the engineers who worked on "actuators," triggering devices installed in all rockets and their various subsystems. The engineers felt that to build an effective actuator they had to consider its technological environment and how it related to larger systems. Thus, it was argued, they were systems engineers.

I began to discern a pattern in the responses. My interviewees spanned four hierarchical levels, and their answers tended to vary with rank. The higher they had moved up the hierarchy at Marshall, the larger their perspective, their conception of the *system*. (I was constantly aware of the hierarchical status of my interviewees. In fact, I could identify it simply by walking into an employee's office because of the ubiquitous status symbol—models of the Saturn V. The larger the model, the higher the status. The one in von Braun's office was so tall that a hole had been cut in the ceiling to accommodate it.) I began to play the devil's advocate in interviews with proponents of systems engineering, arguing that one could justifiably regard the Apollo *Project* as the system rather than Saturn V, Skylab—or the entire space program. This observation was never challenged, but it became clear to me that the Marshall Center was overly oriented toward low-level subsystems engineering. The laboratories, particularly the design laboratories, were too large and independent to be otherwise. As one manager put it, "If we had a lawnmower capability at the Marshall Center, we'd put lawnmowers on all the vehicles." This, of course, created problems for the people who had to integrate the various subsystems.

## The Lead Lab Concept

The way in which the independence of the laboratories was antithetical to the concept of systems engineering can be illustrated by my findings about the lead lab concept. As indicated above, this concept was invented to keep subsystem management in RDO rather than build up new project offices in IO for that purpose. The Astrionics Laboratory was designated as the lead lab for the Apollo Telescope Mount (ATM). My interviews there produced nothing but praise for the concept. In other labs, however, my interviews led to the opposite conclusion. In their opinion, Astrionics' work in other areas was suffering. As lead lab for the ATM, Astrionics was concentrating on the mount to such a degree that it had outraced its own efforts on Skylab's other components. The lab had reached solutions to problems on the ATM which then became fixed parameters that placed constraints on systems the other labs were working on. In addition, Astrionics and other lead labs tended to lag behind on other component work for which they had substantive but not managerial responsibilities. This situation, quite obviously, was antithetical to the systems engineering approach.

While I was preparing to report to von Braun that the lead lab concept appeared incompatible with an increased emphasis on systems engineering, I learned that another university professor doing research and consulting for NASA headquarters had come to the opposite conclusion. His method was to study the research and development of the ATM by taking a "vertical slice" of NASA, moving from headquarters to MSFC and interviewing only those involved in the management of the project. However, he had not taken a horizontal slice at the Marshall Center to see what impact the lead lab concept had on the other labs and for Skylab as a system. He had heard the optimistic reports from Astrionics but had not received the radically different perspectives of the other labs working on Skylab. MSFC employees arranged a long distance telephone call between the two of us, and I was able to convince him that his data were invalid because of his limited sample, which did not take into account the many kinds of interconnections within the organization. There is a general rule of thumb in organizational studies that one must make observations at a minimum of three levels of the hierarchy and more when possible. The lead lab incident related above indicates that there should be an analogous rule for horizontal units as well.

**Another Briefing for von Braun**

On September 16, 1968, I met for three hours with von Braun and his assistant, Jim Shepherd. My data were drawn from interviews at four levels of the hierarchy and the entire horizontal span of the organization. I began by saying that I would not provide detailed answers to all of the 24 questions (many of which were characteristically redundant), but would instead take positions on the major issues, propose some ideas for reorganizing the Marshall Center, and then make some recommendations on the "action items" von Braun had given me six weeks earlier. I felt more relaxed than the first time I had briefed him. We had come to know each other fairly well by then, and I was comfortable now with his give-and-take style. My position was that it appeared to be a propitious time for a reorganization. Though a few of my interviewees were reluctant to change, saying "Let's put a man on the moon before we reorganize," they were distinctly in the minority. I praised the statesmanship of many interviewees who recommended restructurings that would not necessarily ensure the longevity of their own sub-units.

I recommended that the Systems Engineering Office (SEO) be strengthened by adding additional personnel and by repositioning the office in a position of centralized authority within RDO (or the equivalent to RDO in the new scheme of organization). In order to give SEO sufficient authority vis-à-vis the large laboratories, I recommended that the then-current director of SEO, Ludie Richard, be appointed to the position of deputy director of RDO. Richard conveniently met the criteria I had established the previous summer. He was technically competent, represented a new generation of leadership, was of American birth, and was communicatively competent, i.e., articulate, patient, and easy to work with. He was also one of the most highly respected systems engineers at the Marshall Center.

From this new position, Richard would have authority over the design labs and could insure that their plans were "iterated," as they called it, with a central systems engineering office. (Richard's appointment would also solve the bottleneck problem at the RDO level we had discovered in 1967.) By this constant iteration between SEO and all the design labs, a true systems engineering effort could be achieved. I also recommended that the lead lab concept be dropped so that the new SEO office could discourage the autonomous decision making on subsystems which was constraining the other labs.

I went on to sketch the approaches for reorganization that I had considered. After I had indicated which scheme I favored, von Braun pulled out a penciled organization chart and said, "We're close." His schematic was similar to mine. He said this was due to the influence of my previous work and recommendations. For example, his plan included a box labeled AO (for Administrative Operations) parallel to IO and RDO, as I had recommended in 1967 and again in this meeting. Both schematics also included a prominent new line office labeled "Science," which was an attempt to ameliorate the science-technology barrier we had discovered the previous summer.

During the meeting Bonnie Holmes, von Braun's secretary, walked in to report that James E. Webb, NASA administrator, had just publicly announced his resignation and indicated von Braun was free to comment. The director dictated a statement, which Bonnie promptly typed up and returned to him. He asked her to give it to me. He saw that I was puzzled and asked me to check the grammar and style. I did so and pronounced it to be good English, but there was a statement that alluded to some "storms" through which Mr. Webb had steered NASA safely. What does that mean? "The 204 fire, Governor Wallace, and the Alabama environment," he replied.

### Action Items

We then moved on to the host of action items he had asked me to research. My interviews with 14 division chiefs confirmed that they had all been asked by their laboratory directors to provide a Friday Note of each week's activities which were then used to prepare the Monday Notes for von Braun. The division chiefs in turn requested notes from their subordinates (called branch chiefs) and so on. Von Braun's marginalia was also duplicated for the appropriate engineers. He again expressed his satisfaction that such a simple device had imposed a rigorous discipline of organizational communication. Nearly every member of the organization paused at least once a week to consider what information should be transmitted up the line, and they knew that feedback from the director would be forthcoming.

In 1967, I had found indirect evidence that there were serious problems of supervisory communication beneath the branch level of the laboratories. As indicated above, I had recommended that Gary Richetto pursue this potential problem by means of interviews beneath the branch level in two laboratories, Manufacturing Engineering (ME) and Propulsion and Vehicle Engineering (P&VE). Richetto confirmed my hunch: there were problems. Perhaps the most significant was what he dubbed the "reluctant supervisor." Civil Service regulations placed upper limits on grade and salary for research and development personnel. Upon reaching this level, the only route to promotion and increased salary was to become a supervisor. However, the responsibilities of the supervisor were somewhat in conflict with the value premise at Marshall that an engineer should "keep his [or her] hands dirty." As a result, some supervisors accepted promotions without real interest in, or affinity for, their new duties. These supervisors frequently violated common sense principles of communication and supervision.

Following up on Richetto's idea in my interviews with higher-level managers, I discovered that the prototype for the reluctant manager was none other than von Braun himself. With all his talk about the need for keeping their "hands dirty" and his supposed scorn for paperwork and endless conferences in Washington, the director had become the role model for those who accepted the responsibilities of management reluctantly. I wondered how von Braun would react to this criticism. He was surprised and, if anything, intrigued. He slowly repeated the criticism, asked if he had correctly understood it—I said yes—then indicated that would try to improve his image as a manager.

**Other Recommendations**

Von Braun's visits to labs and offices, which I had recommended the year before, had produced the desired effects, and I suggested he keep at it. He wanted to know whether or not he should announce the visits in advance, saying that he suspected that lab personnel created a "Potemkin's Village" when they knew he was coming. I said that I understood people might erect facades by rehearsing their presentations for him, but there would be a lot of disappointment if someone happened to be absent from the lab when he visited. I also recommended that von Braun give another televised speech about the reorganization of MSFC in order to minimize speculation and misinformed rumors.

He had also asked me to look into a controversy over whether the Computation Lab should be allowed to design on-board computers for future space flights. Astrionics had done all such design work in the past and the Comp Lab had been restricted to providing services for the Center. To keep morale high in the Comp Lab, I recommended that it be allowed to do some design work.

The three-hour meeting ended with von Braun requesting that I not reveal his reaction to my proposed reorganization scheme. He wanted to make the final decisions, obtain Washington's approval in principle, and announce the changes himself. This made sense. I had hoped that the rest of the week could be spent at a more relaxed pace in preparation for my drive north to Kent State University. But many of my interviewees wanted to know the results of my interviews and refused to take no for an answer, even when I explained my promise not to reveal von Braun's responses to my proposals. Therefore, the week was as hectic as any other as I ran around the Center, briefing various people on my findings and recommendations but keeping von Braun's reactions confidential.

### The Second Metamorphosis of MSFC

After my academic life resumed at Kent State University, the Marshall Center and I kept in touch. Walt Wiesman informed me that von Braun gave a 90-minute presentation of the new organizational changes on January 16, 1969. The text of his speech was published in a general memorandum entitled "Adjustment to Marshall Organization, Announcement #4." Wiesman sent me a copy.

The reorganization of the Marshall Center was somewhat different from the handwritten version von Braun had shown me. Ernst Stuhlinger, director of the Space Sciences Laboratory (for which, in 1967, I had recommended greater organizational prominence) became associate director of science, reporting directly to von Braun. The staff offices were assigned to the director of administration and technical services (a move analogous to my recommendation for a new AO).

RDO became "Science and Engineering." A new systems engineering directorate was established within this new unit to strengthen systems engineering. Ludie Richard assumed the position I had recommended him for, deputy director, technical, within Science and Engineering. The director of the Astrionics Laboratory, Walter Haeussermann, became director of the new Systems Engineering Directorate. "Mr. Richard will be instrumental in establishing the new Systems Engineering Directorate for Dr. Haeussermann. . . ." von Braun's report read. "The new Systems Engineering Directorate will be established as a line organization with directions and decision authority for overall Center Systems Engineering."

A number of planning offices, including the Advanced Systems Office, were combined into Program Development, where they would concentrate on advanced feasibility studies. IO became Program Management, into which the Saturn IB (an earlier version of the moon rocket) and Saturn V offices were combined as the Saturn Program Office.

I was invited back to the Center for the summer of 1969 in my usual faculty consultant role, but I had been awarded a grant from the Graduate School at Kent State to spend part of the summer in Dublin to continue my research on James Joyce and decided to accept it.

After I got back from Ireland I gathered with friends to watch the moon landing on the evening of July 21, 1969. We were, like most Americans, keen with anticipation, but few people watching were as ego-involved as I. The Saturn V had performed flawlessly in placing the astronauts on the precise trajectory toward the moon. Now the tiny spacecraft had to land them on the lunar surface and bring them back to a rendezvous with the larger spacecraft orbiting the moon. Then we got those first eerie sounds and pictures from the moon.

Armstrong: "Houston, Tranquility Base here. The Eagle has landed." Those words broke the tension for "some sum of billions of eyes and ears around a world which had just come into contact with another world" (Mailer, 1969, p. 335). None of us at our gathering could understand Armstrong's words when he first stepped on the moon, a serious rhetorical disappointment, but we read them later. Mailer (1969) got them down with this terse comment:

"That's one small step for a man," said Armstrong, "one giant leap for mankind." He had joined the ranks of the forever quoted. Patrick Henry, Henry Stanley and Admiral Dewey moved over for him. (p. 352)

*Saturn V launch on the Apollo Program's last mission to the moon, 1972 (NASA photo archives)*

We had redeemed Kennedy's promise, and the nation's mood seemed to be one of regained pride. Some critics argued, however, that it was nothing more than a publicity stunt to distract us from protesting the war in Vietnam. Others complained that it was a waste of money that could have been better spent on social programs. (I worried about that argument until I became convinced, over the years, that cuts in NASA's budgets did not correlate with increases in social programs.) The most incredible reaction to the moon landing came from a large group of American citizens, numbering perhaps in the millions, who did *not believe* the deed had been accomplished. They believed that all the pictures came from a televised simulation on some sound stage. I remember vividly the woman in Florida who expressed this belief with impeccable logic. She said she couldn't pick up television stations in New York, so how could she possibly be getting pictures from the moon?

I later would begin an article about MSFC and the Apollo Project with these lines:

> The Apollo Project was the greatest technological achievement of our society. It worked. During an era of demonstrations, violence, war, assassinations, [riots], scandal, cost overruns and technological failures—it worked. It was also the largest engineering project in history. (Tompkins, 1977, p. 1)

I also described the ways in which Apollo was a success in organizational communication. But that night in 1969, I went to bed happy with the knowledge that the U.S. could do something right and that the Marshall Center had played a major role in the moon landing. At the very least I could say that I had not done anything to botch it all.

Chapter Seven

# A READING OF THE ROGERS
# COMMISSION REPORT

After 1970 I did not hear officially from MSFC for many years, 19 to be exact.[1]  By the early 1970s, my main contacts there were gone.  Von Braun had left for Washington, ostensibly to dream about future space flights and to lobby Congress on behalf of NASA.  Walt Wiesman had chosen early retirement in 1970 in order to devote himself to lecturing and community affairs.[2]  And my life had changed.  After Elaine Vanden Bout Anderson and I co-wrote a book about the tragedy at Kent State University,[3] we decided to get married in 1971.  We lived happily ever after and have since warned our students to be careful about who they choose to be their co-authors!

### *Topoi* and Tradeoffs

I had a new job as chairperson of a new department of communication at the State University of New York at Albany (SUNYA). While there, I kept my summers free for writing monographs about MSFC, which were published in a journal called *Communication Monographs*.  I wrote about a surprise I had experienced at the Space Center: that the neat distinction established by Aristotle between *science*, or demonstration, and *rhetoric*, or persuasion, did not serve me well in trying to understand the organization.  Only the easy decisions at Marshall were made by scientific evidence or demonstration.  The difficult decisions created a rhetorical problem because the solution could not be demonstrated scientifically.  At

MSFC the three master *topoi*, Aristotle's term for possible lines of argument in a rhetorical situation, were

> *reliability, time*, and *cost*. Most if not all, of the arguments given in support of a particular solution had premises anchored in those *topoi*. The optimal solution in these situations could not be demonstrated scientifically. . . . Consequently, the difficult decisions involved some sort of tradeoff [a new word for me in 1967 when I heard it at MSFC] between and among these criteria of reliability, cost, and time. Enthymeme theory [an invention of Aristotle's; the enthymeme is a rhetorical syllogism of which the major premise is drawn from popular beliefs, or in this case, the three main *topoi*], the concept of *ethos*, and rhetorical theory in general help to explain the behavior of the engineers in the discussions leading to a hard decision. It was a rhetorical enterprise. (Tompkins, 1977, p. 25)

This passage will help with the explication of the Rogers Commission Report later in this chapter, but for now it is important to grasp that difficult aerospace decisions involved tradeoffs among the three main *topoi* of reliability (or safety), time (or schedule), and cost.

After nine years of department administration at SUNYA, I accepted an offer to return to my alma mater, Purdue University, in the fall of 1980. W. Charles Redding, the founder of organizational communication and my own Ph.D. adviser, had retired from full-time teaching. Now it was my turn to do some of the advising of Ph.D. students. As mentioned earlier in this book, Purdue identified strongly with the Space Program. Next door to my office was Grissom Hall.

### Skylab and the Space Shuttle

During the 1970s and the first half of the 1980s, I continued to follow the space program with great interest. Walt Wiesman still lived in Huntsville and kept in touch with both the Center and with me. Even though most of the Germans were now gone from the Marshall Center, I had no reason to think the organization was in decline. The Apollo Application Program (Skylab) had gone splendidly and was a source of satisfaction to me because of my earlier involvement. I was particularly moved by the U.S.-Soviet rendezvous in space in 1975 and harbored a small hope that this feat of technological cooperation might help improve relations between the two superpowers. I knew that the MSFC had shrunk in size since its peak during the 1960s, but I knew also that it was busy supervising the R&D of the propulsion system for the space shuttle.

This brings us up to the event with which I began this book, the tragedy of the *Challenger* accident in 1986. While considering the contradictions between past and current practices at MSFC and developing my hypothesis of organizational amnesia, I left Purdue University in the fall of 1986 to accept a position as a professor of communication and comparative literature at the University of Colorado at Boulder. Unexpectedly, there was a space connection at CU, which, like Purdue, claims to have produced more astronauts than any other university. I soon learned that CU's president, Gordon Gee, had led a large party to Cape Kennedy to watch the launch of *Challenger* on February 28, 1986. Ellison Onizuka, a member of the doomed crew, had a Master's degree from the University of Colorado.

## The Rogers Commission Report

After our move to Boulder, the *Report of the Presidential Commission on the Space Shuttle Challenger Accident* (June 6, 1986) became available, as did such books as Malcolm McConnell's *Challenger: A Major Malfunction* (1987), Joseph J. Trento's *Prescription for Disaster: From the Glory of Apollo to the Betrayal of the Shuttle* (1987), and other commentaries. The Rogers Commission concluded that the *Challenger* incident constituted "an accident rooted in history," one that was caused in part by problems in "communication." But the Commission gave no indication that it had any knowledge of the "history of communication" at MSFC.

I obtained a copy of the Rogers Commission Report and read it with great interest, of course. In a recent rereading, I was struck by certain passages in the cover letter to the President. Speaking for the Commission, Rogers wrote:

> Our objective has been not only to prevent any recurrence of the failure related to this accident, but to the extent possible to reduce other risks in future flights. However, the Commission did not construe its mandate to require a detailed evaluation of the entire Shuttle system. It fully recognizes that the risk associated with space flight cannot be totally eliminated.

Each member of the Commission shared the pain and anguish the nation felt at the heavy loss of seven brave Americans in the Challenger accident on January 28, 1986.

The nation's task now is to move ahead to return to safe space flight and to its recognized position of leadership in space. There could be no more fitting tribute to the Challenger crew than to do so. (p. v)

Again we see expressed the "motives" of sacrifice, tragedy, and purpose ("the nation's task") linked as Burke had prophesied and Cheney had documented in his survey of the immediate response to the accident. There seemed to me a contradiction in simultaneously recognizing that the "risk associated with space flight cannot be totally eliminated" and pronouncing that it was the "nation's task. . .to return to *safe* space flight" (italics added). The acknowledgement that the risk could not be eliminated leads one to expect the Rogers Commission might have qualified the absolute term "safe." Another contradiction lay in the rather opaque and confused phrase, "to move ahead to return to safe space flight." Did Burke's notion of purpose, so necessary to tragedy, override other interests within the Commission itself?

On page five of the preface to the report appears an observation that after the landing of the *Columbia* shuttle on July 4, 1982, NASA "declared the Space Shuttle 'operational,' a term that has encountered some criticism because it erroneously suggests that the Shuttle had attained an airline-like degree of routine operation." Even the Commission believed that NASA had been "straining" after its purpose, the element necessary to create a tragedy.

The report describes in detail the components of the shuttle's hardware, the objectives of *Challenger's* flight, the members of the crew and their assignments, and preparations for the flight. The Flight Readiness Review (FRR) for the mission took place on January 15, 1986: "No outstanding concerns were identified in the discussion of flight design, " according to the report (p. 15). In other words, the FRR participants had not been told about concerns with the now infamous O-rings. The short, tragic flight of *Challenger* was summarized in a table on page 18:

| The Flight of the Challenger | |
|---|---|
| The events that followed lift-off were brief: | |
| *Launch time* | *Event* |
| -6.6 sec. | Space Shuttle engines ignition |
| 0 sec. | Solid Rocket Booster ignition |
| + 7 sec. | "Roll program." (Challenger) <br> "Roger, roll, Challenger." (Houston) |
| +24 sec. | Main engines throttled down to 94% |
| +42 sec. | Main engines throttled down to 65% |
| +59 sec. | Main engines throttled up to 104% |
| +65 sec. | "Challenger, go at throttle up." (Houston) <br> "Roger. Go at throttle up." (Challenger) |
| +73 sec. | Loss of signal from Challenger |

The text accompanying this table concludes with the following two sentences: "During the period of flight when the Solid Rocket Boosters are thrusting, there are no survivable abort options. There was nothing that either the crew or the ground controllers could have done to avert the catastrophe." Numerous photographs show the shuttle, the launch, the first plumes of smoke, and the structural breakup of the vehicle which began 73 seconds into the flight.

**The Cause of the Accident**

Chapter IV of the report, "The Cause of the Accident," begins with a collective judgment. "The consensus of the Commission and participating investigative agencies" was that the cause of the accident had been the "failure in the joint between the two lower segments of the right Solid Rocket Motor," (p. 40). No other component was at fault. Back in 1967, Wernher von Braun had explained to me that solid-rocket fuels should not be used in manned flight because they cannot be shut down once ignited. A liquid-fueled engine, however, can be turned off by a valve. Hence, it is impossible to test solid-fuel engines as thoroughly as liquid-fuel engines.

Initial plans for the shuttle, prior to 1970, had called for the use of liquid fuel, but due to cost concerns, earlier designs for the shuttle were shelved. According to the Rogers Report, ". . . solids as boosters for manned flight was a technology new to the agency [in 1971]. Mercury, Gemini, and Apollo astronauts had all been rocketed into space by liquid-fuel systems. Nonetheless, the recoverable Solid Rocket Booster won the nod [of approval], even though the liquid rocket offered potentially lower operating costs. The overriding reason was that pricing estimates indicated a lower cost of development for the solid booster" (pp. 3-4).

Joseph J. Trento has reconstructed the decision processes that produced solid-fuel boosters for the shuttle in his book, *Prescription for Disaster: From the Glory of the Apollo to the Betrayal of the Shuttle* (1987).

President Nixon appointed James Fletcher, a physicist with experience in industry and as the president of the University of Utah, to be the head man at NASA in 1971. As the plans for a solid-rocket shuttle developed, Robert R. Gilruth (a brilliant engineer who had coordinated Project Mercury) and Wernher von Braun (by then at NASA headquarters) strongly opposed the design. Solid-rocket engines, as we have seen, could not be shut down. There was another related reason: the absence of an "ejectable" capsule, which meant that there was no escape system if a problem developed.

According to Trento, Fletcher accepted a compromise on the shuttle budget that would have long-term repercussions when George Schultz, then director of the Office of Management and Budget (OMB) and later Secretary of State under President Reagan, withdrew a 20 percent contingency for that program that Nixon had earlier approved. Trento believes that this compromise probably determined that the shuttle would have to fly with solid-fuel boosters and without an escape system.

Schultz's OMB also recommended that "the Marshall Space Flight Center be closed. To save it, Fletcher. . .gave the very center that vehemently opposed any use of solid rockets for manned flight the assignment of assisting in the development of the solids" (Trento, 1987, p. 115).

Trento notes that Fletcher's decision to award the solid-booster contract to Morton Thiokol was controversial.  While Thiokol's bid was reportedly the lowest, Trento asserts that at least one competing contractor had more experience building large solid boosters (1987, pp. 115-116).  McConnell's book also suggests this and offers a detailed description of the "bitter contract-award dispute" that ensued (1987, pp. 50-61) after Fletcher's decision.  Morton Thiokol is located in Utah, a state in which Fletcher had resided for many years. (Fletcher left NASA in 1977, only to return again as administrator after the *Challenger* disaster; he remained with the agency until 1989.)

The Rogers Report methodically rejects other hypotheses about the *Challenger* accident.  There was no evidence of sabotage; the external tank had not contributed to the cause of the accident; the space shuttle main engines did not contribute to the cause; neither the orbiter nor related equipment contributed to the cause; nothing in the orbiter/payload interface contributed to the accident; the left solid rocket booster and *"all components of the right Solid Rocket Booster, except the right Solid Rocket Motor, did not contribute to or cause the accident"* (p. 53).

The possible failure of other components of this motor were rejected one-by-one before turning to the components of the field joint: the tang, the clevis, and the O-ring.

> *In view of the findings, the Commission concluded that the cause of the Challenger accident was the failure of the pressure seal in the aft field joint of the Right Solid Rocket Motor. The failure was due to a faulty design unacceptably sensitive to a number of factors. These factors were the effects of temperature, physical dimensions, the character of materials, the effects of reusability, processing, and reaction of the joint to dynamic loading.* (p. 72)

Thus, the technical cause of the accident had been identified.

### Contributing Cause

Chapter V, "The Contributing Cause of the Accident," sought to identify the human failures behind the technical failure. The opening paragraph of the chapter begins as follows:

The decision to launch the Challenger was flawed. Those who made that decision were unaware of the recent history of problems concerning the O-rings and the joint and were unaware of the initial written recommendation of the contractor advising against the launch at temperatures below 53 degrees Fahrenheit and the continuing opposition of the engineers at Thiokol after the management reversed its position. They did not have a clear understanding of Rockwell's concern that it was not safe to launch because of ice on the pad. If the decision makers had known all of the facts, it is highly unlikely that they would have decided to launch 51-L on January 28, 1986. (p. 82)

The only way this paragraph can be interpreted is that someone failed to *communicate* the facts prior to launch. Indeed, two paragraphs later the report explicitly identifies this contributing cause as "failures in communication that resulted in a decision to launch 51-L based on incomplete and sometimes misleading information, a conflict between engineering data and management judgments, and a NASA management structure that permitted internal flight safety problems to bypass key shuttle managers" (p. 82).[4]

If someone wanted to conduct an investigation in such a way as to return the country to its manifest destiny, the pushing back of the space frontier, as quickly as possible, there could not be a more suitably abstract and bloodless explanation than to attribute the cause to a "failure in communication." Accept the testimony of a decision maker who says he did not know certain facts, and you have an explanation that does minimum damage to the system. No specific individuals or groups need be blamed. A few people can later be pressured out of their jobs, and the space program can get back to business. (For a similar argument, see Browning, 1988.)

As it turns out, there *were* communication problems involved in the decision to launch. The Rogers Commission Report, however, did not indicate the specific individuals who were at fault. It can be argued that the Commission was guilty of reification, the fallacy of treating organizations as if they were bereft of human beings.

### Readiness Reviews

The doomed flight 51-L, like any other shuttle launch at that time, had to be cleared through five levels of readiness reviews. The system of reviews was complex and confusing to many who followed the Rogers Commission testimony because of the labelling/numbering system. It was confusing also to some who read the report and perhaps to the participants themselves.

Reviews began at Level IV with the contractors. They then ascended to Level III, conducted at three NASA field centers, Marshall (Huntsville), Kennedy (the Cape), and Johnson (Houston). Level II, called the Pre-Flight Readiness Review (also referred to as the Certification of Flight Readiness) was presented to the program manager at Johnson, in which

> . . .each Space Shuttle program element endorses that it has satisfactorily completed the manufacture, assembly, test and checkout of the pertinent element, including the contractors' certification that design and performance are up to standard. The Flight Readiness Review process culminates in the Level I review. (pp. 82-83).

On top of all this was a structured Mission Management Team meeting, L-1, held one day before each launch. This meeting or review closed out action items from the previous level of review and also considered anticipated weather conditions at the launch site and at "abort" landing sites around the globe.

The communication problem identified by the Rogers Commission was that the Thiokol objections to the launch, as well as prior concerns expressed about the O-rings by engineers at both the Marshall Center and Thiokol, *did not reach the Level II and Level I reviews.* The Commission appeared to place the blame with Marshall personnel. The report reproduces the testimony of Lawrence Mulloy, solid rocket booster project manager, about why the weather and O-ring concerns did not reach the higher levels:

> *Chairman Rogers:* . . . Why wasn't that a cause for concern on the part of the whole NASA organization?
>
> *Mr. Mulloy:* It was cause for concern, sir.
>
> *Chairman Rogers:* Who did you tell about this?
>
> *Mr. Mulloy:* Everyone, sir.
>
> *Chairman Rogers:* And they all knew about it at the time of 51-L?
>
> *Mr. Mulloy:* Yes, sir. You will find [it] in the Flight Readiness Review record that went all the way to the L-1 review. (p. 85)

The testimony transcription ends at this point. The paragraph immediately following the exchange is as close as the Commission would come to placing official blame on any individual NASA official:

> It is disturbing to the Commission that contrary to the testimony of the Solid Rocket Booster Project Manager, the seriousness of concern was not conveyed in Flight Readiness Review to Level I and the 51-L readiness review was silent. (p. 85)

By the expression, "contrary to the testimony," the Commission seems to be implying that Mulloy was either lying or mistaken. In any case, it is believed that he failed to adequately communicate crucial information up the line.

The report also contains a long exchange between Chairman Rogers and Mulloy's boss, William R. Lucas, director of the Marshall Center, which has not in my estimation received sufficient attention:

> *Chairman Rogers*: Would you please tell the Commission when you first heard about the problem of the O-rings and the seals insofar as it involves launch 51-L? And I don't want you to go way back, but go back to when you first heard. I guess it was on January 27th, was it?
>
> *Dr. Lucas*: Yes, sir. It was on the early evening of the 27th, I think about 7:00 p.m., when I was in my motel room along with Mr. Kingsbury [Jim Kingsbury, director of Science and Engineering, MSFC]. And about that time, Mr. Reinartz [Stanley R. Reinartz, manager, Shuttle Projects Office, MSFC] and Mr. Mulloy came to my room and told me that they had heard that some members of Thiokol had raised a concern about the performance of the Solid Rocket Boosters in the low temperature that was anticipated for the next day, specifically on the seals, and that they were going out to the Kennedy Space Center to engage in a telecon with the appropriate engineers back at Marshall Space Flight Center in Huntsville and with corresponding people back at the Wasatch division of Thiokol in Utah.
>
> And we discussed it a few moments and I said, fine, keep me informed, let me know what happens.
>
> *Chairman Rogers*: And when was the next time you heard something about that?
>
> *Dr. Lucas*: The next time was about 5:00 a.m. on the following morning, when I went to the Kennedy Space Center and went to the launch control center. I immediately saw Mr. Reinartz and Mr.

Mulloy and asked them how the matter of the previous evening was dispositioned.

*Chairman Rogers*: You had heard nothing at all in between?

*Dr. Lucas*: No, sir.

*Chairman Rogers*: So from 8:00 o'clock that evening until 5:00 o'clock in the morning, you had not heard a thing?

*Dr. Lucas*: It was about 7:00, I believe, sir. But for that period of time, I heard nothing in the interim . . .

*Chairman Rogers*: . . . And you heard Mr. Reinartz say he didn't think he had to notify you, or did he notify you?

*Dr. Lucas*: He told me, as I testified, when I went into the control room, that an issue had been resolved, that there were some people at Thiokol who had a concern about the weather, that that had been discussed very thoroughly by the Thiokol people and by the Marshall Space Flight Center people, and it had been concluded agreeably that there was no problem, that he had a recommendation by Thiokol to launch and our most knowledgeable people and engineering talent agreed with that. So from my perspective, I didn't have—I didn't see that as an issue.

*Chairman Rogers*: And if you had known that Thiokol engineers almost to a man opposed the flight, would that have changed your view?

*Dr. Lucas*: I'm certain that it would.

*Chairman Rogers*: So your testimony is the same as Mr. Hardy's [George B. Hardy, deputy director, Science and Engineering]. Had he known, he would not have recommended the flight be launched on that day.

*Dr. Lucas*: I didn't make a recommendation one way or the other. But had I known that, I would have then interposed an objection, yes.

*Chairman Rogers*: I gather you didn't tell Mr. Aldrich or Mr. Moore [Levels I and II program officials] what Mr. Reinartz had told you?

*Dr. Lucas*: No, sir. That is not the reporting channel. Mr. Reinartz reports directly to Mr. Aldrich. In a sense, Mr. Reinartz informs me as the institutional manager of the progress that he is making in implementing his program, but that I have never on any occasion reported to Mr. Aldrich.

*Chairman Rogers*: And you had subsequent conversations with Mr. Moore and Mr. Aldrich prior to the flight and you never mentioned what Mr. Reinartz had told you?

*Dr. Lucas*: I did not mention what Mr. Reinartz told me, because Mr. Reinartz had indicated to me there was not an issue, that we had a unanimous position between Thiokol and the Marshall Space Flight Center, and there was no issue in his judgment, nor in mine as he explained it to me.

*Chairman Rogers*: But had you known, your attitude would have been totally different?

*Dr. Lucas*: Had I had the advantage at that time of the testimony that I have heard here this week, I would have had a different attitude, certainly.

*Chairman Rogers*: In view of the fact that you were running tests to improve the joint, didn't the fact that the weather was so bad and Reinartz had told you about the questions that had been raised by Thiokol, at least, didn't that cause you serious concern?

*Dr. Lucas*: I would have been concerned if Thiokol had come in and said, we don't think you should launch because we've got bad weather.

*Chairman Rogers*: Well, that's what they did, of course, first. That is exactly what they did. You didn't know that?

*Dr. Lucas*: I knew only that Thiokol had raised a concern.

*Chairman Rogers*: Did you know they came and recommended against the launch, is the question.

*Dr. Lucas*: I knew that I was told on the morning of the launch that the initial position of some members of Thiokol—and I don't know who it was—had recommended that one not launch with the temperature less than 53 degrees Fahrenheit.

*Chairman Rogers*: And that didn't cause you enough concern so you passed that information on to either Mr. Moore or Mr. Aldrich?

*Dr. Lucas*: No, sir, because I was shown a document signed by Mr. Kilminster [Thiokol manager] that indicated that that would not be significant, that the temperature would not be—that it would be that much lower, as I recall it. (pp. 100-101)

### No Automatic Responsibility

As I read this dialogue, I thought back to the communicative practice of automatic responsibility at the Marshall Center in the 1960s (discussed in Chapters One and Three) in which perceived problems were solved and/or communicated up the line. Had automatic responsibility been abandoned or forgotten at MSFC?

Lucas said that between 7:00 p.m., when he was told there would be a telecon to deal with concerns about the cold weather's effects on the O-rings, and 5:00 a.m. the next morning, the day of the launch, he heard nothing about what happened in the teleconference. It could be argued that such apparently passive behavior on the part of the director is surprising, not to mention his seeming lack of curiosity about the teleconference. Passivity might also explain Reinartz's and Mulloy's failure to tell him what happened. Upward communication was what the Marshall Center had been all about in the 1960s. Why didn't Reinartz and Mulloy call Lucas or pay another visit to his motel room? Moreover, Lucas seems to implicitly condemn these two subordinates for failing to inform him of the seriousness of the problem; he had specifically asked them to keep him informed. The condemnation is implicit in his repeated claims that with this knowledge he would have had a totally different attitude, would have even "interposed an objection" to the launch, which, given Lucas's status, would no doubt have canceled it.

There is more that is troubling about this remarkable testimony, which describes activities so at variance with my previous experiences at the Marshall Center. Lucas said that he would have been concerned if Thiokol had come in and said, "We don't think you should launch." This clearly gives the impression that he was unaware that the Thiokol engineers had made such a recommendation, and Rogers replied, "Well, that is what they did, of course, first. . . . You didn't know that?" Lucas answered, "I knew only that Thiokol had raised a concern," again giving the impression that he was unaware that the initial recommendation was against launch. Rogers again asked whether or not he knew about the recommendation against the launch. Lucas then testified that he knew on the morning of the launch that the initial position of some members of Thiokol was "that one not launch with the temperature less than 53 degrees Fahrenheit."

In rereading the above exchange, it seems to me that there is something inconsistent about this series of answers. At first, Lucas acknowledged knowing only that there was some "concern." But the final statement that he knew about the initial recommendation not to launch in the early morning hours before the launch appears inconsistent with his earlier statement, "But had I known that, I would have then interposed an objection, yes." It was not too late on the morning of the launch to raise an objection—or at least a concern.

### Plausible Deniability

Plausible deniability conceivably could also have been at work. This refers to the practice in which the top officials of organizations assert they were not aware of certain facts. It is possible that Lucas did know the facts and testified otherwise. Whether he did or not, his testimony allowed him to maintain the integrity of the Center and its director. Assuming the director did not know, then the Center could not be culpable, and he could implicitly criticize Reinartz and Mulloy for not telling him everything, maintaining that if they had, he would have acted differently. In this scenario, Reinartz and the others might have to go, but the organization would remain intact and have a chance to recover from this tragic and embarrassing episode.

### Four Communication Breakdowns

Commissioner Richard Feynman, Nobel Laureate in Physics and popular author, asked Arnold Aldrich, a NASA official in the Level I readiness review process, about the "cause . . . [of] the lack of communication which we have seen." Aldrich began his testimony by saying there were "two specific breakdowns" (p. 101).

The first breakdown, according to Aldrich, was "the situation that occurred the night before the launch and leading up to the launch where there was a significant review that . . . was not passed forward" (p. 102). That was, of course, Thiokol's concern expressed during the telecon about the weather and the O-rings.

The second breakdown was "the variety of reviews that were conducted last summer between the NASA Headquarters Organization and the Marshall Organization on the same technical area and the fact that that was not brought through my office in either direction—that is, it was not worked through—by the NASA Headquarters Organization, nor when the Marshall Organization brought these concerns to be reported were we involved" (p. 102). Marshall and NASA headquarters were working on the O-ring problem six months before the launch, and no one thought to inform Aldrich and others involved in the readiness review process. (Note Lucas's comment in his testimony about his relationship with Aldrich: ". . . I have never on any occasion reported to Mr. Aldrich" (p. 101).)

Aldrich then thought of a third breakdown: "The Marshall SRB project went forward to procure some additional Solid Rocket Motor casings to be machined and new configurations for testing of the joints" (p. 102). Aldrich added that if budget requests for such changes had come through his office, "it would have been clear that something was going on here that I ought to know about" (p. 103).

A fourth problem occurred to Aldrich. It was similar to what is identified in the literature of organizational communication as *uncertainty absorption* (March & Simon, 1958, p. 165), the communication process by which the qualifiers and exceptions contained in an initial message drop off in subsequent "relays" of the message and are replaced by the more secure inferences of the first receiver. Aldrich explained that "anomaly" reports about the O-rings were logged for early flights, but after subsequent flights "O-ring erosion was not considered to be an anomaly and, therefore . . . there are not [sic] anomaly reports that progress from one flight to the other" (p. 103). As we shall see, Commissioner Feynman would characterize such practices as "Russian roulette."

### Findings

1. The Commission "concluded that there was a serious flaw in the decision making process leading up to the launch of flight 51-L." This indicates a communication problem, since messages expressing the "rising doubts" about the O-rings should have reached the highest levels of the flight-readiness reviews.

2. "The waiving of launch constraints appears to have been at the expense of flight safety. There was no system which made it imperative that launch constraints and waivers of launch constraints be considered by all levels of management." This indicates more communication problems.

Then came the third and fourth findings, rather mild slaps on the wrist of the Marshall Center, which I quote word for word:

3. The Commission is troubled by what appears to be a propensity of management at Marshall to contain potentially serious problems and to attempt to resolve them internally rather than communicate them forward. This tendency is altogether at odds with the need for Marshall to function as part of a system working toward successful flight missions, interfacing and communicating with the other parts of the system that work to the same end.

4. The Commission concluded that the Thiokol Management reversed its position and recommended the launch of 51-L, at the urging of Marshall and contrary to the views of its engineers in order to accommodate a major customer. (p. 104)

The fourth finding made me think back to my interviews in the 1960s about Marshall's practice of "penetration" and its vigilance in forcing contractors to assume the burden of proof in order to guarantee that their products would work. It certainly appeared that some serious changes must have taken place at the Marshall Center.

## Addendum on Ambiguities

Chapter V of the report contained an addendum, "Ambiguities in the Decision Making Process." It concerns testimony given to the Commission by representatives of Rockwell International, the prime contractor for the orbiter. The president of Rockwell's space transportation division, Rocco Petrone (who served briefly as the director of the Marshall Center during the early 1970s) testified that Rockwell was very concerned on January 27, 1986, about the ice on the mobile launcher. They had a series of meetings, following which Petrone called his "program managers over in Florida at 5:45 (PST) and said we could not recommend launching from here [California], from what we [could] see" (p. 115). Petrone also testified that it was his recommendation that it was "not safe to launch."

But the testimony by two of Petrone's subordinates and NASA officials who had conversations with them about the ice led the Commission to conclude "that Rockwell's recommendation on launch was *ambiguous.* The Commission finds it difficult, as did Mr. Aldrich, to conclude that there was a no-launch recommendation" (p. 117, emphasis added).

Two years before this conclusion was reached, Eric Eisenberg (1984) published an article in praise of the concept of "strategic ambiguity," putting forth the idea that communicators protect themselves by using messages that can be construed in two or more ways. The essay attracted an appreciative audience. Those who find the concept of "strategic ambiguity" appealing should read the addendum to Chapter V of the Rogers Commission report. They will be sobered by the possible consequences of ambiguity, whether strategic or not. Ambiguity was a factor in the *Challenger* accident: An unequivocal recommendation not to launch would have averted disaster. Perhaps these ideas about ambiguity should be redefined in regard to the limitations of such communicative practices.

*Icing at the upper levels of the launch tower service structure the morning of the Challenger's last flight (Rogers Commission Report)*

### Russian Roulette

Chapter VI, "An Accident Rooted in History," reviews the original design of the shuttle and the selection of contractors to build it, narrates the history of the controversial field joint and O-rings, and lays the blame for the *Challenger* accident in the original design of the joint. Aldrich's fourth communication problem, the failure to track the anomalies adequately over time, was also identified. Commissioner Feynman's now famous metaphor was included in the findings. He characterized the decision making of NASA as

> a kind of Russian roulette .... [The Shuttle] flies [with O-ring erosion] and nothing happens. Then it is suggested, therefore, that the risk is no longer so high for the next flights. We can lower our standards a little bit because we got away with it last time .... You got away with it, but it shouldn't be done over and over again like that. (p. 148)

Chapter VII documents further problems in organizational communication, as might be expected from its title, "The Silent Safety Program." Reliability and quality assurance offices and labs were found to have been placed under the supervision of the very units they were supposed to have checked, which is not a good principle of organizational communication. Thus, the Commission found another design problem—not in the hardware but in the organizational communication system.

Chapter VIII details the "Pressures on the System." NASA, responding to pressures from customers and its own commitments made to Congress, had created an unrealistic flight schedule. There were too many flights in too little time, with too much "straining" to make the shuttle "operational," i.e., as dependable in its schedule as a good airline. The system was "strained to the limit" in 1985-86, according to this chapter. Spare tires were in critically short supply and parts had to be cannibalized from other shuttles for use in the vehicle being readied for the launch pad. Workers were "fatigued," as were their managers, and a tight schedule did not allow "critical anomalies" to be identified and addressed between flights.

Chapter IX directed attention to "Other Safety Considerations": abort capabilities, thrust termination, ditching, crew escape options, orbiter tires and brakes, the vagaries of the weather, and the launch pad. In reading this chapter, it seemed to me that safety had given way to considerations of cost and scheduling. Using the terms introduced earlier in this chapter, the *topos* or criterion of reliability/safety was overwhelmed by the *topoi* of time/schedule (i.e., don't delay or scrub a launch) and cost (the shuttle must fly frequently to pay its own way). The decision ultimately proved a foul compromise; an artful tradeoff among the *topoi* was not achieved.

### Recommendations of the Rogers Commission

The final unnumbered chapter is devoted to those recommendations unanimously adopted by the Commission. They deal with the need to redesign, test, and verify the faulty solid rocket motor joint, with safety measures, with the shuttle management structure, and with other matters. Recommendation V is relevant to this analysis:

*Improved Communications.* The Commission found that Marshall Space Flight Center project managers, because of a tendency at Marshall to management isolation, failed to provide full and timely information bearing on the safety of flight 51-L to other vital elements of shuttle program management. (p. 200)

A "bulleted" point under this paragraph recommended that "NASA should take energetic steps to eliminate this tendency at Marshall Space Flight Center, whether by changes of personnel, organization, indoctrination or all three" (p. 200).

The Rogers Commission thus apparently chose not to recommend firings, reorganization, and indoctrination as collective solutions, but instead to allow NASA the flexibility of utilizing one or any combination of them to achieve the desired effect. This is the most ironic of all the recommendations: A presidential commission found it necessary to recommend that the Marshall Center improve its system of organizational communication, which, as we have seen in previous chapters, was once the pride of the agency, the government, and the country.

The "Concluding Thought" of the Rogers Commission report refers to NASA as a "symbol of national pride and technological leadership." The Commission "applauds NASA's spectacular achievements of the past and anticipates impressive achievements to come" (p. 201). NASA could now get back to the process of fulfilling its national purpose, its manifest destiny.

Using the new evidence and analyses provided by the Rogers Report and other sources, I began to tighten my case for organizational forgetting. One day, after giving a lecture in a colleague's class in which I contrasted the organizational communication practices of MSFC during the Apollo era to those of the *Challenger* era, a student approached me. He identified himself as Gary Kleiman, a physics major with interest in organizational communication and the space program.

"Have you read the article by Richard Feynman in *Physics Today*?" he asked.

I hadn't, though I had heard about it from colleagues. Kleiman volunteered to bring me a copy. The article was entitled "An Outsider's Inside View of the *Challenger* Inquiry" (Feynman, 1988). As a member of the Rogers Commission, Feynman had come to the same conclusion I had: The *Challenger* accident was rooted in problems of organizational communication. I shall describe Feynman's experiments and his theory of organizational communication in the next chapter.

## NOTES

1. In late April of 1970 I received a call from two members of Ludie Richard's (deputy director of RDO) staff at the Marshall Center. He was having some problems with the new organization, particularly with the systems engineering integration, and wanted to know if I could come down during the summer to help them out. I accepted, wanting not only to help but also to try to gauge the effect of von Braun's absence on the Marshall Center. (He was now at NASA headquarters and Eberhard Rees, his deputy director, technical, had replaced him.) However, due to the crisis at Kent State University that spring, I became involved in a research project that delved into organizational communication problems at the university. (See Note 3 below.) For this reason, I had to cancel my trip to Huntsville.

2. Wiesman has "kept the faith" in organizational communication and is still going strong as the first "Executive in Residence" at the Business School of the University of Alabama at Huntsville.

3. This study of the organizational events responsible for the tragedy (Tompkins and Anderson, 1971) is summarized in Appendix A for the reader who wishes to compare and contrast organizational communication between the Marshall Center and Kent State University.

4. In a fact-checking telephone conversation on September 2, 1992, between Roger Boisjoly and Claude Teweles, the publisher of Roxbury Publishing Company, Boisjoly indicated that some of the detailed information contained in the Rogers Commission Report about the performance of the O-rings was not available prior to the accident. He claimed that no overall chart or record was kept of all flights indicating the outside temperature at the time of launch and the condition of the O-rings after the boosters were recovered. This data, Boisjoly said, was scattered throughout Morton Thiokol and NASA. In September and October of 1985, Boisjoly claimed that he had specifically requested this information so that a statistical analysis could be done in order to identify the probability of O-ring failure. Only in the aftermath of the *Challenger* tragedy was this analysis done, on the behest of the Rogers Commission. Only then did it become clear that in any flight launched below 60 degrees Fahrenheit, the O-rings began to deteriorate. Boisjoly indicated that had he had this kind of documentation in hand prior to the launch of Flight 51-L, he would have had a stronger case for convincing his superiors and NASA to cancel the launch.

## Chapter Eight

# FEYNMAN'S TWO EXPERIMENTS

Despite Richard Feynman's Nobel Prize in Physics (1965) and his bestselling book, *"Surely You're Joking," Mr. Feynman,* he is best known to space buffs for a simple but dramatic experiment he conducted with a rubber washer and a cup of ice water.

### The First Experiment

The Rogers Commission heard testimony about the O-ring, a rubber gasket that was supposed to contract and expand within a "field joint" (so called because the boosters were assembled in the field) to prevent dangerous leakage of hot gases from the solid fuel boosters. During the infamous teleconference discussed earlier, the decision about whether or not to recommend a launch hinged partly on the weather at the Cape and its potential effect on the O-rings.

On the morning of Flight 51-L, the weather was colder than at any previous launch of a shuttle, and some engineers argued that they were, therefore, outside the "envelope" of experience. Icicles hanging from the launch tower, if sucked into the rocket engines, could be a threat to the flight. Would the cold weather affect the performance, the resiliency of the O-rings? As described above, some Morton Thiokol engineers feared it might. In his testimony, Lawrence Mulloy of the Marshall Center claimed the evidence was "uncomplete," as Feynman put it, and he pressed the Morton Thiokol engineers to prove that the cold weather would prevent the O-rings from functioning effectively.

## The O-ring and the Ice Water

At a climactic point in the hearings, a model of the field joint, complete with the inserted O-ring, was passed from panelist to panelist. Feynman had made a trip to a hardware store to prepare for this moment. When the model reached him, he pulled out a clamp and a pair of pliers. Feynman then extracted the O-ring with the pliers, squeezed it with a clamp, and plunged it into a cup of ice water. He announced the results of his experiment:

> I take the clamp out, hold it up in the air, and loosen it as I talk: "I discovered that when you undo the clamp, the rubber doesn't spring back. In other words, for more than a few seconds, there is no resilience in this material when it is at a temperature of 32 degrees. I believe that has some significance for our problem." (Feynman, 1989, pp. 151-153)

This strikingly simple, dramatic experiment demonstrated that cold weather was bound to affect the performance of the O-rings. The Morton Thiokol engineers who had raised doubts about the O-rings had been right, particularly Roger Boisjoly, but their own managers had overridden them in an effort to make the recommendation which they, the Morton Thiokol managers, thought their NASA teleconference partners wanted to receive. That recommendation, of course, was to launch the shuttle the following morning.

Only the readers of Feynman's article in *Physics Today*, which he expanded for his posthumously-published second book, *"What Do You Care What Other People Think?"* (1989), know about Feynman's second experiment. It was an experiment in organizational communication.

### The Second Experiment

Although Feynman was a brilliant scientist, as a member of the Rogers Commission he had trouble understanding the thinking and language of the engineers from NASA and the contractors. Their penchant for alphabet soup acronyms was mind-boggling: SRB meant solid rocket booster, SSME stood for space shuttle main engine, LH for liquid hydrogen, LOX for liquid oxygen, etc. This is another instance of the fifth problem of communication I had presented to von Braun and his staff back in 1967: the barrier between science and technology. Scientists and engineers simply spoke different languages.

As a result of his communication difficulties with the engineers who testified before the Rogers Commission, and particularly with those who had been promoted into management positions, according to his book, Feynman felt he needed to break away from the insulated atmosphere of the Rogers Commission. He had begun to suspect that there might be a management problem behind the technical problem of the O-rings. He wanted face-to-face communication with ordinary NASA workers and engineers, to talk to them without the inhibiting presence of their bosses.

Feynman spoke with a group of workers, who were initially fearful of talking to a member of the Rogers Commission, and asked them detailed questions about their jobs. They willingly described their problems. Furthermore, they claimed that they had tried without success to communicate these problems to their supervisors. Happily enough for the astronauts in the Apollo Program, upward-directed communication at the Marshall Center had received high priority under von Braun. The system Feynman was examining did not seem to work in the same way.

It was at the Marshall Center that Feynman conducted his second, less well-known experiment. He had heard from a NASA manager that the probability of a failure for a shuttle engine was 1 in 100,000. Astounded by this figure and how it was arrived at, Feynman asked to talk to some Marshall Center engineers without the presence of their manager. The manager showed up nonetheless, bearing a huge report intended to satisfy Feynman. The manager justified his presence by explaining that he *was* an engineer—an engineer with managerial responsibilities.

After getting nowhere, Feynman was subjected to a formal presentation he had neither requested nor wanted to hear. He suddenly stopped the presentation and made a simple request, asking his briefers to write down on pieces of paper the probability of booster engine failure in a shuttle flight. The three engineers' probabilities were close: 1 in 200, 1 in 200, and 1 in 300. The Marshall manager refused to give a numerical probability. After some intense prodding, he came up with a figure close to the estimate Feynman had received from the other NASA manager—1 in 100,000. Feynman and the engineers were incredulous.

Feynman concluded that there was a serious communication barrier between the engineers and their managers. The Nobel

Laureate in Physics was now doing "orgcom" research, which he called his "particular adventure." The adventure was one of "investigating the lack of communication between the managers and the engineers who were working on the engine" (Feynman, 1989, p. 190).

In *"Surely You're Joking," Mr. Feynman*, Feynman boasted that the California Institute of Technology, where he spent most of his career, had rejected a proposal to establish a department of psychology on the grounds that the field was not "scientific" enough for Cal Tech. Ironically, however, he fell back on social scientific theorizing in order to cope with the issues that emerged during the Rogers Commission investigation.

### Feynman's Theory of Organizational Communication

In the "Afterthoughts" section of Feynman's essay on the *Challenger* investigation, "Mr. Feynman Goes to Washington: Investigating the Space Shuttle *Challenger* Disaster," he offers his own theory, although he was not confident that it was valid (perhaps because of his inexperience in explaining *social* phenomena). Feynman explains NASA's problems of communication in this way:

> When NASA was trying to go to the moon, there was a great deal of enthusiasm: it was a goal everyone was anxious to achieve. They didn't know if they could do it, but they were all working together.
>
> I have this idea because I worked at Los Alamos, and I experienced the tension and the pressure of everybody working together to make the atomic bomb. When somebody's having a problem—say, with the detonator—everybody knows that it's a big problem, they're thinking of ways to beat it, they're making suggestions, and when they hear about the solution they're excited, because that means their work is now useful: if the detonator didn't work, the bomb wouldn't work.
>
> I figured the same thing had gone on at NASA in the early days: if the space suit didn't work, they couldn't go to the moon. So everybody's interested in everybody else's problems.
>
> But then, when the moon project was over, NASA had all these people together: there's a big organization in Houston and a big organization in Huntsville, not to mention at Kennedy, in Florida. You don't want to fire people and send them out in the street when you're done with a big project, so the problem is, what to do?

You have to convince Congress that there exists a project that only NASA can do. In order to do so, it is necessary—at least it was *apparently* necessary in this case—to exaggerate: to exaggerate how economical the shuttle would be, to exaggerate how often it could fly, to exaggerate how safe it would be, to exaggerate the big scientific facts that would be discovered. "The shuttle can make so-and-so many flights and it'll cost such-and-such; we went to the moon, so we can *do* it!"

Meanwhile, I would guess, the engineers at the bottom are saying, "No, no! We can't make that many flights. If we had to make that many flights, it would mean such-and-such!" And, "No, we can't do it for that amount of money, because that would mean we'd have to do thus-and-so!"

Well, the guys who are trying to get Congress to okay their projects don't want to hear such talk. It's better if they don't hear, so they can be more "honest"—they don't want to be in the position of lying to Congress! So pretty soon the attitudes begin to change: information from the bottom which is disagreeable— "We're having a problem with the seals; we should fix it before we fly again"—is suppressed by big cheeses and middle managers who say, "If you tell me about the seals problems, we'll have to ground the shuttle and fix it." Or, "No, no, keep on flying, because otherwise, it'll look bad," or "Don't tell me; I don't want to hear about it."

Maybe they don't say explicitly, "Don't tell me," but they discourage communication, which amounts to the same thing. It's not a question of what has been written down, or who should tell what to whom; it's a question of whether, when you *do* tell somebody about some problem, they're *delighted* to hear about it and they say "Tell me more" and "Have you tried such-and-such?" or they say, "Well, see what you can do about it"—which is a completely different atmosphere. If you try once or twice to communicate and get pushed back, pretty soon you decide, "To hell with it."

So that's my theory. Because of the exaggeration at the top being inconsistent with the reality at the bottom, communication got slowed up and ultimately jammed. That's how it's possible that the higher-ups didn't know. (Feynman, 1989, pp. 213-215)

This passage provides a "primitive" theory of organizational communication by someone outside the field. By primitive I have in mind two meanings: first, that it is "unsophisticated" or underdeveloped.  No organizational theorist I have ever read wrote the way Feynman did.  The second meaning in this context is a philosophical or epistemological one.  A primitive theory deals with basic assumptions and first-order inferences.  Feynman's theory of organizational communication is so fecund, so pregnant with possibilities, that it deserves a chance to deliver its implicit messages.  It needs explication.

### Feynman's Theory Explicated

Feynman's theory is limited to a single case.  But it is quite clear that he believes it applies to other cases as well, at least certain aspects of it.  A good theory about a specific organization can provide insights into other organizations.  Let us try, then, to amplify Feynman's theory and enumerate the important lessons it contains that transcend NASA and apply to some other, if not most, organizations.

**The Lesson of Communication.**  Feynman saw that the best way to understand NASA was in terms of communication.  The explication of organizational communication in the second chapter of this book makes it unnecessary to repeat the basic arguments here.

**The Lesson of Interdependence.**  Feynman calls on his experience at Los Alamos and his understanding of NASA during the Apollo project in trying to explain NASA during the shuttle program.  He seems to be saying that if one member or unit within a larger organization fails, all units fail.  If one succeeds in solving a problem, all succeed and benefit.  This is the basic insight of the "systems" approach to complex organization.  In fact, some would say this is the only important insight the systems approach provides (an idea Barnard had first expressed in 1938).

Some organizations are more interdependent than others, however.  The examples Feynman uses are highly interdependent organizations.  Department stores, for example, are less interdependent than space centers.  The ready-to-wear section will not necessarily succeed or fail in relation to what happens in kitchenware.  No single department's red ink is likely to bring down the entire store.

**The Lesson of Enthusiasm, Commitment, and Identification.**
Feynman correctly observes that when these conditions are present
to a high degree, people care more and communicate more openly
with others in the organization. Organizational identification and
commitment are concepts I have researched and theorized about for
the past 20 years. My interest started with the enthusiasm, commitment, and identification I witnessed at MSFC and came to experience myself. I have researched and theorized about these concepts
during the past ten years in association with George Cheney, also at
the University of Colorado at Boulder. We have stood on the
shoulders of two intellectual giants, one a humanist—Kenneth Burke,
winner of the National Medal for Literature in 1981—and the other
a scientist—Herbert A. Simon, the only Nobel Laureate (Economics)
who has written on organizational communication. They convinced
us that the process of identification is the most important factor in
understanding communication, human relations, and organizations.
Our own research and theorizing have reinforced this conviction (see
Cheney & Tompkins, 1987; Tompkins & Cheney, 1985; Tompkins &
Cheney, 1990). Feynman discovered the concept by experience and
intuition.

Nonetheless, Feynman does not warn of the fearful consequences
of identification and commitment that Cheney and I discovered: that
a high degree of commitment and identification can be dangerous,
particularly when it is of the unquestioning variety. Hitler and his
Nazi followers provide a classic example. The fanatic commitment
of some Nazis made the unthinkable not only "thinkable," but as
history has recorded, "doable." The allied opposition to Nazi
Germany was itself a kind of identification by antithesis, as Kenneth
Burke has expressed it (Burke, 1972, p. 28). This identification by
antithesis no doubt contributed to the feeling Feynman experienced
in the Manhattan Project that he celebrates in his own essay. That
project produced, of course, the atomic bombs dropped on Nagasaki
and Hiroshima.

Cheney and I are also concerned about the degree to which U.S.
society in the 1980s and 1990s displays an overidentification with the
corporation. How much damage has the unqualified commitment to
the company done to the family and the community? Feynman's
theory needs to be qualified in this regard as well.

**The Lesson of Analyzing Organizations as Parts of Organizational Sets.** The concept of the organizational set (see Perrow, 1979) was applied in earlier chapters to the Marshall Space Flight Center. Feynman quickly realized what it took organizational specialists almost 100 years to discover: It is not possible to have a full and well-rounded understanding of a "focal" organization without analyzing its relationship to its environment—and an organization's environment is made up primarily of other organizations. This was the problem of "external interfaces" I was trying to understand at the Marshall Center in 1967.

Thus, the organizational set is made up of suppliers and clients, controllers and constituents. For example, if a contemporary state university represents a focal organization within an organizational set, the interfaces are many and complex: students, current, past (alumni), and potential; government agencies and private foundations which must be persuaded to cough up large sums of money for various departments' research projects; potential benefactors who must be identified and cultivated; bids by vendors eager to supply computers, laboratories, and other equipment which must be carefully scrutinized; faculty which must be recruited and persuaded to stay; the favor of state governments and boards of regents/directors which must be curried for the basic necessities. A complete list of all components of the set would take up too much space for this book to detail. Barnard observed that society itself is a network of organizations, a set of sets we might say, which provides the "structure" of society. He also argued that nearly every organization is situated in a subordinate relationship with at least one other organization (Barnard, 1938).

Feynman saw NASA in a crucially subordinate relationship with Congress. The complications of its relationship with the executive branch, contractors, and the voting, tax-paying citizens might also be considered. Further complicating the organizational set is the loop between voters and Congress and so on.

**The Lesson of the Relationship between External Communication (Persuasion, Rhetoric, Public Relations) and Internal Communication.** The messages that organizations communicate to their external audiences constrain and affect their internal audiences and vice versa. Many of the messages that are ostensibly directed outward (for instance, those that establish and maintain the organizational image) are just as important to the internal audiences, i.e., the employees (Cheney, 1991). A few years ago, a business organization tried to improve its institutional image by an aggressive advertising campaign in which it asserted over and over that "We listen." The little dramas they broadcast usually portrayed an executive of the company listening empathetically to a customer. I talked to a graduate student who knew many of the employees at one of the company's local plants. She said the commercials made them "mad as hell" because the executives of the company had never listened to *them* so carefully.

If Feynman's thesis is correct that NASA *apparently* needed to exaggerate the benefits and economies of the shuttle to Congress, then these claims may have also been heard by NASA's own employees. Those employees would have had three choices: (1) to try to fulfill those exaggerated claims; (2) to communicate to their superiors that it would be difficult if not impossible to realize them; or (3) to avoid communicating their problems to their superiors. Managers who make exaggerated claims run the risk of believing their own rhetoric. They then have the choice of encouraging people to talk about their problems—as was done during the von Braun era—or of discouraging any defeatist messages from their employees.

Similarly, corporations that make exaggerated claims about their products or services can run into unintended difficulties with employees who know better. Credibility and trust can be expected to be among the first casualties in such a system.

**The Lesson of Plausible Deniability.** After spelling out his theory, Feynman said, "The other possibility is that the higher-ups did know, and they just *said* they didn't know" (Feynman, 1989, p. 215). In this strategy of plausible deniability, management—the "big cheeses," to use Feynman's term—can be kept informed of questionable practices in subtle, even tacit, ways. Then if things go badly, they can later deny with plausibility that they were ever aware of the misdeeds.

The strategy of plausible deniability appears to have been manifested in President Nixon's unsuccessful defense in the case of Watergate and may have been employed in President Reagan's successful defense of the Iran-Contra affair and the arms-for-hostages scandal (see Browning, 1989). This lesson is interesting but almost irrelevant in the case of the *Challenger* disaster for a simple reason:

The effects on the organization are the same for the Marshall Center whether the big cheeses knew or not. Even if higher-ups in MSFC had known the problems their subordinates were having with the shuttle, such a condition would still contradict the organization's history of nurturing open and upward-directed communication. From this perspective, the higher-ups *ought to have known* and acted on that knowledge. If they did not know, then they violated their own history.

Whether Marshall's management was ignorant of the O-ring problems because it had inhibited the upward-directed transmission of those problems, or did know about the problems but pretended otherwise, the system failed in both a technical and moral sense. To know about a technical problem that can cause the loss of human life, and then fail to act upon that problem, is also a failure of communication and morality. Marshall management knew about the O-ring problem; that is well documented. The failure of communication in the decision to launch *Challenger* was the failure to exercise automatic responsibility—to solve the problem or see that it was communicated up the line, rather than encouraging Morton Thiokol to recommend the flight.

## Chapter Nine

# HUNTSVILLE REVISITED

It remained for me to conduct my own "experiment," to gather direct evidence which could either confirm or reject the organizational forgetting hypothesis. In the fall of 1989, I decided that it was time to test the hypothesis directly. Almost five years had passed since the *Challenger* accident. The investigations had long been completed, their recommendations implemented, and the shuttle was flying again. Surely enough time had passed so that a visit to the Marshall Center would not be construed as interfering with ongoing activities or the reform of the organization.

### Reestablishing Contact with MSFC

On October 26, 1989, I wrote to the director of the Marshall Center, T.J. "Jack" Lee, introducing myself and recalling my previous association with MSFC, and enclosed articles I had published in *Communication Monographs* (Tompkins, 1977; Tompkins, 1978) based on my experiences at Marshall. I proposed returning to the Marshall Center between late October of 1989 and April of 1990. My plan was to interview Lee and other management personnel about current communication practices at the Center. I quote from my letter:

> The results [of the proposed study] would ultimately be communicated to the academic world by means of convention papers and articles (after sending the first draft to you for a response). The interview results would be anonymous; no interviewee would be identified with any specific answers, and my previous work at

MSFC and other organizations has taught me how to avoid "traceability." The questions would be similar to my original diagnostic study, asking what is working well and what isn't. Those who have been at MSFC for a long time would also be asked about changes they have perceived over time.

I received a response from Director Lee dated November 30, 1989. The first paragraph read:

> I believe that your proposal to continue your study of organizational communications at the Marshall Space Flight Center is consonant with our long range goals. Since information flow is so vital to the Agency, we must learn our strengths and weaknesses in this area, so that we can preserve the former and address the latter.

The second paragraph formally invited me to the Marshall Center and identified J.A. "Woody" Bethay, executive assistant to the director, as my point of contact. Remembering Bethay's name from my previous assignments at the Marshall Center, I called him. We agreed that I would interview 16 of the top managers at the Marshall Center on January 9 and January 10, 1990—one hour per interview. Bethay supplied me with brief biographies of each manager, the strategic plan of the Center, a brochure celebrating the 25th anniversary of the Marshall Center, and all of the organization charts published from 1969 to 1989, which allowed me to trace the structural changes in the organization since my work there in 1967 and 1968.

While scanning the *Strategic Plan Progress Report: A Reflection on 1988. . . A View Toward 1989,* I learned that MSFC employment was down to 3,340 people, less than half the number employed when I had consulted to the organization in 1967. Several passages jumped out at me from the *Progress Report.* In addressing the Center's commitment to excellence, the document stated that this "attitude and a probable increase in the number of civil service personnel and support contractors should help us *penetrate* our projects in more technical depth and thus be better able to anticipate and resolve problems" (emphasis added). *The writer of this passage seemed to understand von Braun's concept of penetration,* I thought and wondered if it was still in use.

The last page of the report was devoted to the Marshall Center's "Guiding Principles," a commitment to: Excellence; Importance of our People; High Standards; Equal Opportunity; Teamwork; High

Quality, Safety, and Reliability; Cooperation; New Challenges; Diversity; and Communications—"[to] assure open and effective communications with our people, government and industrial partners, and with the public."

The "Introduction to Marshall Space Flight Center," printed in the Center Telephone Directory, gave a short history of the organization and listed current and future projects. The then-current projects included: the space shuttle, the space station *Freedom*, the Hubble space telescope, the orbital maneuvering vehicle (described as a "space tug" to maneuver other spacecraft on orbit), and the tethered satellite system, among others. Indeed, it was claimed that the Center "is working on more projects today than at any time in history." *More projects with half the personnel,* I thought, wondering how that set of complications had affected organizational communication.

I flew into Huntsville on January 8, 1990, and caught a ride on the van provided by my hotel. The sleepy, rather seedy town of the 1960s was gone. Instead, I found a bustling, sprawling metropolis with countless new hotels, motels, and restaurants. The Carriage Inn, once the finest Huntsville had to offer, was boarded up. After checking into my hotel, I called Woody Bethay's office to let him know I had arrived. Then I called my old friend, Walt Wiesman, and invited him and his wife Erica out for dinner the following evening. We had a lovely reunion.

The next morning, I arrived early enough to register for a NASA visitor's badge and took the elevator up to the ninth floor. I caught myself half-expecting to bump into von Braun in the familiar corridor, as had happened so often in the past.

### The Interviews

Interviews were conducted with the following people. (The reader may wish to locate the interviewees on the organizational chart on the next page so as to evaluate how well the sample represents the top and middle sections of the structure. Note that German surnames no longer constitute a dominant majority.)

Joseph A. Bethay, Executive Assistant to the Director
J. Wayne Littles, Deputy Director, MSFC
Susan McGuire Smith, Chief Counsel, MSFC
Robert G. Sheppard, Director, Institutional and Program Support, MSFC
C. Donald Bean, Director, Administrative Operations Office, MSFC

William B. Chubb, Director, Information and Electronic Systems Laboratory, MSFC

Robert S. Ryan, Assistant to the Director, Structures and Dynamics Laboratory, MSFC

Armis L. Worlund, Deputy Director, Propulsion Laboratory, MSFC

Paul H. Schuerer, Director, Materials and Processes Laboratory, MSFC

Einar A. Tandberg-Hanssen, Director, Space Science Laboratory, MSFC

George F. McDonough, Jr., Director, Science and Engineering Directorate, MSFC

Fred S. Wojtalik, Manager, Hubble Space Telescope/Advanced X-ray Astrophysics Facility Projects, MSFC

Thomas J. "Jack" Lee, Director, MSFC

James M. McMillion, Director, Systems Analysis and Integration Laboratory, MSFC

J. H. Newton, Deputy Director, Test Laboratory

This sample represented the top three layers of management and a rather complete sample of the horizontal differentiation or specializations at the Marshall Center. Moving from office to office, I was stunned by the openness of the interviewees. Although I had experienced the same phenomenon in 1967 and 1968, times had changed. So had I. No longer an employee of the Center, I was an outsider this time, here at my own initiative and expense. I had thought that after the *Challenger* tragedy and the probing, job-threatening investigations, these managers might well have chosen to be more reticent.

Instead, they opened up to me. For my part, I promised them anonymity in the sense that I would not identify them by name or title in writing up their comments for my report or in any papers written for publication. Copies of the report would be circulated to all interviewees. As I was leaving one office, the interviewee called down the hallway to me, "See you again in 20 years!"[1]

The interviewees made mainly positive remarks about the current system (and many negative remarks about the previous administration). I reconstructed my interview notes as soon as possible, coding them for themes, e.g., the general state of health and strengths of the current system, current problems, and, of course, practices of the past.

Although my initial proposal said nothing about an immediate report to the Center, Woody Bethay said it would be helpful. I agreed. He asked me to call from the airport when I was scheduled to leave on Thursday morning, January 11, to give him my general

# NATIONAL AERONAUTICS AND SPACE ADMINISTRATION
# GEORGE C. MARSHALL SPACE FLIGHT CENTER

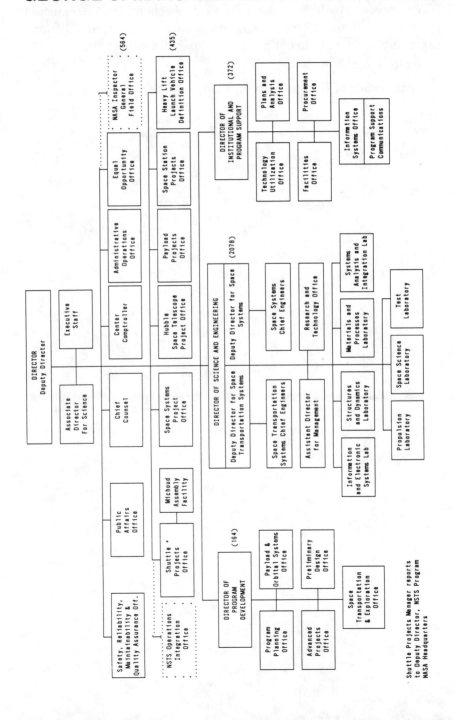

Shuttle Projects Manager reports to Deputy Director, NSTS Program NASA Headquarters

impressions. I did so and indicated that they were positive. There were some problems that could be pursued by means of a question-naire survey, much like the one Gary Richetto had conducted beneath the branch level over 20 years earlier, but overall I found organizational communication at the Marshall Center to be in a state of vigorous good health.

The results of the study are described in the next three chapters.

## NOTES

1.  Before this book went to press, Roxbury Publishing Company submitted passages to its attorney for review.  The lawyer recommended that certain of the quotations from unidentified interviewees be "fact-checked" or verified with the sources directly by the publisher.

I wrote a letter to 13 interviewees (who, among them, had made all of the remarks Roxbury had marked for verification), asking each for permission to reveal what was said to me in 1990 to the publisher of Roxbury, Claude Teweles. I added that Teweles had also promised to keep all responses confidential. I also enclosed a form on which they could check off whether or not they were willing to have Teweles call at their convenience.

The envelopes began to show up in my mailbox over a two-week period in the late summer of 1992.  Twelve of the thirteen answered my request (the thirteenth had not said anything that had to be checked).  Ten indicated they were willing to have their quotations verified.  Two declined and supplied reasons.  The first wrote that he/she had not realized at the time of the interview that the results would be published, implying that it was her/his impression that the study was conducted solely for internal use at MSFC. "For that reason," the letter continued, "I was extremely open in my comments to you and prefer that they remain within the NASA 'family.' " I wrote back, that in my letter to Director Lee in 1989 I had made it clear that I intended to publish the results as I had done after my earlier experience at MSFC (Tompkins, 1977; 1978).  The manager wrote me again, indicating that I was free to use all comments except for two critical remarks, accurately remembered after two-and-a-half years, which had been marked for fact-checking or verification.

The other manager who checked the "no" option gave a different reason: "It was my belief that quotations would not be used at all.  The context of how quotations are used may not have the intent or meaning of the statements made."  The first sentence was clearly the result of a misunderstanding; the second sentence is true in a general sense, but its application to this specific case could have been checked in the verification process.  The result of these two interviewees' decisions was that two short quotations, one from each interview, were excised from the book. The loss of these quotations does not weaken significantly the bases for the conclusions drawn.

The other ten managers checked the "yes" option but wanted to be treated in different ways.  Two asked me to fax them the quotations I had planned to use before they would check the form. I did so, and both agreed to verify the quotations to Claude Teweles (after minor changes requested by one of them). Teweles called them and they verified the quotations as accurate.

Some interviewees accepted the quotations without even a single change: "That sounds like me," one interviewee told Teweles. Others requested changes in the choice of words, one of whom said in essence, "I probably said that, but I'd rather express it this way now." In two cases the interviewees, alerted now to legal considerations, realized in retrospect that they could not *prove* statements they had made to me. In one case the statement was dropped; in the other the interviewee asked to change the quotation to express a perceived consensus among the Marshall managers at the time.

In short, the overwhelming majority of quotations were verified as accurate some 31 months after they had been made to me. In qualitative research such as this study, authors do not often write about "reliability" and "validity," terms usually reserved for quantitative studies. This exercise in verification provides a kind of "replication" or repetition of the study, with the happy consequence of turning up the same findings in 1992 as in 1990.

In fact, Teweles enjoyed the process, experiencing some of the excitement and satisfaction of social-scientific research, even stimulating the interviewees to amplify old observations and provide new insights which have been incorporated in the final version of the book. The author wishes to express gratitude to Claude Teweles for his willingness to participate and his sensitivity in conducting the verification process.

# Chapter Ten

# THE LUCAS ERA AT MSFC

An organization often experiences profound changes when its founder retires or otherwise passes from the scene. Wernher von Braun was not only the founding director of the Marshall Space Flight Center, he was also a charismatic figure. The sociologist Max Weber expressed the crisis for charisma in the question: How to avoid mere routinization after *the* person of the organization is gone? When von Braun transferred from MSFC, the organizational changes were minimized initially because his long-term associate and deputy director, Eberhard F.M. Rees, replaced him. Rees was, of course, a member of the German Rocket Team who had helped von Braun develop a unique system of organizational communication.

## A Brief History of Leadership at MSFC

The long-term resentment toward the German team, centered in Washington, D.C., would soon find effective leverage, however. In fact, according to Ordway and Sharpe, von Braun was seen by some as forced out, "kicked upstairs," when he transferred to a relatively meaningless position at NASA headquarters. He believed he had to leave for the good of the Center. He also realized that other NASA bureaucrats resented his popularity with the public, and that the resentment stemmed partly from his power as the director of the largest NASA field center and, perhaps mainly, from the fact that he was German (Ordway & Sharpe, 1979, p. 401).

## 'Papa' Rees

The rather retiring Rees would be resented for the last two of these reasons. A former member of the Paperclip 120, Rees was older than von Braun and thus acquired his paternal nickname. Rees himself retired in January of 1973, and the rest of the Germans would retire within a few years.

## Enter Rocco Petrone

As described in Chapter One, Rocco Petrone replaced Rees as director of the Marshall Center.[1] Transferred to that top post at MSFC from NASA headquarters, Petrone was the first "outsider" to lead the organization even though he had worked with Marshall personnel during their days with the Army at the Redstone Arsenal.

It would be difficult to determine exactly what charges Petrone was given from NASA headquarters when he took over at the Marshall Center. In fact, I did not question my interviewees about Petrone or his leadership; the remarks made about him were volunteered without any prompting on my part to characterize the Lucas era as qualitatively different from the von Braun-Rees and/or subsequent eras.

One of my interviewees described Petrone as a "hatchet man" who was determined to "weed out" all of the Germans, to "cut out the fat" and, to mix metaphors, the "deadwood." Another manager referred to Petrone's "obsession" with "pushing the Germans out." According to this manager, Petrone's methods created a "persecution complex" at the Marshall Center. Communication suffered, another manager explained, because the director appeared mainly concerned about "cut-backs." One interviewee said, "Petrone's main job was to destroy the Germans and break the backs of the labs. The labs were almost autonomous until he came along. [Petrone] stripped the administrative functions and put them into a management organization within Science and Engineering."

## William Lucas Moves Up

William Lucas replaced Petrone in 1974. As indicated in an earlier chapter, I had met Lucas in 1967, interviewing him when he was a young lab director, the only American-born engineer to head a major lab at that time, and again in 1968. I had seen him in action at Staff and Board briefings. The man was insightful, helpful, and highly knowledgeable about von Braun's philosophy of organizational communication. In fact, he served as director of the Marshall Center longer than von Braun, from 1974 to 1986, until, according to my interviewees, he resigned because of the shuttle disaster.

I read Malcolm McConnell's book, *Challenger: A Major Malfunction* (1987), sometime after it appeared, paying particular attention to Chapter Eight, "The Men from Marshall." It offers a relentlessly harsh profile of Director Lucas, describing him as "authoritarian," a "tyrant," and "autocratic." McConnell relied on only four sources who asked to remain anonymous, but they claimed to have accumulated decades of experience working and communicating with Lucas.

In his depiction of Lucas, McConnell paints a portrait of a man whom one would not have expected to emerge as a leader in the system of organizational communication created by von Braun. The account takes some pains to distinguish between Lucas's and von Braun's managerial styles:

> Ironically and contrary to popular press myth, Lucas had not acquired his "Teutonic" management style from Wernher von Braun and the "Hunsville" [sic] Germans; in fact many observers saw Lucas's leadership style as the exact opposite of von Braun's. Where von Braun had been a charismatic visionary who instilled loyalty through a personal magnetism, Lucas was a coldly distant (and often rigid) master bureaucrat. He believed in doing things according to regulations. Interpreting the regulations was his personal prerogative. (McConnell, 1987, pp. 106-107)

McConnell illustrates his profile with a story about Lucas which was related to him by a Huntsville observer who wished to remain anonymous. The story was apparently confirmed to the author by other sources. One day the director reportedly observed a number of personnel jogging during their lunch break, and he asked why. An aide explained that they were running to fight the stress and tension of the launch schedule. Lucas quickly calculated that they could not possibly have time to eat, run, shower, and change clothes during the 30 minutes allowed for lunch. Therefore, he reportedly issued an oral warning, to be passed down the line, prohibiting such exercise. McConnell also relates another account of this story from a different anonymous source. In this version, Lucas's reason for the ban was his concern over Army Ballistic Missile Agency personnel noticing Marshall people taking time off from work.

Several of my interviewees volunteered statements of respect for Lucas. Some praised his engineering ability, others his activities in the Baptist Church, and several said that once away from the Center and out of his organizational role as director, Lucas could be genial in one-on-one interpersonal communication. I personally recall him as pleasant and helpful during our meeting back in the 1960s.

More importantly, from an organizational perspective, several interviewees expressed gratitude for Lucas's handling of the challenge from Washington during the 1970s. Recall that, according to my interviewees, his predecessor, Rocco Petrone, had forced out the Germans in the early 1970s and had also begun personnel cuts that would ultimately reduce the Marshall Center from a force of about 7,300 people in 1967 to the 1990 level of 3,600. (Later, we will consider the consequences of this reduction in force on subsequent events.)

"It must have been terrible for Bill Lucas to watch people going out the door in droves," one interviewee commented. "This place is conscious of the fact that it could happen again." It is likely Lucas abhorred the thought of such a reduction. Who wants to be in charge of a radically shrinking organization? Some of my interviewees believed that Washington seriously considered abolishing the Marshall Center altogether in the mid-1970s. According to Trento, "The OMB [Office of Management and Budget] was recommending that the Marshall Space Flight Center be closed " (1987, p. 115). The managers I interviewed felt that for much of the government, the Apollo Project *was* the space program. When Neil Armstrong stepped onto the moon, the Space Race was won, the program over. Lucas devised a strategy for combatting this plan—if indeed such a plan did exist in Washington—by diversifying the Center's activities and foregoing the use of support contractors.

Diversifying meant that the Marshall Center would dilute its massive specialization in boosters, engines, and propulsion, and find other ways of contributing to the space program, e.g., by producing payloads such as the Hubble Telescope. In their bestselling book, *In Search of Excellence* (1982), Peters and Waterman examine the lessons learned from America's best-run companies. One of those lessons is: "Stick to your knitting." (We shall return to Lucas's strategy of diversification for a reconsideration of its long-term effects.) Foregoing the use of support contractors meant that the Marshall Center personnel would save money by doing more of the "dirty work" of R&D themselves, devoting less effort to the monitoring of contracts. On the other hand, their technical depth was significantly reduced, making it impossible to penetrate prime contractors to the degree they had in the past.

Together, Lucas's strategies illustrate how far an organization will go to ensure survival. They are credited by some with stabilizing the Marshall workforce at about 50 percent of its peak employment. Apart from these expressions of respect and gratitude, however, many of my interviewees were critical of Lucas. They pointed to his inability to maintain an effective system of organizational communication (what Chester Barnard called the first executive function). This criticism, coupled with the acknowledgement that Lucas was effective in one-on-one situations, particularly when off the Marshall turf, illustrates that organizational and interpersonal communication require very different abilities. Some people possess both sets of skills (e.g., von Braun); others have one or the other—or neither. The acquisition of one set does not necessarily guarantee the other.

**Colleagues' Assessments of Lucas.** The following remarks were made by my interviewees. The comments are nearly literal transcriptions, with some editing and paraphrasing to provide context.

- It's not hard to get up here [to the ninth floor of Building 4200] and become isolated. Dr. Lucas lost touch. We were not being effective in downward communication and did not make people comfortable coming up the line. Dr. Lucas sincerely wanted to know, but he didn't get the information he should have. The ninth floor is hallowed ground.

- I feel bad about saying this, but people were afraid to bring bad news [to Lucas] for fear they would be treated harshly. They didn't want to be chewed out. It was kill the messenger. There was a tendency to push things down, to keep the lid on problems; no news is good news. Lucas was not sinister or nasty—it was just his management style. It seemed apparent to everyone that to reinstill our organizational pride, it was best that Dr. Lucas leave.

- Lucas was a dead fish. Cold, vindictive, he would embarrass people publicly. It was very hard to go to him with a problem—you could expect no sympathy. He could chill you with that hostile expression of his: "Good grief." Dr. Lucas related poorly to the press and his superiors.... He never acknowledged we made a mistake with *Challenger* but left his key subordinates swinging in the wind during the investigations. . . . Dr. Lucas resigned under pressure.

- I thought the world of Dr. Lucas, even though he was so rigid and formal. People were afraid to raise problems with him. We started canning and preprogramming what went up to Dr. Lucas. We were afraid of his response. He'd jump all over people if what they said didn't suit him.

- Dr. Lucas's team presented an image of strength. As such, they gave the impression they didn't like to hear bad news. When they did, they'd say we didn't anticipate the problems and solve them. The messenger gets shot, in other words. It takes a strong messenger under those circumstances. That caused us to put the shiniest face on everything we could, put on the biggest smile. I don't want to go up there to the ninth floor and get shot down, so they got less than totally accurate information. You delay, you put the best face on it. If he expects you to be perfect, you're going to flunk. If you carry a problem to Dr. Lucas, he would demand, out of frustration, "How many more of these are out there?"[2]

- Dr. Lucas's group expected us to be conversant about every technical detail. They made us apprehensive, reluctant to volunteer information. To volunteer an opinion subjected you to uncomfortable critiques. So, you didn't volunteer. We suffered embarrassment and humiliation. Your career could be in jeopardy. Lucas constrained communication. There were too many managers trying to master too much detail. . . .

- My feeling was that Dr. Lucas was secluded. He ate his meals on the ninth floor. It was not easy to get through to Lucas. He was protected. . . . And then they [Lucas, Kingsbury, Mulloy, Reinart] had to leave after *Challenger*. They deserve some blame for *Challenger* because of their communication style.

- Communication with Lucas was more constrained than with von Braun, not as open, but you could get through if you wanted to. My opinion is that if somebody was forceful he could have been heard.

- Communication for a year or two or more before *Challenger* was a problem.

- The pre-*Challenger* period was the worst we've seen in communication. There was a fear on the part of people to surface problems at a high level: kill the messenger. I'm at fault for not surfacing problems. I saw it in meetings with Dr. Lucas—people humiliated in front of peers and contractors.

- Lucas wanted information filtered. His communicative style was intimidation. The way he did business didn't encourage people to bring up problems. Before a formal review, he wanted people to tell him what was going on. He didn't want to hear about it for the first time in a formal review.

These comments from top and middle managers establish something close to a consensus that Lucas's communication style produced an ineffective system of organizational communication, one that led Marshall further from von Braun's methods. This picture of isolation and defensiveness, along with the theme of "kill the messenger," is antithetical to the Ideal Managerial Climate (Redding, 1972), described in Chapter Two, that I saw during the von Braun era. In a sense, one could say it is amazing that the Marshall personnel completed 24 successful shuttle flights before the *Challenger* disaster in this kind of organizational climate. It was, as Feynman has said, a kind of Russian roulette.

**Patterns of Organizational Behavior.** These verbal depictions bring to mind the concepts and typology of the neurotic organization (de Vries & Miller, 1984) discussed in Chapter Two. Of the five types of organizational neuroses—the paranoid, compulsive, dramatic, depressive, and schizoid—no single type seems an exact fit to the state of organizational affairs during either the Petrone or the Lucas administrations. But that is the way ideal types often function in reality. However, looking at *combinations* of elements from several types can be useful in understanding the neuroses of an organization. In applying these labels, I wish to stress the following disclaimer: The section below is *not* intended as a psychological analysis of any individuals' personalities. Rather, it is an analysis of an *organization* and patterns of *organizational* behavior, primarily communicative in nature, that led to the unsatisfactory functioning of the Marshall Center during these two administrations.

As described earlier in this chapter, due to reductions in force, a number of people at MSFC during and after Petrone's brief reign believed—apparently with good reason—that NASA headquarters was out to "do them in." But the reductions in force were only part of the cause for this "persecution complex" (to quote an interviewee) atmosphere. There were also rumors that the Center might close down. The subsequent attempt to save the Center through diversification could be read as a "paranoid" strategy on the part of the organization. (Note that the word "paranoid" is not used here in a necessarily pejorative sense; paranoia is also a healthy reaction to a situation that may imperil an organization's survival.) As de Vries and Miller (1984) wrote, "One strategy that may be used quite frequently by paranoid firms is product-market *diversification*. Here the attempt is to reduce the risk of exposure to, or reliance on, any one environment" (p. 27). According to de Vries and Miller's model, the paranoid organization is interested in finding out what its problems are through an emphasis on organizational intelligence. However, this does not fit Lucas's reported aversion to hearing about problems, at least toward the end of his administrative tenure.

Although Lucas may have been averse to hearing about problems, on the basis of several interviewees's comments and McConnell's findings (1987), it could be argued that his administration exhibited a "preoccupation with trivial details" (de Vries & Miller, 1984, p. 24). One could postulate that this reflects an organizational "obsession" with monitoring and controlling internal operations (as opposed to an interest in the external environment, which is the case with a paranoid organization). Monitoring and controlling are descriptive terms commonly used to characterize a compulsive organization. Though considered by some as "coldly distant" (McConnell, 1987, p. 107), at least Lucas was one of the "family," had moved up the ranks, and was not perceived as wishing harm to the organization. Indeed, Lucas was trying to save the organization, hence the "compulsiveness" of his administration.

### Communication as a Factor in the *Challenger* Accident

Could the communicative style of MSFC have been a factor contributing to the *Challenger* accident? I had not planned to put that question directly to my interviewees. But it seemed to be a natural one to pose during six of the interviews because of the concerns I heard expressed.

Here is what the six I asked had to say:

- I don't know. Lucas's style did intimidate a lot of people. I'm not sure, but society requires us to say "yes"—we fire the football coach when the team doesn't win.[3]

- Yes, the communication problem was a factor—but not the night before. We knew about the O-rings, but I'm not sure the problem was communicated to the right people. And it was not clear who was to be *the* project director, the Center director or someone else. (emphasis added)

- Was it a factor? My opinion is that is probably a true statement. We developed a feeling, "Well we've had 25 flights and we weren't going to have a failure." We ignored or put off the problem.

- Was it a factor in *Challenger*? We all knew about the O-ring problem. We met in August and had a solution, but Lucas and Hardy were under pressure to be on time with the flights. To hold up a flight was difficult. The level of fatigue was dangerous. . . . The teleconference got turned around. When challenged, Thiokol, rather than standing behind their data, told the government what they thought it wanted to hear. . . . Yes, there was a communication problem.

- There were four factors that I see: (1) There was some basis in Lucas and his style; (2) some basis in the goals from Beggs [the NASA administrator who determined the frequency of shuttle flights] and his advertising to the public; (3) some basis in the misinterpretation of the O-rings—we were misreading the hardware; and (4) if Thiokol had said "We don't want to fly," then there would have been no flight.

- Was communication a factor in the *Challenger* accident? I worry about that a lot. My impression is that Thiokol was opposed to the launch at the engineering level. They were surprised at the stance of the Marshall managers. Always before, the Marshall managers would make sure that it was okay to launch. The teleconference was atypical. We needed more openness in the agency than we had then. We've seen the results doing otherwise.

I asked, "What results?"

The manager said, "*Challenger*."

### Roger Boisjoly's Response

While I was writing this book, Roger Boisjoly visited the University of Colorado to give a lecture.[4] Boisjoly was the Morton Thiokol engineer who had recommended against the launch of *Challenger* during the teleconference the night before blast-off. He and his engineering colleagues at Morton Thiokol went to the teleconference prepared to recommend against a launch. As discussed in an earlier chapter, according to the Rogers Commission Report, Marshall Center representatives were reportedly "appalled" by the recommendation and asked them if they wanted to wait "until April" to launch. Where was the communication failure in this incident?

Boisjoly and his colleagues argued that they could not recommend the launch because they were "outside the envelope"—they had no data on how the O-rings would perform at such a low temperature. The NASA officials refused to accept this recommendation and talked the Thiokol managers into reversing it. The NASA officials were wrong, but they were not ignorant of the facts. Their communication failure was in not communicating Boisjoly's initial recommendation and the extent of his and other Thiokol engineers' grave concerns up the line. They violated the principle of automatic responsibility.

In summary, it seems clear that ineffective communication was a significant factor in the *Challenger* failure. There were other factors, to be sure, but problems in communication have to be included.

## NOTES

1.   Petrone's name was mentioned in Chapter Seven of this book in connection with the Rogers Commission.   Petrone was by then a top executive of Rockwell, the contractor for the orbiter.   He testified that he recommended against the last flight of *Challenger* on the basis that ice was present before the launch.   The Rogers Commission Report concluded that "Rockwell's position on launch. . .was not clearly communicated to NASA officials in the launch decision chain during the hours preceding 51-L's launch" (p.116).

2.   During the publisher's fact-checking in 1992, this interviewee added that "Lucas wanted the Center to do the very best job at all times.   But when pushing for that, some people interpreted that he didn't want to hear about problems."   This manager felt that Lucas ultimately defeated his own purposes because "what he intended to say wasn't received by the people listening.   Not only what we *say* is important, but how we *act*.   People aren't just listening to us, but *reading* us as well."

This interviewee also added the following comments about Lucas: "He never got on my case or chewed me out.   But you couldn't go to his office and put your feet up.   You couldn't just say, 'Let's just talk about it [a problem].'"   It was more comfortable, this manager said, to make "a polished presentation. . . .   And it was never Bill, always Dr. Lucas."

3.   During the publisher's fact-checking in 1992, this interviewee made the additional comment that "self-imposed pressure within the agency had more to do with causing the *Challenger* accident than communication per se."

4.   I spent a number of hours with Boisjoly and attended his speech and question-and-answer period. He gave his permission for me to use anything he said (except for one anecdote which he plans to use in his own book). Boisjoly related that he told the truth in his testimony to the Rogers Commission, as opposed to answering questions "yes" or "no" and volunteering nothing, which, he claimed, had been the advice of his managers at Thiokol. He then lost his job at Thiokol. Residents of the town he lived in, who had once elected him mayor, now began to shun him and his wife, Boisjoly said, and many members of his own church refused to speak to him. A dead rabbit was placed in his mail box. On several occasions while taking long walks near his home, he said, vehicles swerved as if to hit him. Boisjoly then experienced post-traumatic stress disorder. (He later founded his own consulting engineering company.)

## Chapter Eleven

# ORGANIZATIONAL FORGETTING

### Perceived Problems in the Current Organization

There is additional evidence relevant to my hypothesis of an organizational memory loss at MSFC. During my interviews I asked each individual to describe any problems he or she perceived in the current organizational communication system. In addition, nearly every interviewee was asked to comment on the key principles and practices of organizational communication at the Marshall Center as developed under von Braun: automatic responsibility, penetration, and the Monday notes. In discussing contemporary problems, some of the interviewees mentioned these principles without my having to bring them up, which thereby provided two indications of the degree to which those concepts were practiced, i.e., those "prompted" and those "unprompted."

Four interviewees, for example, mentioned problems associated with the current status and practice of automatic responsibility. These four were knowledgeable about the principle's history and could define it in a way consistent with my understanding of it—an understanding gathered from conversations with and memoranda by von Braun. One of the four mentioned that the demands of a diverse matrix organization managing many projects made the practice of automatic responsibility more difficult than it was in the old days of fewer projects and a simpler matrix. In 1990, the diversity of projects underway at the Marshall Center made it more difficult for individuals to have the technical competence or authority to assert or invoke automatic responsibility. Two of the four interviewees indicated that the organization sometimes seemed to encourage, contrary to the spirit of automatic responsibility, an attitude of "I'll let the other guy worry about that problem." One interviewee noted, "In those days [of] von Braun and the German philosophy. . .[there were] no clear lines of authority and responsibility. There was redundancy and infighting. You got to talk and argue. That allowed people to know what's going on. Today the organization is leaner, has clearer responsibilities. . . .   We are more isolated."

Problems associated with the practice of penetration were also volunteered by three interviewees.   Penetration, as described in previous chapters, is a practice that dates back to the Centaur and Apollo Projects and involves the aggressive infiltration of organizations external to the Marshall Center, primarily its contractors. Penetrating personnel would report back to Marshall management about problems and projected delays on the part of contractors. There was also an internal version of penetration practiced at MSFC in the 1960s discussed in Chapter Three. As noted previously, the external practice of penetration was initiated to ensure that MSFC would be a "smart buyer" on behalf of U.S. taxpayers. By penetrating contractor organizations, the Marshall Center knew what it was buying and could anticipate potential problems—better in some cases than the contractor itself.

However, the 50 percent reduction in force and diversification in the number of projects managed had combined to create a situation in which fewer people were forced to monitor more tasks. This made it more difficult to penetrate each contractor group. One manager said, "We're spread too thin [to maintain past levels of penetration]." Another manager commented, "We became almost too diverse." A third said, "Times are different now. Under von Braun, it was a time of birth. We had new and exciting challenges but were focused on one major goal. Now we are diversified. That makes communication more difficult. We have pockets of individuals dedicated to one project. That is the main difference."

## Penetration

When directly questioned about penetration, only six interviewees could define the practice. A typical example of an informed answer was, "The Marshall Center is different.   We do penetrate the contractor. We follow through and it's right we do so because (1) we have 30 years of experience; contractors come and go; (2) we have to be smart buyers and penetration helps us become that." One of those six, however, believed that MSFC was "too thin" in human resources to penetrate as deeply as in the past.

Two interviewees understood the concept and thought it had been downgraded or transformed into a weaker communicative practice over the years. One of them discussed penetration in the context of the *Challenger* tragedy and concluded that, during that period, the "workload increased and the workforce decreased to the degree that we didn't penetrate the contractor." Another interviewee gave a similar explanation: "We had gotten away from that [penetration], had gotten into more of a mode of contract monitoring than penetrating. We lost a lot of that—we didn't have the resources to penetrate as in the past." Three people did not know the term and asked the interviewer for a definition. Once informed, one interviewee then said, "I never heard the term, but we do practice it."

## Automatic Responsibility

Thirteen managers were asked about the current practice of automatic responsibility. Eight said that the principle was currently in effect, and five said they had never heard of the concept. The eight who said it was still in effect were asked to define it; four of them gave definitions that were vague or inaccurate. For example, one interviewee defined automatic responsibility as "stepping in for the [lab] director when he's unavailable," which clearly misses the mark. Thus, only 4 out of 13 could answer that question. Those four added that the status of the concept had changed over the years. One said it currently had a "weakened" status, partly because of limited resources for dealing with a diverse array of projects. Another said the practice "went out" during the Lucas era. A third said Lucas didn't emphasize it and added the speculation that perhaps it was because Lucas wanted to be in on all decisions. In short, automatic responsibility had been forgotten by most managers in the best position to remember it, and the practice had thus fallen into disuse.

## Monday Notes

The practice called Monday Notes was another matter. Every manager asked about this communication device could define in detail its practice and background rules. The interviewees informed me that the Monday Notes were now called Weekly Notes. They also pointed out some other changes that involved more than simply a change in names.

Von Braun's practice had been to write in the margins of each note before reproducing and returning the entire package of notes to each contributor. In 1990, the director no longer wrote in the margins; instead, notes were communicated up the line via electronic mail. The loss of open feedback from the boss may also have been a matter of the current director's style, but we can cite this as an inevitable tradeoff involved in adopting new communication technologies.

Other changes involved some screening of items by the manager positioned between the note-writer and the director. Under the open atmosphere of Thompson and Lee, however, this was not thought to present a problem. As was discovered in my earlier studies, the note-writers varied widely in their methods for generating the content of the Weekly Notes. Some required notes from their direct subordinates, while others invited any and all employees in their labs or offices to provide information. Evaluative comments about the Weekly Notes system were highly favorable.

### Factors of Organizational Forgetting

Apart from the continued practice of the Monday Notes in their new form as the Weekly Notes, it seems clear from the above that there was a fairly serious degree of organizational forgetting over the years, as well as an erosion of strength in some of MSFC's more traditional communicative practices. My assumption in drawing this conclusion is that the senior management group, the 15 people I interviewed, should be the best informed people about the use of these concepts in the organization.

How can this organizational memory loss be explained?

## Public Memory

"Public memory," wrote the eminent anthropologist Mary Douglas, "is the storage system for the social order" (1986, p. 70). Douglas discusses the concept of "structural amnesia," but explained that anthropologists are less inclined to wonder why people forget than to ask why they remember. Douglas's best explanation of collective or structural forgetting/remembering is that whatever is functional or advantageous to the system is remembered; that which is dysfunctional is forgotten. This is not a fruitful explanation if one believes that the von Braun system of organizational communication was functional for MSFC—unless, of course, it was dysfunctional for the Lucas administration, which, according to many of my interviewees, allowed some of the practices to be forgotten and fall into disuse.

My interviews made clear that (1) the forgetting began during the Petrone era, and (2) it was a *selective* forgetting. Some concepts have almost completely passed away—penetration and automatic responsibility—while the Monday Notes still survive, albeit in a somewhat different form and under a new name.

The Weekly Notes survived because they constituted a regularly recurring, habitual activity. As we shall see, however, there was a significant change in the content of the notes under Lucas. According to my interviewees, the notes became "sterile" and lost their previous "charm" as an informal, open forum where contentious issues could be addressed. (There is a certain security in routine for people in a risky business. Bureaucratic routine creates the illusion that all is well. When the memos are flowing regularly and on time, who will worry that the system is flawed or that the content is deceiving? In Mussolini's Fascist regime in Italy, at least the trains ran on time.)

Penetration suffered a different fate. As mentioned, Lucas had fought to save the Marshall Center during the 1970s through a strategy of diversification. Some of my interviewees had comments about the effects of diversification on the practice of penetration at a time of shrinking resources, with fewer people to monitor more projects and contractors. Trento (1987) put it more strongly: "By the end of 1980, NASA's capability to technically verify any contractor's work had all but vanished" (p. 176). Clearly, it became less and less

feasible to practice penetration at MSFC, particularly since management was not stressing it. Organizational forgetting began to set in.
The job was to monitor the contract; penetration was forgotten or
abandoned.

The demise of automatic responsibility suggests a different
possible explanation. Based on my interviewees' responses, it
seemed a near consensus that Lucas did not like to hear about
problems coming up the line. Some managers admitted that they did
not volunteer information about problems for fear of becoming a
"dead" messenger. The success of automatic responsibility depends
on the willingness of engineers to identify new problems and
volunteer to solve them; if they cannot solve them, it is their
responsibility to communicate the information up the line. Based on
the interviewees' description of the communicative style under
William Lucas's administration, it would appear that automatic
responsibility could hardly have been attractive to those who would
have had to practice it. In fact, this style seemed to encourage
people to take less responsibility for problems, not more.

Under the hypothesis of organizational forgetting, one might
argue that Rocco Petrone's reductions in force could have provided
the "shock" or trauma—a kind of "organizational amnesia"—that
drove the practice of automatic responsibility out of use. The
communicative style subsequently practiced under Lucas's administration, as well as its diversification plan, could have contributed to
driving the concept out of use as well.

**Attrition**

There is another factor that helps to explain this case of
organizational forgetting: attrition of the enculturated workforce.
Von Braun, the creator of the system, left the Center in 1970.
Walter Wiesman, coordinator of internal communication, retired in
the same year. Eberhard Rees retired three years later, and the rest
of the Germans either left during Petrone's brief tenure (1973-74) or
retired soon after that. These people had all been in influential
positions and more deeply immersed in the Marshall culture than
anyone else.

Many others were forced out by the reductions in force. As of
this writing, at least 50 percent of those nurtured in the von Braun
culture are long gone. Moreover, one third of the 1990 work force

was hired after the *Challenger* accident. A manager in one of the laboratories told me that one third of his/her employees had been with the organization for an average of only one year. "The challenge," she/he explained, "was how to communicate the culture of the organization to them."

## Organization and Change

I submit that my "long-distance" hypothesis of organizational forgetting is supported by both the indirect and direct "experiments" of January 1990 presented in this and the preceding chapter.

The selective memory loss could be explained by several possible factors, not least of which was the communicative style of Lucas's administration, a style that, as described by my interviewees, would appear antithetical to many value premises of the "old" culture. Even the successful attempt to save the Center with a strategy of diversification could have contributed to the organizational amnesia and forgetting. An organizational culture is likely to endure if its leader acts out its values in the everyday practices of the organization. The interviewees felt by and large that Lucas did not "enact" the culture as a role model; indeed, they believed that many of the communication practices during this period ran counter to the tenets of the old culture.

Many of us think of organizations as entities that retain the same identity or essence over time. Social theorists have shown that some organizations have persisted for 200 years or more, even though the founders and other original members are no longer alive. The Supreme Court, it is argued, is still the Supreme Court even though the original justices are long dead.

The case of the Marshall Space Flight Center forces me to question that common assumption. NASA is still a young organization, only 34 years old at the time of this writing. The Marshall Center is only 32 years old—but that is old enough for an organization to have a history. The size, culture, leadership style, mission or purpose, and communication philosophy of the original organization were so different from those of the Petrone and the Lucas administrations that a case could be made that they represent two different organizations or, at least, two stages or phases of the same organization.

# Chapter Twelve

# DEATH AND REBIRTH

"My own view of the Marshall Center relies on the Greek concept of hubris," remarked one of my interviewees, "and the tragic flaw of this organization was its pride and arrogance. The *Challenger* tragedy had to produce a big let-down. Many of us knew at least some of the astronauts, and we grieved them. We knew that it was our propulsion system that had failed. For six, eight, nine months we felt isolated. Johnson [NASA's Manned Flight Center in Houston] was not kind; they rubbed salt in our wounds with statements like 'Marshall killed our astronauts.' Then the Rogers Commission began its investigations; its prosecutorial, cross-examining style was more typical of a grand jury than an investigation. We hit rock bottom. People still grieve. It's hard to deal with the subject."

## Mourning

As I listened to the interviewees, I began to realize that they had gone through a period of grieving or mourning. John Bowlby has identified four stages of mourning:

> Observations of how individuals respond to the loss of a close relative show that over the course of weeks and months their responses usually move through a succession of phases. Admittedly these phases are not clear-cut, and any one individual may oscillate for a time back and forth between any of them. Yet an overall sequence can be discerned.

The four phases are as follows:

1. Phase of numbing that usually lasts from a few hours to a week and may be interrupted by outbursts of extremely intense distress and/or anger.

2. Phase of yearning and searching for the lost figure lasting some months and sometimes for years.

3. Phase of disorganization and despair.

4. Phase of greater or lesser degree of despair. (1980, p. 18)

As de Vries and Miller point out:

There is considerable agreement in the literature that the process of dealing with the loss of a loved one is the model after which all other forms of loss are patterned. And loss necessitates mourning. A disturbance of the organizational status quo precipitates a comparable process. It causes the loss of old and familiar patterns of functioning and administrative relationships as they are replaced with new ones. Working through, mourning, and change thus appear to be intimately connected. (1984, p. 156)

People at the Marshall Center went through something similar to these four stages or phases, some experiencing them more intensely than others. Because I had not anticipated the topic, I did not routinely question my interviewees about grieving and mourning. Many said nothing to me about such feelings, but those who did talk about the subject attributed such feelings to others. Therefore, I assume such feelings were fairly widespread.

There was certainly a numbing effect immediately after the accident. There was also yearning, searching, and anger. A period of disorganization followed, when Lucas and the other shuttle managers resigned. Then came the reorganization; perhaps rebirth is not too strong a term to use. The process of "working through" the tragedy also produced some profound changes in organizational communication.

In her classic study, *On Death and Dying* (1969), Elisabeth Kübler-Ross describes two different stages of the grieving process: denial and acceptance. Based on the testimony given to the Rogers Commission by officials at MSFC, it appears that initially the Marshall Center's official stance was a form of denial, a refusal to acknowledge any responsibility for the *Challenger* accident. However, in 1990, my interviewees were quick to acknowledge institutional responsibility, even guilt and culpability.

The managers I interviewed spoke of feeling wounded and bleeding. Others chose the imagery of fatal or near-fatal wounds to the organization and its members. Cynthia Stohl of Purdue University suggested to me in a conversation that they were mourning a "double death." They were grieving not only the death of the astronauts, but also that of a once-proud organization, the George C. Marshall Space Flight Center.

### Rationality and Emotion

"There has to be a period for grieving," explained a different manager. "Some people just can't talk about it now." I was quite surprised in some of the interviews by the intense, cathartic nature of my interviewees' discourse. As Max Weber pointed out in the early part of this century, modern bureaucracy is based on the principle of rationality. Rationality, the calculable, is justified on the grounds of superior efficiency. The rational justification or authority for bureaucracy requires it to exclude emotionality from its discourse.

Roger Boisjoly said in a network television interview that he almost "lost it" during the teleconference. "I was becoming emotional," he said, as if it were an improper feeling to experience, not to mention one to express.

MSFC, as a space center rooted in the premises of science and engineering, probably placed more emphasis on rationality than most bureaucracies, even if its members sometimes deceived themselves in their quantitative expressions of confidence in their technology. Thus, it was considered "out of place" for many of the Marshall people to discuss their emotions with each other, to express their guilt and grief about the "double death."

### Purging the Guilt

As the contemporary American sage, Kenneth Burke, has shown over and over again, we often search for scapegoats to purge ourselves of our collective guilt. So it was with the Marshall Center. "The purge was necessary, at least in part," an interviewee told me. "Lucas, the shuttle managers, the teleconference people had to go. We cleaned house." They had to go, I was told, because they were no longer able to lead the Marshall Center.  Burke would no doubt submit that a renewed sense of community, consubstantiality, and identification would be difficult to achieve without such a purge.

### J.R. Thompson: A Transformational Leader

After the period of purgation, a remarkable transformation began to take place.  A replacement for Lucas had to be found. Some bet that T.J. "Jack" Lee would be named.  Having been moved up to serve as the acting director after Lucas left, Lee was a long-time insider who had transferred from the Army's Redstone Arsenal to the Marshall Center when it was established in 1960.  He had been named deputy director of MSFC in 1980.

But Lee was bypassed, this time at least, in favor of J.R. Thompson.  Thompson was both an insider and an outsider.  He had worked at the Marshall Center during the von Braun era and had a reputation as a good engineer.  His scholarly credentials were good enough for him to have left the Marshall Center for a faculty appointment at Princeton University.  He was familiar with the problems of the shuttle and of the Center because he had been involved in the Rogers Commission's investigation of the *Challenger* accident.

James McGregor Burns (1978) has made the distinction between two kinds of leaders: transactional leaders and transformational leaders.  Transactional leaders keep things going as they were in the past.  They pragmatically make deals with people, scratch their backs to get things done.  Transformational leaders, on the other hand, produce dramatic changes, see new visions, and inspire people to achieve greater heights.  There is no doubt that von Braun was such a leader.  I believe that J.R. Thompson also enacted the role of transformational leader in the two years he directed the Marshall Center.

"J.R.'s appointment as director was a masterstroke," an interviewee said.  "He was one of our own but not tainted by association with the *Challenger* accident."  I heard nothing but praise for Thompson's efforts to re-create the organization.  The following are some of the comments my interviewees made about that effort.

## Colleagues' Assessments of Thompson's Leadership

- J.R. convinced people he would do his damnedest to stimulate communication. He had an open door. He was the right personality at the right time. He placed a great stress on the team, the "we." J.R. was also open to and effective with the press, other NASA centers, headquarters, and contractors.

- J.R. opened up the ninth floor. He even had a Christmas reception up there.

- He had a feel for what to do. He was a cheerleader who worked around the clock fixing the problem. He was upbeat and positive, assuring us that we would return to flight. He opened up MSFC. He even wore a Santa Claus suit at one of his Christmas receptions. J.R. opened meetings with "What are the problems?" That sometimes led to debate and controversy, something we hadn't seen in a long time. . . . People loved J.R.. . . . Our emotional health now is that we're older and wiser, confident and proud.

- J.R. gave us openness. On balance, he was a breath of fresh air.

- J.R. was kind of a von Braun. He used a lot of the same approaches—an open door, perfectionism; he wanted it right and would work all night to get it.

- J.R. figured, I think, he could work hard enough to fix whatever problem you tell him about. He was open, more so than Lucas. There had to be a change.

- J.R. was one of our own and didn't place blame. He reminded us of our strengths, that we are in a high-risk business. He gave us updates on the closed-circuit television. He came out to the labs for meetings. And did walk-throughs in the lab. We have opened up communication significantly.

- It was quite a change with J.R. Thompson. He spelled out there should be better communication. He even ate in the cafeteria and came down here [to the labs] once a month. Morale is good, much higher than at any time since 1974. It perhaps reached a peak with J.R. People even work in the evening without overtime. . . . Communication is a strange beast. It is reasonably okay now.

- J.R. reached out to people. He dressed as Santa Claus for a Christmas reception and everyone came.

- With von Braun communication was always good. Not as open under Lucas, but with J.R. and Jack [current director T.J. Lee] it's back to the original.

- There was a tremendous change in morale and communication. It's really unbelievable. He [Thompson] even stopped the executive luncheons and ate in the cafeteria. If you had a problem you could sit down with him and talk about it. Everybody noticed it.

- His appointment was good—in the family but also outside. His background fit us, and he knew us well. A complete stranger might have produced different results. J.R. *got us safely in the air again.* He also had institutional concerns about communication—communication within the Center, intercenter communication, and communication with headquarters.

- J.R. and Jack got out to the offices and labs. That was not done with Dr. Lucas. After *Challenger*, the Rogers Commission mentioned our problem of communication—we made a conscious effort to fix it, especially upward communication. Part of it was due to our new leaders. J.R. was convinced a communication effort was needed and was very effective at it. Some thought he did too much PR, but I think it was necessary. He had gatherings with every employee and created a sense of teamwork. We needed it.

- J.R.'s positive attitude was necessary. That started the healing process. . . . His message? It happened. Let's make sure it doesn't happen again. His message? Let's communicate. We made a major redesign of the field joints (that housed the O-rings). Morale is good. Why? Because we fixed the *Challenger*.

Note the subtle distinctions between the forms of address in the above comments: "J.R." versus "Dr. Lucas" or "Lucas." Note also the remarks about the return to flight and the healing process; I believe they have a double meaning, a metaphorical as well as a literal one. The shuttle did fly again, and, in a way, the Marshall Center did as well. My guess is that J.R. Thompson appreciated both levels of meaning because he so clearly understood the *symbolic* import of his role as a leader in trying to revitalize the organization.

Was it nothing more than a gag that J.R. played Santa Claus? I doubt it. In any case, he distributed some precious gifts: rebirth, new confidence, improved morale, and, most importantly, reopened channels of communication.

## Necessary and Sufficient Conditions

Since revisiting the Marshall Center in January of 1990, I have tried to infer and enumerate the factors involved in bringing back to life an ailing organization. "Necessary and sufficient conditions" may seem a pretentious phrase, but it does reflect what I have attempted to specify in the following three conditions:

1. *There has to be change in leadership.* At MSFC, it can be argued that if the top administrators had not resigned after *Challenger,* they would have had to be fired. No human is perfect, nor is any human creation such as a complex organization. As indicated above, Kenneth Burke taught that it is characteristic of human beings, both individually and collectively, to seek out scapegoats to rid themselves of guilt when things go wrong. It is frightening but true that nothing unites people as much as a common enemy, be it an Adolph Hitler, a Saddam Hussein, the Germans, the Japanese, or the Russians at various times in our history, a competitor, a cross-town team, or even our own unsuccessful football coach.

There are other reasons why there had to be a change of leadership at MSFC. As described earlier in this book, some members of the organization apparently believed the Lucas administration's organizational communication practices to be responsible to some degree for the *Challenger* accident. The Rogers Commission cast a cloud of doubt over his administration's leadership. The feeling expressed by many of my interviewees was that Lucas could not have led the Marshall Center back to recovery. He lacked, they believed, the communicative skills and style, the *ethos*, to get the organization back into space.

2. *The new leadership has to possess certain characteristics.* The first is *purity,* i.e., an unsullied record. This is a corollary to the first condition to some extent. Lucas was perceived by many as tainted for his role in the *Challenger* disaster; Thompson was not. The second characteristic is *trust,* or rather, the ability to inspire trust in others. Thompson had this ability, and it did not hurt him after all—indeed it seems to have helped—that he had worked effectively at the Marshall Center during the von Braun era. He was a member

of the "family," a distant relative perhaps, and his long sabbatical at Princeton enhanced his purity.

Thompson must have understood and appreciated the importance of communication, particularly in its *systemic, stylistic,* and *rhetorical/symbolic* dimensions.  By *systemic,* I mean that he surely realized the system of organizational communication had to be rebuilt—particularly the upwardly-directed channels.  His ability to inspire trust was crucial in this respect.  Thompson also took care to send the word down the line that he wanted more open communication downward, hence the open door, the visits to labs, and the information update addresses on closed-circuit television.

By the *stylistic* dimension, I mean Thompson's ability to set an example of openness and accessibility, to *enact* the kind of communication he wanted to encourage.  Thompson had to demonstrate that messengers with bad news would not become victims.  The "What are the problems?" approach with which he opened his meetings illustrates that style.

The *rhetorical* dimension refers to his persuasive efforts to rebuild the Marshall Center's self-respect, to help members of the organization regather their collective identity.  There is a cluster of social scientific theories that are generally labeled under the term "identity or impression management."  Kenneth Burke and Erving Goffman are two representative theorists of this school or approach to human action.  Their claim is that we humans are constantly involved in managing the impressions other people gain of us.  We go to great lengths to manipulate how others perceive us.  I suggest that the expression "reverse identity management" is more applicable in this situation, the notion that J.R. Thompson's discourse "managed" the employees' impressions of themselves to help them regain their identity of competence and excellence.  Thompson's words were crucially important here: His continuing message was that "we" can fix the problem and fly again. Thompson had the *right rhetorical stuff.*

It was also crucial that Thompson articulated a certain responsibility on the part of the Marshall Center for the *Challenger* disaster. One cannot help to heal a wound that has not been identified and diagnosed.

Finally, it was important that Thompson had high standards. Some called him a perfectionist.  He did not coddle the Marshall people in their grief. He let it be known that he wanted things right and that he expected others to work alongside him all night if necessary to get it right. Together they could fix any problem through high standards and hard work. This requirement is identical to the fifth factor in Redding's Ideal Managerial Climate discussed in Chapter Two: an emphasis upon high-performance goals.

3. *An organization must undergo a "redemptive praxis."* Redemption means a release from blame or guilt; praxis means the exercise of an art, science, or skill. By combining the two concepts I hope to suggest that we cleanse, even heal, ourselves by good work and good works. One top MSFC manager said, "One hundred and fifty of us gathered the day after the accident to get to work on the problem. We worked seven days a week from January to Easter." Another manager responded to a question about why morale improved so dramatically in this way: "We fixed the *Challenger*."

By exercising their arts, sciences, and skills in the pursuit of excellence—the fixing of the space shuttle—the people of MSFC healed themselves and flew again.

## Chapter Thirteen

# J.R. THOMPSON'S RESPONSE

While analyzing the necessary and sufficient conditions at MSFC discussed in Chapter Twelve, I came to realize that there was only one person who could either validate or refute my conclusions: J.R. Thompson himself. Thompson had left the Marshall Center in 1988 to accept a position as associate administrator of NASA. Walter Wiesman had written to him about my work, so I decided to approach him about my analysis. In the spring of 1991, I wrote to him at NASA headquarters in Washington, D.C., detailing my objectives. Indicating that I was working on a book about the Marshall Center, I summarized what my interviewees had told me about his leadership, and explained how I was trying to isolate the factors that had brought the Marshall Center back to life.

### A Telephone Interview

Two weeks later I received a phone call from Thompson's secretary. She said he was agreeable to a telephone interview. The interview took place on May 16th. I clamped the receiver between ear and shoulder and got ready to take copious notes. Thompson broke the ice by suggesting that we call each other "J.R." and "Phil." He mentioned that we might have bumped into each other in 1967 or 1968, when he worked in the Propulsion and Vehicle Engineering Laboratory, directed at the time by William Lucas. (He had also worked closely with Hans Paul, a division chief in P&VE whom I had interviewed in 1968.)

Thompson briefly described his background. He had joined the Marshall Center in 1963, worked on the Saturn series of rockets and on Skylab, served as manager of the shuttle main engine program, and was chief engineer of the Center when he left for Princeton in 1983.

I then explained that it was generally my practice to guarantee anonymity to my interviewees, but since in this case the subject was his own leadership, that would not be possible. His remarks would have to be for the record. I did say, however, that if he found himself telling me something not for attribution, I would honor any such request. He accepted the conditions by saying, "I don't anticipate saying anything you can't use." And he didn't.

It was my goal, I said, to understand the period of his leadership at the Center when he tried to rebuild the organization. I asked him to describe the situation at Marshall when he arrived in 1986 and what he tried to do about it.

J.R. Thompson began his account by saying he had an advantage when he took over on September 26, 1986—his past experience at the Marshall Center. "I knew their capability. . .knew it was a first-class center." He considered his job to be one of getting "the train back on the track." Shifting metaphors, Thompson said he tried to "turn the wick up" to help Marshall personnel gain greater confidence in themselves and to get the leadership group "to take the reins."

He felt it was necessary at the time to "open up the review process, to encourage differences of opinion." He even admitted trying to "provoke" such differences. He had read and heard a lot about the Marshall Center after he left in 1983—that it was a "so-called closed shop."

"I had trouble relating to that," he remarked. When he had worked at the Marshall Center, Thompson said, he never felt stifled by the Center management. As manager of the shuttle main engine program, Thompson had spoken to William Lucas nearly every night. "I never felt I couldn't give him what he needed. I felt open communication helped me and never found the system stifling."

Despite his own experience with Lucas, Thompson did acknowledge that the "closed shop" image was a serious problem. "That perception had to be busted wide open," he volunteered. He felt then that he had to encourage past strengths and the expression of the "natural" tensions that characterize the R&D of space vehicles. He went out of his way to find dissenting views.

I mentioned that many of my interviewees had remarked on how he had opened his review meetings. "Yes," he said, " 'What are the problems?' You had to know what was not going well, where the problems are."

In relating his perceptions of the Space Center in 1986, Thompson took great care to avoid any criticism of Lucas. He emphasized that he had not experienced any communication troubles while serving under him in earlier years. J. R. Thompson is by reputation, and by my own experience of him, an open and assertive communicator, one who sounds as if he is not easily intimidated or inhibited by authority. He did admit, however, that others had problems with Lucas, that there was a perception the system had to be "busted wide open."

**A Test of the Necessary and Sufficient Conditions**

Thompson's careful ambivalence continued when the time came for me to explain the factors in my own analysis. He agreed that there had to be a change of leadership if the organization were to be revived. "Yes," he said, "without being critical, there had to be a change."

In regard to the first of the four characteristics I had postulated for a new leader—that he be an "outsider" untainted by association with the *Challenger* accident—Thompson again agreed. "True," he said. It was a "plus" to have the new leader brought in from outside. He reminded me that, although he had been gone for three and a half years, his past experience with the organization was "also important"—particularly the fact that he had worked in propulsion. The biggest problem to be fixed was the solid rocket motor. In saying this, he confirmed the next factor—the ability to inspire trust by virtue of his "family" membership. He even used the word "trust" and emphasized the importance of being able to inspire trust.

The next attribute was the need to understand and appreciate the importance of communication in its systemic, stylistic, and rhetorical/symbolic dimensions. When I put the first requirement, the systemic problem, to him, Thompson said without hesitation that "anybody could tell that had to be the first order of business." How to do it was the question, he added. "You can't write a memo announcing that henceforth there will be an open communication system. You've got to stimulate, probe, call on them by name, provoke their discussion." The system, Thompson said, will then "bootstrap" itself. "Once you've got the guy to express his concern, he'll tell you what else he's worried about." By "bootstrap," Thompson apparently meant that one successful action will motivate another, similar act and, thereby, create a kind of momentum for the new or changed behavior.

"I made it clear that it was not a democracy," said Thompson. "We're not after that. But I didn't want to be cheated" [of vital information].

We then turned to Thompson's communicative style. He recalled that back in the days when he was in charge of the shuttle main engine program, he had spent much time in the labs, where he had come from. "And I still felt comfortable in their backyard." He said he "enjoyed" getting out to hear the engineers talk about their work and their problems.

Thompson indicated that Jack Lee (who had briefly served as acting director after Lucas resigned and before Thompson was appointed) had already stopped the executive lunches on the ninth floor by the time Thompson arrived. Thompson said he simply decided to follow Lee's lead. He went down to eat in the cafeteria "with co-workers rather than executives, with technicians and clerical people. They have good taste. You get the pulse of the Center from them." Thompson said he regarded the cafeteria conversations as opportunities to build cohesiveness and confidence. He mentioned the Christmas parties in the same vein. He was easily talked into wearing the Santa Clause suit, he said.

"Who talked you into it?" I asked.

"Probably my secretary. I knew the benefits. It seemed natural; I enjoyed it."

We then turned to my hypothesis that it had been necessary for him to "manage the identity" of the Marshall Center personnel to help them regain confidence in their skills. Thompson agreed, saying this was "the first order of business." He then spoke at some length about the actual tasks he put before the Marshall personnel. They redesigned the solid rocket motor. They got the technology right.

Then they built it, "built in some flaws and put it through a rigorous test program." Thompson's strategy was to take risks on the test stand, not during flight.

At first I did not understand the purpose of building in flaws before the tests. Thompson explained that they sliced up the O-rings and ran tests that way; they put cracked blades into the engines, "wound up" the motors on the test stand, and were elated when they "didn't fail." The tests proved the durability of their design. I found this to be an interesting strategy but began to wonder whether Thompson had lost the connection to the question about managing identity. Then he made the link with the familiar metaphor, "confidence bootstraps" (i.e., the verb "to bootstrap"). When the models hold up during such rigorous tests, he said, people begin to realize that they "are not just lucky." He described it as being almost like a "high." "In the process you've built up the confidence of the engineers. I played that up."

We then turned to the characteristics to which others had attributed Thompson's success: high standards and the willingness to work long and hard to achieve them. Some, I added, even described him as a perfectionist. He agreed.

"I enjoy work," he said. "I worked a lot of hours. I like tough problems." They started to work early in the morning, he said, and stopped only when "the learning curve flattened." His strategy of rigorously testing the new design also reflected this perfectionist streak.

**Redemptive Praxis.** I asked Thompson's opinion of my redemptive praxis theory, apologizing for my academic jargon, and explained what I meant. He grasped it immediately and agreed, saying, "Time heals also. It did take us a couple of years to heal. The people in place were capable. That was never an issue. We had to get to the heart of the problem. We tested and we had setbacks. We almost relished them." Thompson then said that "it was not just me. They were all off and running."

And then they began flying again. "All the redundancy" that had been built into the new motors worked. At the time of our interview, he said there had been 15 successful flights since *Challenger*, which meant that 30 solid-fuel boosters had worked successfully. They had worked so well that the hot gases had not breached even the first of five new barriers designed to contain them.

Thompson thus validated the analysis of the factors necessary and sufficient to revive an ailing organization—at least in terms of MSFC. "Have I missed anything?" I asked.

"No, I think you've got it—keep it balanced," Thompson said.

We continued talking. He seemed to want to add emphasis to certain points by means of repetition and restatement, and as he talked, certain additional questions came naturally to my mind. For example, I mentioned that I had been told by one interviewee that Lucas refused to acknowledge any responsibility on the part of the Marshall Center for the *Challenger* failure. Thompson, on the other hand, was said to have done so openly. I asked whether or not he thought that act was important.

He believed that it was: "You've got to be able to say it out loud without pointing blame. Early on, I took the blame for the Center." He could do so because he had worked there for 20 years, even though he had been involved in the shuttle main engine, not the solid-fuel propulsion systems that failed on the *Challenger*. It came easy to Thompson to admit a failure. With almost a sense of pride, he said, "I have been associated with more test failures than anyone in NASA." Thompson convinced me that the admission of failure on his part, and the accepting of the Center's responsibility for the *Challenger* accident, should be stressed more heavily than I had originally done. He added that the admission was "double edged," because by saying it out loud he also warned the public that it would not be the last failure, a double meaning not missed by his Marshall Center audience either. Accidents are inevitable in such a risky business.

### Redundancy

Thompson had spoken so frequently about redundancy in the hardware that I mentioned having once written that von Braun's system of organizational communication had imitated the technology they were using at the time. The reviews, the Monday Notes, and other channels had provided the system with communication redundancy.

Thompson concurred and felt this was important. He went on to provide an example: the Quality Assurance Program he had put into place. The redundancy in such a system "encourages tension," he said. Then you "stir the pot." Had he used von Braun as a model in developing his own style and system? "Not intentionally," Thompson said, but he assumed that he had done so "subconsciously." It would have been difficult not to "pick up" some of von Braun's practices. *Was it transference?* I wondered. Perhaps, to use Thompson's word, it happened "subconsciously."

The Monday Notes came up as another example. Thompson indicated that he had found upon his return that the content of the Notes had become "sterile." He had let it be known that he wanted them to be contentious. "I enjoyed most, I respected most, a good, solid, technical argument."

### Causes of the *Challenger* Accident

Toward the end of our interview, it seemed natural to ask Thompson for his assessment of the *Challenger* tragedy. What were the causes or factors in the accident? Thompson said, "The cause was technical." The booster would eventually have failed—even in warm weather. The design did not allow a "sufficient margin of error on the seals."

Thompson added an organizational factor. NASA had fallen into a "trap." The shuttle was supposed to pay an increasing proportion of its own way with each flight. That meant more and more flying, less and less testing. "You learn more from a failure than a success, but you should *do it on the ground*." Thompson's first action, therefore, was to "turn up the wick on the testing program."

I could not resist a final question: "Had faulty communication been a factor in the *Challenger* accident?"

"Too many people commented on that [for it] not to be a problem," he replied. Thompson repeated that he had always communicated with Lucas, but "others did not." Communication was "quite a problem."

### Summary and Interpretation

In summary and interpretation of the interview, J.R. Thompson clearly validated the analysis offered above. He identified most of the conditions without prompting. In addition, he was remarkably similar to von Braun in placing such high value on organizational communication. Like von Braun, Thompson cherished conflict,

.ent, and dissent, although both tried to keep it "constructive." .ompson's attempt to eliminate the "sterility" of the Monday Notes, to encourage "good, solid technical argument" reminded me of the lab director who told me in 1967 that argument gave the Monday Notes their particular "charm." Thompson helped restore the organizational memory of the Center and revive the practices that had served the organization so well during the von Braun era.

Thompson's remarks also indicate that he was very much aware, had been self-conscious of his activities to revive the organization, to get the train back on the track. It was my impression that he perceived the organization at the time of the *Challenger* accident much as many of my interviewees had—even though he had not personally experienced the problems and took pains in our conversation "not to be critical."

It thus seems conclusive that the communication system was a factor in the *Challenger* accident. Rebuilding the Marshall Center also meant rebuilding its system of organizational communication. And although my analysis and Thompson's validation apply only to one organization, I believe it is fair to say that it is applicable to other organizations as well.

## Chapter Fourteen

# THE MEANING AND FUTURE OF THE SPACE PROGRAM

I am somewhat optimistic about the future of the Marshall Space Flight Center, particularly in view of J.R. Thompson's successful efforts to revive the organization. In the long run, as some wag said, we are all dead. So it is with organizations, as I believe this narrative indicates. Some of the country's leaders have proposed "privatizing" the space program, an idea I feel is misguided. Yet it demonstrates my point: These leaders presumably would simply do away with NASA or at least reduce it to the mere allocation and monitoring of contracts.

No matter how successful an organization might become, there is always the potential threat, as we have seen, of routinized complacency and the institutional forgetting of those very principles that allowed the organization to achieve greatness.

Chapter Thirteen showed how J.R. Thompson achieved something like an organizational miracle in his two years as director of the Marshall Center. The nation and the space program, including both NASA and MSFC, owe him a debt of gratitude. (Thompson, like von Braun before him, transferred from MSFC to NASA headquarters in 1989.)

Jack Lee became director of the Marshall Center in July of 1989, six months before I interviewed him as part of my 1990 study. Because of my promise of confidentiality, I cannot reveal anything Lee told me. I can, however, comment on what others had to say about him. It is to his credit that he opened up the Center to my inquiry in the same way von Braun had done in 1967. That demonstrates that he is both secure in what he is doing and desires to improve organizational communication at Marshall.

Lee worked under von Braun, Lucas, and Thompson. He undoubtedly learned some important lessons about communication during the Center's ups and downs. Lee was given credit by the interviewees for continuing the reforms begun under Thompson, as witnessed by the comments quoted in Chapter Twelve. For example, the statements of appreciation for his visits to the labs and offices noted that Lee accompanied Thompson. "With von Braun communication was always good," one manager noted. "Not as open under Lucas, but with J.R. and Jack, it's back to the original." Thompson also gave Lee credit for some important reforms, including, for example, the discontinuation of the executive luncheons.

Here are some additional comments that were made about Lee's leadership: "The current director [Lee] is accessible and decisive," said another manager. "I can't ask for more from a boss even though I don't always get what I want." "There is much less tension in our relationship with headquarters," offered a manager in a good position to know.

### A New Decade

When I revisited the Center in January of 1990, television sets in the cafeteria on the first floor of Building 4200 replayed the successful 33rd shuttle launch. After I finished my first day of interviews on January 9, I picked up a copy of *The Huntsville Times*. The headline was "Columbia Starts '90s with Roar." The mission was to put a Navy communication satellite into orbit and retrieve an 11-ton orbiting science laboratory.

"I don't think I've ever seen a cleaner countdown and launch," said Richard Truly, administrator of the National Aeronautics and Space Administration, as quoted by an Associated Press writer in the *Times*. "What a marvelous way to start the '90s."

It was a good beginning for the new year and new decade, but the next 12 months produced a record of results which were mixed at best. Ten shuttle flights were originally scheduled for 1990; only six took place. On the other hand, that was the highest number since 1985, the year before the disaster. Hydrogen leaks halted two shuttle flights for several months during the summer of 1990. The leaks were reportedly caused by faulty workmanship, inadequate tests, and other problems. But the big failure was the much-heralded launch of the Hubble space telescope.

The Marshall Center had a major responsibility for the Hubble Project. The space telescope, together with other telescopes placed in orbit, were supposed to give us deep and multidimensional glimpses of phenomena never directly perceived before. The launch was successful, but the telescope's flawed mirrors prevented proper focusing. NASA promptly blamed the contractor, the Perkin-Elmer Corporation, as well as lax supervision. Due to budget constraints, there had been limited penetration of the contractor and limited testing of the telescope prior to launch. Relevant to our earlier analysis, one must reflect on the difficulty of monitoring and penetrating contractors while at the same time pursuing a strategy of diversification in an increasingly complex organizational matrix—especially after a reduction in force.

There are other signs that NASA no longer commands the admiration, respect, and support it did in the 1960s.

### 'NASA Aura Dims'

"NASA Aura Dims as City Fights Rocket Test." This headline for a story in *The New York Times*, December 15, 1990, dateline Bay St. Louis, Mississippi, describes how far NASA's trajectory of popularity and prestige has fallen since the apogee of the 1960s. This story is about the same Mississippi Test Facility that I visited in 1967. Times have changed.

> Back in the 1960's, when the space program started testing rocket motors in a big tract of swamp near here, many people felt proud about the loud noises and smoke plumes in their woods.
>
> Those kinds of feelings for the National Aeronautics and Space Administration are now rare. What once was a symbol of America's scientific superiority has lost prestige everywhere due to some spectacular failings, and along this stretch of the Gulf Coast the space agency is now commonly viewed with fear and distrust.
>
> The dispute here is over a plan by the agency to test a new rocket motor for the space shuttle. Despite repeated assurances from NASA, many residents fear that the tests, each of which will release 350 tons of chemicals into the woods, about 12 miles from

Main Street, will pollute the environment and endanger the public. (Suro, 1990, p. 22)

The Mississippi Test Facility used to be an extension of the Marshall Space Flight Center. It is now an independent facility known as the John C. Stennings Space Center (named for the state's Senator who fought hard to bring NASA budgets to Mississippi). As mentioned in Chapter Three, the Hancock County site was chosen to test the rocket engines of the mighty Saturn V because it was believed no one lived in the area. As bulldozers cleared the desolate area for the test facility, however, workers found numerous illegal stills used to make moonshine. Today the stills are long gone, and MTF may be on the way out as well.

NASA seems to have lost its rhetorical grip on the public imagination, the grip necessary to generate its financial support. This slide began during the Nixon administration, when NASA was unable to create a consensus among its constituents about what should come after the Apollo and Apollo Applications Programs. The scientific community eschewed manned flight in favor of deeper probes into space. (Is this not a contemporary example, at least in part, of the science-technology barrier I discovered in 1967?) Even though unmanned probes of the cosmos probably produce more knowledge for big science, the drama of manned flight and particularly the trips to the moon captured the audiences. The future of the space station is still in doubt. From month to month, week to week, Congress has taken different positions: approval, disapproval, qualified approval for a scaled-down version, then a new, modified disapproval. Astrophysicists and astronomers would prefer that it not be built, in the hope that this course will make more money available for their interests, the unmanned probe of deep space. This is a questionable assumption.

On February 13, 1992, Richard H. Truly resigned as administrator of NASA. A former astronaut and retired Navy vice admiral, Truly brought the shuttle back to safe flight. But according to a *Los Angeles Times* article by L. Dye, headlined "Head of NASA Resigns Post Under Pressure," Truly reportedly locked horns with the White House over space policy and was forced out.

Truly was committed to the shuttle and the troubled space station project *Freedom*; the White House's National Space Council had sought to influence NASA toward sending humans to Mars and establishing a permanent base on the moon, projects about which Truly had doubts.

> Others had doubts about Truly's ability to lead the agency; other sources said Truly lacked the charisma and the leadership needed to win congressional support for NASA's programs and recharge an agency that has seemed adrift in recent years. He has had to carry that burden alone because of the abrupt resignation last fall of his deputy, J.R. Thompson, a gregarious leader who complemented Truly's low-key profile.
>
> The departure of the top two leaders could lead to major revamping of the agency, something that has been recommended repeatedly by numerous commissions. (Dye, 1992, p. A34)

On March 11, 1992, President Bush nominated Daniel S. Goldin, an executive of the aerospace contractor TRW, Inc., to replace Truly as administrator of NASA. An article by William J. Broad in *The New York Times* the following day reported that Goldin was expected to be more receptive to White House views than was his predecessor. An anonymous White House source was quoted as saying of Goldin, "He's obviously outside the NASA culture" (Broad, 1992, p. A1).

Goldin is also reportedly expected to develop tighter bonds with the private sector. He is an expert in space robotics; at TRW he was involved in such projects as Brilliant Pebbles and Brilliant Eyes, space satellites which are portions of the Strategic Defense Initiative or "Star Wars."

I was troubled by J.R. Thompson's departure from the agency because he had earned my respect through his performance in revitalizing the Marshall Center and by his openness in my interview with him six months before his resignation.

I watched Goldin in a television interview with Robin MacNeil of PBS after the astronauts successfully reorbited an errant satellite in May of 1992. He seemed knowledgeable, at ease, and quietly impressive as he assured his viewers that NASA in the future would seek a "balance" between "human and robotic" projects. The press also reported that Goldin was keen to achieve von Braun's brightest dream, a trip to Mars and back by U.S. astronauts.

A profile of Goldin's activities between April and August was published by *The Los Angeles Times* on August 5 (Pasternak, 1992).

During that four-month period, Golden had shaken up NASA. He began soliciting opinions from the 24,000 employees of the agency, asking why the U.S.A. needs a space program. Goldin said he intended to hold town hall meetings on the subject all across the country.

In frequent pep talks, Goldin told NASA employees they are going to have to do more with less money: *"Fasterbettercheaper"* came out of his mouth as one word (Pasternak, p. A12). He had set "red" teams against "blue" teams in order to come up with cost reductions both sides could endorse. All of this activity by Goldin received mixed reviews: Some thought it was just the thing to make NASA soar again; others felt it bordered on the "absurd" (Pasternak, p. A1).

Where Goldin plans to lead the agency is not completely clear, although he "says he is excited about the prospect of visits to Mars, talked about since the post-World War II days of Wernher von Braun" (Pasternak, p. A 12). Goldin also tipped his hand about an organizational change of interest to the subject of this book—communication: "He has also vowed to trim bureaucratic layers that he believes create unnecessary delays. 'NASA headquarters,' he said, 'is going on the UltraSlimfast diet' " (Pasternak, p. A12). Chapter Two of this book, written long before Goldin was appointed to NASA, discussed the need to cut layers from U.S. organizations in the interest of improved communication and effectiveness. Goldin apparently discovered the same need within NASA. (And in a late-August verification phone call with one of the 1990 interviewees, Claude Teweles learned that plans to reduce layers of management were being discussed in Huntsville and at all of NASA's field centers.)

## Is the Space Program Worth It?

Was the Apollo Project a worthwhile national effort? Many have complained that the money that funded it would have been better spent on social programs and unmanned flights. Norman Mailer tried to make sense of the moon shots. Alvin Kernan, an emeritus professor of humanities at Princeton University, recently wrote a book (1990) announcing *The Death of Literature*. In it, he summarized Mailer's effort:

Norman Mailer in *Of a Fire on the Moon* portrayed the first landing on the moon in 1969 as an assault by science on humanistic literature and the arts, preempting the god of poetry, Apollo, for the name of the mission, and transforming the traditional symbol of the romantic imagination, the moon, into a lifeless scientific object. The overwhelming achievements of the scientific approach to knowledge were making it impossible for writers like Mailer any longer to claim that literature offered much understanding, or was even useful in any way. He dramatized this loss of artistic confidence by showing that before the mighty power of science it became nearly impossible for the writer Aquarius-Mailer to write his novel asserting the truths known to the imagination. The Manson family in California, the drugged youth at Woodstock, Teddy Kennedy at Chappaquidick, once Mailer's allies in the radical left, all failed the liberal-romantic cause in the fateful summer of 1969. The artist alone was left to defend the imaginative and the vital against the assaults of science with his novel. But he is too demoralized to fight back in the manner of Byron or Hugo, and the best he can do is to produce, with great heavings and gruntings, a tangled "factive" composite of NASA press releases, autobiographical fragments, reports of the moon shot for *Esquire*, a great deal of self-analysis, technologese, and some rambling philosophizing asserting that the landing of men on the moon was probably a good thing in the long run for humankind. (pp. 204-5)

Kernan asserts that NASA and its Apollo missions, other events, and trends in literary criticism have produced a "changed world in which literature as it has been understood in the romantic and modern eras no longer can function, no longer has a place, in the end ceases to exist" (p. 207). This analysis seems too pat, too simple, and too negative to satisfy me. For one thing, Mailer, if not Aquarius, knew that the Apollo program was more a triumph of engineering than an "assault by science" on humanistic literature and the arts. And Mailer seemed to be more concerned that NASA preempted the name of Apollo, the *sun*-god of the ancients, for a trip to the *moon* than he was disturbed by the fact that Apollo was also the patron of music and poetry. Outrageous as he may be at times, is it fair to Mailer to describe the Manson family as his "allies"? Moreover, the moon is not always the traditional symbol of the romantic imagination. Tennyson sang of the "dying moon." It is the "cold fruitless moon" in *A Midsummer Night's Dream*. Shakespeare also wrote these lines for *Othello*:

It is the very error of the moon;
She comes more near the earth than she was wont,
And makes men mad.

In *Romeo and Juliet* the bard has Romeo swear by the moon, provoking this response from Juliet:

O! swear not by the moon, the inconstant moon,
That monthly changes in her circled orb,
Lest that thy love prove likewise variable.

I have no doubt that literature will continue to exist, that it will continually renew itself. I agree with Mailer that Apollo 11 was good for humankind.

In the summer of 1990, the White House appointed an advisory committee to report on the future of the space program. The Augustine Committee (named for its chair, Norman R. Augustine of the Martin Marietta Corporation) issued its report in mid-December of that year. The report recommended the narrowing of the space station's objectives, the development of a new alternative launch vehicle to the shuttle, and a higher priority for scientific objectives. It also observed that NASA was suffering from organizational aging. One of the symptoms was a cautiousness or aversion to risk. Although there is doubtless some truth in this observation—perhaps an aversion to *vision* is a better diagnosis—it is nonetheless a curious conclusion. Cautiousness is a natural reaction to the *Challenger* disaster. What astronaut would desire a riskier program? The hypothesis of memory loss established by this book is, however, a characteristic of the aging noted by the Augustine Committee; the agency should be on guard against hardening of the arteries.

### Meaning by 'Metaphoric Engineering'

The best way I know to explore the meaning of the space program is to contemplate the metaphors used by and about NASA. Chapter One of this book relied on George Cheney's (1987) analysis of the media coverage of the *Challenger* accident and its use of such metaphors as "frontier," "mission," and "manifest destiny" to justify the continuation of the space program. In this chapter, I rely on Patricia Nelson Limerick's (1989a) analysis of these same metaphors used by and about NASA during the past three decades. Although Cheney's and Limerick's papers were written independently, they provide a symbolically symmetrical set of bookends for *Organizational Communication Imperatives.*

Patricia Nelson Limerick is a professor of history who wrote a book entitled *The Legacy of Conquest: The Unbroken History of the American West* (1987), in which she turned upside-down Frederick Jackson Turner's famous thesis that the American frontier was closed in 1893. Limerick argued that Turner's reason—the 1892 census indicated that there were two persons per square mile living in the U.S.—seemed a bit arbitrary. Why not three persons? More importantly, Limerick showed that the major issues in the Western United States in the 1980s were identical to the issues in 1892: water shortages, boom and bust economic cycles, illegal immigration across the Rio Grande, and uneasy race relations.

Limerick's book became something of a sensation and changed the writing of Western U.S. history. She was invited to address a NASA conference in 1989 and came up with an intelligent and funny speech that was well received: "Imagined Frontiers: Westward Expansion and the Future of the Space Program." She admitted at the beginning of her talk that she was not a historian of the space program and was even, in her own words, technologically helpless. If NASA had stayed on its own terrain of engineering, she said, she would not have had anything to say, but because the promoters of space travel had invaded her terrain—the history of the American West—a showdown at High Noon was unavoidable.

Limerick did admit to skills in "metaphoric engineering," and allowed that, had she been consulted about NASA's intended use of the "new frontier" metaphor in the beginning, she would probably have advised against it. But after three decades of speeches, reports, and public relations campaigns linking their frontier to hers, Limerick concluded it would do a world of good to historians and space engineers alike to take the frontier metaphor seriously. She accepted the premise that metaphors are important because they create meaning and affect human behavior and that a well-used metaphor can give one a new range and force of options and alternatives.

She then gave an example of an unthoughtful metaphor: President Reagan's speech on the Fourth of July, 1982. The occasion was the landing of the space shuttle *Columbia*, which Reagan compared to the "driving of the Golden Spike which completed the first transcontinental railroad." Limerick was struck by the fact that Reagan and his speech writers thought it was a happy comparison and were apparently unaware that when the railways were joined at Promontory Point in 1869, the chief executive of the Central Pacific, Leland Stanford, "proved unfamiliar with a sledgehammer, and could not hit the Golden Spike." There was more:

> Ronald Reagan also did not know, or care, that one half of the first transcontinental, the Union Pacific Railroad, went bankrupt twenty-five years later in the depression of the 1890s, or that the other half, the Central Pacific, even though it became more prosperous, did so by keeping a stranglehold on Pacific Coast traffic, charging all that the traffic would bear, through its affiliate the Southern Pacific, the company known as the Octopus, the company whose chief attorney was widely understood to hold much greater power in the state of California than the so-called governor did. With all that prosperity, the Central Pacific still played out a prolonged drama in trying to get out of the interest payments.
>
> Add to this the far-reaching corruption in Congress that came out of federal aid to railroads, and add the rough and even brutal working conditions on the railroad, especially for the Chinese working on the Central Pacific in the Sierras in winter (we didn't bother to keep track of how many died, the construction manager said later; we knew we could replace them); add it all together—executive misbehavior, large-scale corruption, shoddy construction, brutal labor exploitation, financial inefficiency—and it's a wonder that when the President compared the shuttle landing to the Golden Spike someone from NASA didn't hit him, to defend the organization's honor. It's a wonder no one—no shuttle pilot, mission coordinator, mechanic, or technician— said, "Now cut that out—we may have our problems, but it's nowhere near that bad." (Limerick, 1989a, pp. 5-6)

Limerick then compared the old frontier model with that produced by the New Western History. In the old model, everything ended in 1890 when the entire continent was settled and civilized—a nice tidy happy ending. The new model, by contrast, holds that little has changed, that the West is full of ghost towns, failures, and unresolved consequences: "of minesites leaching toxic chemicals into streams and rivers, of demoralized conquered people trapped by alcoholism and unemployment on reservations, of over-allocated streamflow and depleted groundwater, of periodic fires in forest lands that only the silliest of optimists would call 'managed' " (p. 9).

The old frontier model was exactly the wrong metaphor for NASA because it created *complacency*, a belief in Hollywood happy endings. (In fact, Limerick might have used *Star Wars*, both the film and the defense program, as an exemplification of the wrong application of the frontier metaphor.) Instead, Limerick argued, the space program needed a metaphor that would keep NASA alert to the dangers of the true conditions of the frontier. Quoting from a study of the future of space exploration commissioned by NASA, Limerick showed that the authors seemed to believe that Columbus opened access to the New World. Didn't they know that people emigrated to North America from Asia some 10,000 to 30,000 years before Columbus? Didn't they know that Columbus found almost no gold, that he killed off the natives with disease and forced labor, and returned to the Old World in chains after one of his voyages? When they suggest "that we follow in Columbus' footsteps, do they have *even a clue* as to where those footsteps went?" (p. 11).

Like Cheney's study of the media coverage of *Challenger* conducted two years earlier, Limerick's study of space rhetoric revealed the dangerous traces of Manifest Destiny. She warned: "Watch out for this Manifest Destiny business; it is a lot trickier than it looks. Commit yourself to a *destiny*, and you are handing over your free will; you are *volunteering* for compulsion; you are *destined* to do them, not because you have reflected, pondered, and chosen to do them" (p. 12).

Limerick maintained that history does not always support the assumption that new frontiers provide rich resources which, with a little ingenuity, can be transformed into "new wealth." "A mine, it was often said, is a hole in the ground into which a fool drops his money" (Limerick, 1989a, p. 13). Historical research into Nevada's Comstock Lode, for example, concluded that the investments were larger than the returns. Thus, it is far from axiomatic that the new frontier is bound to yield rich resources and new wealth.

Limerick's criticism of the old/new frontier metaphor is perhaps at its sharpest in contrasting the lofty good intentions of NASA's planners with the tragic realities of the past and in contrasting NASA's resolution to expand the space frontier in a peaceful manner, all the while respecting the equality and integrity of alien life forms, with what happened in the conquest of the West, "the reality of Indian devastation by disease, alcohol, loss of territory, and coercive attempts at assimilation" (p. 14). And although those space aliens depicted in movies and novels are not always sympathetic creatures, Limerick admitted having twinges of compassion for their future as she contemplated our desire to start searching for the infinite resources out there and to create new wealth and new jobs for humans among those space aliens. Limerick felt obligated to find a way to warn the aliens, to tell them "to keep their many eyes on their wallets, when they hear these admirable intentions invoked" (p. 14).

Limerick concluded her speech by challenging NASA to develop a metaphor that deepens rather than trivializes its enterprise, a metaphor to keep them alert to the possibilities of disasters, traps, and unintended consequences. She warned that it isn't always possible to come up with clear plans and clear sets of goals that can be adhered to—"you don't know where you're going until you start going there" (p. 15).

> So that would be my advice: When people demand that you set forward your plans and goals in definite ten-year increments, smile patiently; you can even fill out their forms with platitudes if they insist; but put your real energy into getting a metaphor that you can trust, a metaphor that won't betray you by leading you into complacency or compulsion. When you consider the pool of applicants for that metaphor, let the real Western history be one of the candidates. (Limerick, 1989a, p. 16)

There is a postscript. Limerick (1989b) also gave a short paper at the end of the conference called "Reflections on Attending a Conference of Space Scientists and Space Policy Planners, September, 1989." After having laid her cards on the table during the first talk, this time she heard not a word of frontier imagery from any of the other participants—perhaps out of their own self-consciousness. It was as if she had banished that "f-word" from the others' discourse, driven it into hiding. So, she had to find other words to pay attention to. She found it in an "m-word" and its variant form: "mission." If people have missions, what can you call them other than *missionaries*? she suggested. Think of NASA people as missionaries, she continued, and they "appear as what they are— creatures of a stiff and brittle faith, warding off infidels, and never understanding why the heathen don't have the sense to convert" (p. 3). Limerick might well have borrowed a quotation from Charles

Dickens' *Bleak House*, in which the financially bankrupt Mr. Jellby struggles to give his daughter Caddy some profound advice. After several false starts, he finally gets it out: "Never have a Mission, my dear child."

Then Limerick moved into *my* terrain, the realm of organizational communication:

> This institutional failure to communicate, this reluctance to communicate, this hostility to communication—is the most troubling impression I've gotten from these sessions, most troubling because it is so reminiscent of the failed communication Richard Feynman described in his reflections on the Challenger disaster, and because this shutting down of conversation, with the expletive "NASA-bashing," certifies that this is an agency *no one can help*. If someone doesn't figure out this one, if someone can't get the message through to NASA that this defensiveness, this complete unwillingness to face open appraisal, is self-destructive and deeply shortsighted, then I think the party's over, and I would then shift to a "people at a wake" metaphor for this gathering. (Limerick, 1989b, pp. 3-4)

One purpose of this book is to point out the value of communication, the dangers of defensiveness and unwillingness to face open appraisal.

### A Proposal

I wish to make a recommendation in regard to the future of the space program. I believe we should once again give the highest national priority to the space program. The reason for my belief is this: There is an unsuppressible human drive to extend the biosphere. The U.S. will continue to have a space program. Although the Japanese have recently made noises about developing their own program, the voters in the U.S. will not tolerate falling back into second or third place. They may chose a Honda over an automobile made in Detroit, but they will not tolerate the Rising Sun on Mars, for example, before the Stars and Stripes are planted there.

The question then is, what kind of space program should the U.S. have? I believe that NASA may be back on track and on its way to becoming the organization that it once was. This process should be encouraged. Excellent organizations provide us with models of communication from which we can learn—and which other organizations can emulate. In our current age of organizational anxiety, there is a growing fear that no matter what our business organizations do, they cannot match the Japanese in efficiency, quality, and commitment. My proposal is that we make a national commitment, not unlike Kennedy's commitment to the Apollo Project, to help NASA regain its untarnished excellence of the past. I submit this proposal not only to bring about a first-rate space program, important though that goal is, but also because the country needs to have an organizational model of excellence, a yardstick, an exemplar from which other enterprises can learn.

Margaret Mead, the late anthropologist, saw today's organizational problems coming some time ago. In a televised Congressional hearing, she supported NASA and the space program because they alone seemed to uphold standards of technical excellence at a time when she saw an increasing shoddiness in American commercial products. Nothing else seemed to work right except our rockets.

### Upward-Directed Communication

The Los Angeles riots, which erupted while this book was being put to bed, remind us again that in many ways the societal structure of the U.S. is unsound. Like the eruptions in Watts and Detroit in the 1960s, this event shocked us all into the realization that many of those who are "down" do not identify with the larger, white-dominated hierarchy. Although much of the activity after the Rodney King verdict must be interpreted as opportunistic criminality, the initial outrage in Los Angeles and other communities is clearly a form of upward-directed communication by people who lack other means of expressing their discontents. Many local (and largely white) television reporters covering the disturbances acted as if they were reporting from a foreign war zone. Their lack of familiarity with South-Central Los Angeles reflected the extent to which they were not used to paying much attention to its residents.

One of the more distinguished students of race relations in the United States is an African-American professor of political science and history: Manning Marable. Marable is also a journalist; his column "Along the Color Line" appears in many newspapers across the country.

On June 3, 1992, a column by Marable appeared in my local newspaper under the title, "Los Angeles Riots Point Up Nation's Race/Class Fault Line." The title prepares the reader for an analogy between the San Andreas fault and the deep division between the social/racial levels in the U.S. In Marable's estimation, the Rodney King riots were merely tremors, not the big "quake" we can expect in the future.

Earlier in the book I applied von Braun's analogy of an "earthquake prediction system" to the Detroit riots of 1967. I had not thought through the analogy as carefully as did Marable. The jagged fault line is a vivid image for what I have been blandly calling the divisions of our organizational and societal hierarchies.

Marable also sees the communicative nature of the eruptions in Los Angeles. Dismissing as superficial the interpretation that the disturbances were caused primarily by the Rodney King verdict, Marable also sees them as a "message":

> By taking to the streets, they are crying out to society: "We will be heard! We will not be ignored, and we will not go away quietly. And if the system refuses to listen to us, we intend to burn it to the ground." That is the meaning of Los Angeles. (Marable, 1992, p. 8A)

I suspect it is not a mere coincidence that NASA's greatest successes occurred at a time that the agency, and particularly its largest field center in Huntsville, believed open channels of communication to be the key to effective organization and management. Von Braun's philosophy of management was one of organizational communication. The emphasis of his "earthquake prediction sensors" metaphor was on upward-directed communication. Problems were to be rooted out and faced, not discouraged. Messengers with bad news were rewarded, not killed. That is the meaning of automatic responsibility, the Monday Notes, penetration, and the consciously-created redundancy of communication channels.

One of the objectives of this book has been to describe the organizational cultural values and practices that allowed the United States to keep John F. Kennedy's commitment to land a man on the moon and return him safely to earth. It is my hope that there will never be a recurrence of the kind of organizational memory loss that contributed to the *Challenger* accident.

## A Final Metaphor

I close with another metaphor about the meaning of the space program. It appears in the definitive political history of the space age, Walter A. McDougall's (1985) . . . *the Heavens and the Earth:*

*A Political History of the Space Age*, although it is not original to McDougall. I reproduce here the first two paragraphs of the book in which McDougall presents what he calls the most provocative of all analogies contrived to convey the meaning of the Space Age:

> Three hundred sixty million years ago, we are told, there lived a fish we call *Eusthenopteron*. It frequented the murky shallows of rivers in Pangaea, the vast supercontinent that was later to divide, like a living cell, into North America, Europe, and Asia. Over the course of millennia, climatic changes gradually dried up its rivers. But the Crossopterygians, the transcendental elite to which *Eusthenopteron* belonged, were both stubborn and blessed, hence candidates for metamorphosis. They already sported lobe fins for "walking" on the bottom of their late-Devonian streams and prototype lungs for gulping air in case of foul, stagnant water. In time, *Eusthenopteron*'s muscular fins tugged it across mud flats that once, as streambeds, had marked the absolute boundary of its fishy universe. Now the viscous channel revealed itself to be a cradle, and then a platform to a new universe of solids and gases. Animal life had come to the land. In time our analogous friend became an amphibian, *Ichthyostega*, although the new name is a human conceit that *Eusthenopteron* would probably resent.
>
> In A.D. 1961 *Homo sapiens*, in turn, left the realm of solids and gases and lived, for 108 minutes, in outer space. Life again escaped, or by definition extended, the biosphere. The earth's crust and canopy of air became another platform to a new universe as infinite as soil and sky must have seemed to *Eusthenopteron*. The opening of the Space Age was another cleavage, more sharp than blunt, in natural history. It took an era for marine fugitives to populate the land. But by the end of the 1980s some human beings will be constantly in space, if only as scientists, soldier-spies, or telephone repairmen. By the middle of the next century human colonies may be populating earth's neighborhood. Of all the analogies contrived to convey the meaning of the Space Age, therefore, the amphibian adventure of the Devonian period is the most provocative. (McDougall, 1985, p. 3)

There is a footnote at the end of this passage, and only the most curious reader might turn to page 466 to learn the original source: "Wernher von Braun proposed this analogy at the time of Apollo 11, while others spun variations on the theme of Columbian voyages and President Nixon spoke of the moon mission as the 'greatest week since creation.'"

I believe von Braun's metaphor of a "new universe" deepens rather than trivializes our understanding of the Space Age. It is not inconsistent with Limerick's "frontier" metaphor, but if we do retain both analogies, let us also remember of which frontier we speak, of the nature and realities of the Western frontier and the space frontier. And we should not forget the lessons of Limerick's "metaphorical engineering": that the *real* frontier was not one big happy Hollywood western ending; instead, it was fraught with dangers and disasters, failures as well as successes.

In my description of the Marshall Center's rebirth after the *Challenger* accident, I stressed that a new, flightworthy bird emerged out of the ashes of the accident. It is also an important lesson of human organization that the phoenix had to transform itself into ashes *before* it could be reborn. We must not forget the lessons of the past if we are to avoid a repetition of the cycle.

# Appendix A

## A SUMMARY OF THE TOMPKINS-ANDERSON STUDY OF KENT STATE UNIVERSITY

*I wrote a book with Elaine V. B. Anderson about the tragedy at Kent State University that occurred on May 4, 1970, entitled* Communication Crisis at Kent State: A Case Study. *A summary of their study is included here so that comparisons between Kent State and MSFC can be made by the reader who wishes to take a break from the narrative.*

### Academic Year 1969-1970

The academic year 1969-70 was quieter than my first year at Kent State, much quieter, in fact, than at other universities in the country. It was also becoming apparent that there were serious problems of organizational communication at Kent State University. That old problem of the "invisible boss" was discussed frequently by faculty and students, but in a much more serious and less nostalgic way than at MSFC. The administration had also radicalized a conservative student body by breaking promises in its treatment of the Black United Students and the Students for a Democratic Society.

Jerry Hayes, a newly appointed assistant to the president, meant to do something about the problem. He had heard about my courses in organizational communication and my research for NASA and asked for help. I did what I could. Walter Wiesman was coming up from the Marshall Center to give a lecture, and I suggested the two get together to talk about how Wiesman's program of internal communication could be adapted to Kent State.

Hayes ultimately retained Wiesman as a consultant.  I still believe that given a bit more time, Hayes could have improved the organizational communication system at the university and helped make it a better organization.  But the tensions soon found their expression again.

## The Cambodian Incursion

In late April of 1970, the United States government revealed that the country had expanded the Vietnamese war by an incursion into Cambodia.  President Nixon addressed the American public on television on the evening of Thursday, April 30, 1970, in an attempt to justify the apparent reversal of his policy to wind down U.S. involvement in the conflict.  Walt Wiesman happened to be visiting Kent State University for a conference on organizational communication and a consulting trip for Hayes.  We watched the televised speech that night at my townhouse.  At its conclusion, Wiesman presciently observed that the speech had not done its job, that we could expect big trouble.

## Street Action and the Ohio National Guard

The next day an estimated 500 persons attended a rally at the grassy center of the KSU campus.  Word had it that there would be some "street action" in downtown Kent, Ohio, that night.  The rumor proved correct.  Store windows were smashed, a bonfire was set ablaze, and police cars were pelted.  The mayor of Kent declared a state of emergency and ordered the bars downtown that were primarily patronized by students to be closed.   Angry students and other customers, most of whom were innocent of any wrongdoing, were turned out into the streets and herded toward the edge of the campus, where they dispersed.

Late the following afternoon, the mayor of Kent secured a commitment from the Ohio National Guard to come to the aid of the city and campus.  The Guard arrived in time to see the sky lit up by flames from a burning ROTC building at the university.  Troops were deployed on campus to the surprise of university officials who reportedly had not been consulted in the mayor's decision nor informed of it.

On May 3rd, KSU students returning from a weekend away were shocked to find the campus ringed by armed guardsmen and military vehicles. The university president, who had spent the weekend out of town, also returned. That night a crowd gathered on the edge of campus, and it was announced that the president of the university and the mayor would meet with them. When the crowd was later informed that the two officials would not meet with them after all (even though the president was on his way to the scene), they felt double-crossed. They cursed and threw rocks at guardsmen and police, who responded with tear gas. Injuries were sustained on both sides.

Early in the morning on May 4, 1970, I warily crossed a line of guardsmen on the way to my office. A glass door to the building had been shattered. Posted on another door was an injunction prohibiting destruction to the campus. There was a hand-scrawled poster on a first floor bulletin board calling for a rally on the campus at noon. I asked the departmental secretary to call the provost's office to find out if classes had been canceled. The answer was no, classes were meeting as usual.

Virtually everyone who was alive in 1970 knows what happened at Kent State University at noon that day. The rally took place, and the guardsmen tried to break it up. In the confusion that ensued, four students were killed and nine wounded by the guardsmen's rifles. As the news flashed around the world, most campuses closed in protest. Many thought President Nixon would soon be facing a war at home in addition to the one in Vietnam.

## A Communication Analysis

Soon after the tragedy, the president of KSU appointed me to serve as the chair of a task force on communication and as a member of The University Commission to Implement a Commitment to Non-Violence. I called the Marshall Center and canceled my trip to Huntsville, where I had been invited back for another summer consultancy. It was our purpose to examine the role of the university in this series of events. How well did KSU operate as a communication system during the crisis? With help from colleagues I began a research project in which we interviewed the president, 4 vice presidents, 9 deans, 29 chairpersons, 120 faculty members, and 225 students. I wrote a report and a set of recommendations for the commission.

We asked the interviewees what they knew during the crisis. Although 58 percent of the faculty was aware that a rally was scheduled for noon on May 4th, only 44 percent knew the rally had been prohibited. Of the students, 75 percent knew about the rally and 56 percent had heard it was prohibited. Only 37 percent of the faculty and 34 percent of the students were aware that the guardsmen had live ammunition in their weapons. Importantly, 53 percent of the faculty and chairpersons said they would have behaved differently had they known the facts. They said they would have used their influence to cool down the situation and dissuade students from a confrontation.

Why did these organizational members know so little during the crisis? The president of the university, operating on faulty upward communication, had apparently left town on Friday for the weekend without delegating authority to an acting president. The academic vice president/provost, who should have been in charge during the president's absence, indicated he was unaware that the president had left town.[1] As far as we could determine, only two attempts were made by the administration to communicate vital information to the university community during the crisis. The first was a statement read over the campus radio station that very few heard. The second was the release on Sunday, May 3, of 12,000 leaflets indicating that the governor had taken control of the campus and was prohibiting demonstrations and rallies. These were placed mainly in student mailboxes in dormitories, which most students don't check on Sundays. These two forms of communication, we found, were almost totally ineffective.

We also found that the informal organization responsible for promoting the Monday rally was far more effective in communicating than the formal organization (the university) was in trying to communicate that it was prohibited. As we noted in our book:

> The academic-chain-of-command did not function effectively. The Provost (Vice President for Academic Affairs) was ill (and ill-informed); his Associate Provost was in California attending a convention. The Dean of Education was in Europe, the Dean of Business Administration was also in California. The remaining deans received no official word about the crucial issues. And so forth for chairmen and faculty. (p. 39)

As a result, regular lines of authority were not used during the crisis.

But the most controversial of our findings was that it was the KSU administration, *not* the Guard, who had insisted on breaking up the rally. This had occurred at a joint meeting before the shootings. We were stunned. Everyone had assumed that the Guard had given orders to the administration, not the other way around. The administration's rationale was that because it had distributed the leaflets, it would appear inconsistent if the Guard didn't break up the rally. (The Scranton Commission, charged with investigating the incident, was never able to determine who was responsible for giving the order to open fire.)

Somewhere in Kenneth Burke's wide-ranging discussion of human motives, he points out that all too often we behave as we do merely because one act motivates another. The act of distributing the leaflets became the administration's motive for stopping the rally. In other words, one act that was ineffectual motivated another that proved tragic. Moreover, the leaflet was factually inaccurate in attributing the prohibition on rallies to the governor.

The definitive history of the Kent State tragedy was written two years later by Peter Davies (1973), with access to FBI files and other information unavailable to us in 1970-71. It validated our communication analysis of the Kent State tragedy.

> The root problem at Kent State was lack of communication, and as the days passed, this problem grew more and more grave, as Phillip K. Tompkins and Elaine. . .Anderson show [in *Communication Crisis at Kent State*]. When finally the students demanded a meeting, they were answered with tear gas, and in turn the guardsmen were answered with rocks. With everyone shouting at one another, no one could be heard, until the forces unleased by official ineptitude, inflammatory political rhetoric, and arson crystallized into a burst of gunfire. (p. 28)

In summary, Kent State University suffered a breakdown in communication during those fateful days in May of 1970. The president was invisible, authority was not delegated, and the lines of communication were not used. Why? We asked our interviewees to describe the routine functioning of KSU. Somewhat to our surprise, we learned that even routine functioning was also characterized by ineffectiveness. As we concluded in the book (Tompkins & Anderson, 1971):

. . .the disintegration of Kent State University during the crises of
May, 1970, can be traced to certain organization-communication
*imperatives* which were present in the routine functioning of the
university: a highly centralized and indecisive administration which
operated "blind" because of inadequate upward-directed communication; a President with little appreciation for his communication
responsibilities; the absence of a two-way system of communication
designed to integrate all segments of the rapidly expanded university; academic officers who were shut out of administrative decision-
making. . . . (pp. 119)

Our final conclusion was that the university president "had failed
in his first function as an executive: *to develop and maintain a system
of communication.*  His inability to delegate authority to his Vice
Presidents allowed the latter to refer to themselves as 'assistants to
the President.' The academic officers, the deans, were almost
unanimous in the judgment that they had been blocked from
providing 'academic input' into the central administrative decision-
making process" (Tompkins & Anderson, 1971, p. 120). I have not
repeated all of the details included in our book, but it is conceivable
that this incident might have had a considerably happier ending with
more effective organizational communication and executive functioning. Other, larger, more open and radical universities weathered the
storms of that period without fatalities.

## Comparative Case Studies

The Kent State tragedy provides a case study to compare with
this book's depiction of the Marshall Center.  The contrast is stark,
as practices of organizational communication at these two institutions
varied widely.  In fact, MSFC and KSU in 1970 appeared to be
dialectical opposites: One gave organizational communication the
highest priority; it can be argued that the other gave it no priority at
all.  One organization encouraged and nurtured upward-directed
communication; the other, according to the results of our study,
either ignored or discouraged it.

It is conceivable, for example, that Kent State University could
have benefitted immensely if it had experienced the factors isolated
in the "necessary and sufficient conditions" analysis (presented in
Chapter Twelve) immediately after its tragedy.  One of the conditions was met.  There was a change of leadership not long after the
tragedy, and the outgoing president mentioned his inadequate

communication abilities during his resignation statement. Unfortunately, the next leader manifested few if any of the abilities and intuitions of a J.R. Thompson. The university's administration continued to deny any responsibility for the slain and wounded students. Enrollments dropped, and little attempt appears to have been made to enhance the identity of a demoralized faculty.

I conclude this section with an invitation to readers to test this analysis on ailing organizations from their own experience.

## NOTES

1. This information was provided by the academic vice president and provost of the university.

## QUESTIONS FOR DISCUSSION

Compare and contrast the Marshall Space Flight Center and Kent State University in terms of organizational communication.

1. What differences between the two organizations were observed?

2. Could the tragedy at Kent State been avoided with better organizational communication? How?

3. Compare Kent State in 1970 with MSFC of the pre-*Challenger* period.

## Appendix B

# QUESTIONS AND EXERCISES FOR DISCUSSION, ESSAYS, AND CLASS PROJECTS

The following material has been provided to facilitate the use of this book in college and university classes. The questions, suggestions, and exercises may be assigned by the instructor. If so, the assignments assume that students are organized in small groups or participate in classroom discussions of the reading material. Students may also wish to refer to these questions in study groups for purposes of reviewing, and/or as a way of understanding the author's intentions.

### Chapter One. THE *CHALLENGER* ACCIDENT

A. According to studies of the diffusion of news concerning the *Challenger* accident, this was a memorable event:

1. How did you first hear about the *Challenger* accident?

2. Did the news of the accident reach you via organizational communication, that is, by means of either formal or informal channels of an organization?

3. What were your subjective feelings about the accident?

4. Conduct a small survey of people in your age group. Compare the results to the results collected by other members of your group or class. How representative were your own responses? Were there any long-range effects?

B. According to Tompkins, the *Challenger* accident constituted a tragedy.

1. Does this event fit your definition of a tragedy? Why or why not?

2. Go to the library and consult some reference works dealing with tragedy in life and literature. Compare these definitions to the *Challenger* accident.

3. What are the three most important organizational tragedies of your lifetime? Justify your choices.

**Chapter Two. THE IMPERATIVE OF STUDYING ORGANIZATIONAL COMMUNICATION**

A. Tompkins uses four stories or anecdotes from his experience and reading to help illustrate principles and concepts of organizational communication.

1. Explain the concepts, principles, and lessons illustrated by each story.

2. Come up with four more anecdotes from your own or others' experiences.

   a. Do your stories have the same "morals" as the ones discussed by Tompkins?

   b. Are they different? If so, what new lessons about organizational communication can be articulated?

B. Go to the library and look up discussions of Sigmund Freud's concept of transference.

1. Do you agree with Tompkins that transference is a part of one's "normal" experience with organizations? Why or why not?

2. Do you agree that transference can cause problems for the individual and the organization? Defend your answer.

C. Tompkins argues for the need to reduce the layers of management, called "relays" by Peter Drucker, in many contemporary organizations.

1. Pick a paragraph at random from a book that has not been read by your classmates. This paragraph will serve as the

"message" for the following communication experiment. Now send 16 people out of the room to wait silently until you are ready for them; 12 of them will play the role of "layers" of management in a "tall" organization. The others four will represent the layers of a "short" organization.

Call in the first person from the tall organization. Read the message aloud to that person. Then call in the second person and have the first person repeat the message to the second from memory. Continue this procedure until the 12th person has received the message from the 11th. Then ask the 12th person to express his or her understanding of the message to the class.

Next, repeat the procedure with the shorter, four-person organization. You and the rest of the class are now in a position to answer the following comparative questions about the effectiveness of the two "organizations."

2. Compare the results of the two communication events, looking for answers to these and other questions.

a. How long did it take for the message to move through each chain of relays?

b. Which chain produced more omissions from, additions to, and distortions of the original message?

c. What implications do your observations have for large organizations?

d. If an organization has to lay off managers and other employees, what is the most humane way to do it?

(i) Consider questions of timing, channels, participation, channels, and feedback.

(ii) General Motors announced that 21 of its plants would be closed and 74,000 of its employees would be laid off in the future. The announcement was made one week before Christmas of 1991. Go to the library and look up accounts of how and what GM did to communicate its decisions. Should human considerations weigh as heavily to a corporation as financial ones do?

**Chapter Three. THE MARSHALL SPACE FLIGHT CENTER AND THE APOLLO PROGRAM**

A. Tompkins kept a journal during his involvement with NASA's Marshall Space Flight Center. It was useful to him in writing this book. Keep a journal for one week, recording significant messages sent and received. At the end of the week, prepare an analysis of your entries. Prepare to give either an oral or written report of your analysis.

1. In a group or class discussion, compare your entries and analyses with those made by other students (oral vs. written, etc.).

2. If any of the events recorded are of common events (such as exchanges that took place in the class all of you are taking), compare them closely.

3. If any of these events are recorded in significantly different ways, discuss the implications for the idea of an organizational memory.

B. Tompkins displays and discusses the organizational chart of MSFC:

1. Draw an organization chart representing your college or university.

2. Be sure to include every layer, including your instructor and yourself. (A campus telephone directory will help).

3. Compare your chart with those produced by your group members or classmates.

a. Do they agree?

b What do the lines connecting the boxes symbolize or stand for?

c. How many layers or relays are there between you and the president of your campus?

d. Could your college and university be organized in a different way? Is there a way to reduce the number of layers and bring the administration closer to the faculty and students?

e. Some students of organization believe organizational charts should be made of concentric circles. Experiment with this form and decide whether or not it is a good idea. (Hint: does eliminating the "up" and "down" metaphor help or hinder one's understanding of structure?)

C. Tompkins discusses the Monday Notes, automatic responsibility, and penetration in this chapter.

1. Define each concept or practice.

2. Identify the strengths and weaknesses of each.

3. Discuss the extent to which each concept or practice could be adopted by other organizations.

## Chapter Four.  SOME PROBLEMS OF COMMUNICATION AT THE MARSHALL CENTER

A.  Tompkins found ten problems in organizational communication at the Marshall Center.

1. Which ones were the most serious problems?

2. Which ones are most likely to be found in other organizations?

3. Which ones can you verify as problems in organizations you have experienced or heard/read about?

B.  Identify three problems of organizational communication at your college or university.

C.  Why does Tompkins discuss race relations and the Detroit riots in a book about organizational communication?

## Chapter Five.  STAFF AND BOARD BRIEFING

A.  Tompkins offered recommendations about the ten problems to Werhner von Braun and his associates at MSFC.

1. Did any of the problems seem insoluble or impossible to solve?

2. Are problems of organizational communication (and recommendations to improve them) discussed as openly in most organizations as they were at MSFC?   Be specific.

3. Prepare a list of recommendations for the president of your college or university addressing the three problems of organizational communication you identified earlier.

## Chapter Six. REORGANIZING THE MARSHALL CENTER

A. Tompkins begins this chapter with von Braun's speech to Marshall Center employees about the reductions in force.

1. What is your evaluation of the methods von Braun used in announcing the cuts?

2. Are these methods still useful for the "restructuring" of organizations today?

3. Compare von Braun's approach with the ideas you came up with in discussing the problem of cutbacks in Chapter Two.

4. Define and evaluate pros and cons of horizontal and vertical organizational research. How would you apply it in studying your college, university, or some other organization?

## Chapter Seven. A READING OF THE ROGERS COMMISSION REPORT

A. The discussion of the Rogers Commission Report allows the reader to compare and contrast organizational communication at the Marshall Center at two different points in time, in the 1960s and the 1980s.

1. What differences can you identify?

2. What passages in the Rogers Commission testimony and text indicate support for the hypothesis of organizational forgetting at the Marshall Center?

## Chapter Eight. FEYNMAN'S TWO EXPERIMENTS

A. Dr. Feynman describes his famous O-ring experiment. Go to a hardware store and buy two pieces of an O-ring. They are also called "sealants" because they are used to seal a circular joint shut, preventing gases from leaking through the joint. Also purchase two small clamps. You will need only one additional accessory in order to conduct an experiment for your class. The steps to follow are these:

1. Bend both of the pieces of the O-ring and hold them in that position with the clamps.

2. Place one of clamped pieces of O-ring in a glass of ice water. (This will approximate the temperature in Florida at the time of the fatal launch.)

3. Leave the piece in the water for ten minutes or so while holding the other in your hand.

4. Take the clamps off of both pieces of the O-ring and let members of the class observe the difference in time it takes for them to return to their original state. What does this demonstrate about *Challenger*?

B. Feynman's second experiment involved organizational communication. He concluded that the engineers' managers did not know what they, the engineers, knew about the probabilities of failure for the shuttle.

1. How persuasive is Feynman's experiment in communication?

2. Assuming that Feynman's conclusions are correct, what possible motives could explain the gap in understanding of such probabilities between the engineers and their managers?

## Chapter Nine. HUNTSVILLE REVISITED

Was MSFC in 1990 the same organization that it was in 1967? Or did each represent a different organization?

## Chapter Ten. THE LUCAS ERA AT MSFC

A. There is a conflict between the organizational theory that stresses the "system" or "structure" as being determinate, and the theory that stresses individual people and/or psychology.

1. Which approach makes better sense of the organizational world? Support your answer with examples from the study of MSFC.

2. Which approach does Tompkins seem to stress?

3. Is it possible to achieve a theoretical balance between the two approaches? (Hint: A quick glance at a model of the communication process will help.)

**Chapter Eleven.** ORGANIZATIONAL FORGETTING

A. Tompkins argues that MSFC suffered from a form of organizational memory loss and "amnesia" in the period leading up to the *Challenger* accident.

1. If the organization did suffer from amnesia, what could be identified as the shock or trauma that "metaphorically" brought on the condition?

2. At times Tompkins speaks of organizational forgetting, at other times of amnesia. What is the difference? Could both explanations be applicable? If so, how?

3. Other than a shock or trauma, what other communicative practices could induce organizational forgetting?

B. Were problems of organizational communication responsible for the *Challenger* accident?

**Chapter Twelve.** DEATH AND REBIRTH

A. The Marshall Center is characterized as placing a great emphasis on rationality. Some employees had difficulty, as a result, in expressing their emotions about the *Challenger* accident.

1. What is the proper place of emotionality in a scientific-engineering organization?

2. Read Burns (1978) on the distinction between transformational and transactional leaders. Then draw up a list of historical and contemporary organizational leaders who seem to fit each category.

B. J.R. Thompson was described by his colleagues as having helped bring MSFC back to life.

1. List the characteristics Thompson seemed to possess that made it possible for him to achieve this transformation.

2. List the steps that he took to make the transformation possible.

C. Tompkins defines the his thoughts on necessary and sufficient conditions for bringing back to life a failed or ailing organization.

1.  Summarize (in your own words) those necessary and sufficient conditions.

2.  Do some library research on other organizations that have experienced such a rebirth. Decide whether or not Tompkins' conditions above were present.

## Chapter Thirteen.  J.R. THOMPSON'S RESPONSE

A.  Why did Tompkins interview J.R. Thompson?

1.  Did Thompson's comments validate or invalidate Tompkins' findings? Support your answer.

2.  How many of the strategies Thompson used at MSFC could be applied to an ailing business organization?

B.  Redundancy is a concept introduced in this chapter.

1.  Define redundancy.

2.  Can redundancy apply to channels as well as to messages? Support your answer.

## Chapter Fourteen.   THE MEANING AND FUTURE OF THE SPACE PROGRAM

A.  Tompkins attempts to justify the continuation of the U.S. space program in this chapter.

1.  Organize a formal debate in your class with two speakers supporting and two rejecting the following proposition: "It is resolved that the U.S. space program should be accorded the highest national priority."

2.  If the space program is maintained in the future, should it be devoted to manned or unmanned spaceflight?   Or both? Support your answer.

B.  Tompkins believes that metaphors give meaning to organizational activity and existence.

1.  Make a survey of metaphors people use in speaking about contemporary organizations. (Hint: Sports teams and military activities are two widespread metaphors to listen for.)

2. Do the metaphors currently in use bring out the best of our organizational life?

3. Organizations have been compared to teams, armies, families, space stations, garbage cans, and the human nervous system. Create your "own" organizational metaphor and develop it in detail; be sure that communication is emphasized.

4. Can one metaphor capture the characteristics of organization?

C. This book is organized by means of a double "plot" with a common idea or concept.

1. What is the major plot?

2. What is the minor plot?

3. What is the common idea or concept?

4. Discuss the quotation from Manning Marable in this chapter.

a. To what extent do you accept his thesis that the Los Angeles riots were communicative in nature, that they constitute a "message" from those at the bottom to those above them?

b. Discuss in depth the "fault line sensors" and "earthquake prediction system" as they pertain to big cities in the U.S.

## REFERENCES

Barnard, C. (1938). *The functions of the executive.* Cambridge, MA: Harvard University Press.

Bion, W. (1959). *Experiences in groups.* London: Tavistock.

Broad, W. (1992, March 12). Bush nominates TRW executive to lead space agency to new era. *The New York Times,* pp. A1, A9.

Browning, L. (1988). Interpreting the *Challenger* disaster: Communication under conditions of risk and liability. *Industrial Crisis Quarterly, 2,* 211-227.

Browning, L. (1989, August). *Managing blame in the Iran-Contra affair: The role of plausible deniability.* Paper presented at the Academy of Management, Washington, D.C.

Bowlby, J. (1980). *Loss.* New York: Basic Books.

Burke, K. (1966). Mind, body, and the unconscious. In K. Burke (Ed.), *Language as symbolic action* (pp. 63-80). Berkeley, CA: University of California Press.

Burke, K. (1969). *A rhetoric of motives.* Berkeley, CA: University of California Press. (Originally published 1950)

Burke, K. (1972). *Dramatism and development.* Barre, MA: Clark University Press.

Burke, K. (1984). *Permanence and change.* Berkeley, CA: University of California Press. (Originally published 1935)

Burns, J.M. (1978). *Leadership.* New York: Harper & Row.

Cheney, G., & Tompkins, P.K. (1987). Coming to terms with organizational identification and commitment. *Central States Speech Journal, 38,* 1-15.

Cheney, G. (1987, February). *The linkage of sacrifice and purpose in the rhetoric of the Challenger disaster: Media accounts and the reinforcement of a national "mission."* Paper presented at the annual convention of the Western Speech Communication Association, Salt Lake City, UT.

Cheney, G. (1991). *Rhetoric in an organizational society: Managing multiple identities.* Columbia, SC: University of South Carolina Press.

Collier, P., & Horowitz, D. (1987). *The Fords: An American epic.* New York: Simon & Schuster.

Davies, P. (1973). *The truth about Kent State: A challenge to the American conscience.* New York: Farrar, Straus, Giroux.

De Vries, M., & Miller, D. (1984). *The neurotic organization: Diagnosing and revitalizing unhealthy companies.* New York: Harper Business.

Douglas, M. (1986). *How institutions think.* Syracuse, NY: Syracuse University Press.

Drucker, P. (1988, January–February). The coming of the new organization. *Harvard Business Review,* 45-53.

Dye, L. (February 13, 1992). Head of NASA resigns post under pressure, *The Los Angeles Times,* pp. A1, A34.

Eisenberg, E. (1984). Ambiguity as strategy in organizational communication. *Communication Monographs, 51,* 227-242.

Feynman, R. (1986). *"Surely you're joking, Mr. Feynman!".* New York: Bantam Books.

Feynman, R. (1988, February). An outsider's inside view of the Challenger inquiry. *Physics Today,* pp. 26-37.

Feynman, R. (1989). *"What do you care what other people think?"* New York: Bantam Books.

Goldhaber, G., & Barnett, G. (Eds.). (1988). *Handbook of organizational communication.* Norwood, NJ: Ablex.

Heilbroner, R. (1990, September 10). Reflections: After communism. *The New Yorker,* pp. 91-100.

Hirschman, A.O. (1970). *Exit voice and loyalty.* Cambridge, MA: Harvard University Press.

Jablin, F. (1979). Superior-subordinate communication: The state of the art. *Psychological Bulletin, 86,* 1201-1222.

Jablin, F., Putnam, L., Roberts, K., & Porter, L. (Eds.). (1987). *Handbook of organizational communication: An interdisciplinary perspective.* Newbury Park, CA: Sage.

Kanter, R.M. (1983). *Men and women of the corporation.* New York: Basic Books.

Kanter, R.M. (1983). *The change masters.* New York: Simon & Schuster.

Kernan, A. *The death of literature.* New Haven, CT: Yale University Press.

Kiianmaa, A. (1991). *The woman who couldn't swallow.* Paper presented at the Conference on Narrative and Organizational Studies in Communication, Keystone, CO.

Kübler-Ross, E. (1969). *On death and dying.* New York: Macmillan.

Lasswell, H. (1965). *World politics and personal insecurity.* New York: Free Press.

Levering, R., Moskowitz, M., & Katz, M. (1984). *The 100 best companies to work for in America*. New York: New American Library.

Limerick, P. (1987). *The legacy of conquest: The unbroken past of the American West*. New York: W.W. Norton.

Limerick, P. (1989a). *Imagined frontiers: Westward expansion and the future of the space program*. Unpublished manuscript.

Limerick, P. (1989b). *Reflections on attending a conference of space scientists and space policy planners, September, 1989*. Unpublished manuscript.

Lukes, S. (1974). *Power: A radical view*. London: Macmillan.

Mailer, N. (1971). *Of a fire on the moon*. New York: New American Library.

Marable, M. (1992, June 3). Los Angeles riots point up nation's race/class fault line. *Boulder Daily Camera*, p. 8A.

McConnell, M. (1987). *Challenger: A major malfunction*. Garden City, NY: Doubleday.

McDougall, W. (1985). *. . . the heavens and the earth: A political history of the space age*. New York: Basic Books.

McGregor, D. (1960). *The human side of enterprise*. New York: McGraw-Hill.

March, J., & Simon, H. (1958). *Organizations*. New York: John Wiley.

Mayer, M., Gudykunst, W., Perrill, N., & Merrill, B. (1990). A comparison of competing models of the news diffusion process. *Western Journal of Speech Communication, 54*, 543-553.

Nieburg, H. (1966). *In the name of science*. Chicago: Quadrangle Books.

Noller, D. (1991). *Beyond a buzzword: An empowerment perspective*. Unpublished manuscript.

Ordway, F., & Sharpe, M. (1979). *The rocket team*. New York: Thomas Y. Crowell.

Pacanowsky, M. (1989). Communication in the empowering organization. In J. Anderson (Ed.), *Communication yearbook 11* (pp. 356-379). Newbury Park, CA: Sage.

Pasternak, J. (1992, August 5). When the sky isn't the limit. *The Los Angeles Times*, pp. A1, A12, A13.

Perrow, C. (1979). *Complex organizations: A critical essay*. New York: Scott, Foresman.

Peters, T., & Waterman, R. (1982). *In search of excellence*. New York: Harper & Row.

Pettey, G., Perloff, R., Neuendorf, K., & Pollick, B. Feeling and learning about a critical event: The shuttle explodes. *Central States Speech Journal, 37*, 166-179.

Preston, R. (1991). *American steel.* New York: Prentice Hall.

Redding, W.C. (1972). *Communication within the organization.* New York: Industrial Communication Council.

Redding, W.C. (1985). Stumbling toward identity: The emergence of organizational communication as a field of study. In R. McPhee & P.K. Tompkins (Eds.), *Organizational communication: Traditional themes and new directions* (pp. 15-54). Newbury Park, CA: Sage.

*Report of the Presidential Commission on the space shuttle Challenger accident* (June 6, 1986).

Richetto, G. (Ed.). (1968) *Conference on organizational communication.* Huntsville, AL: MSFC/NASA.

Simon, H. (1976). *Administrative behavior* (3rd ed.). New York: Free Press.

Sloan, A.P. (1964). *My years with General Motors.* New York: Doubleday.

Suro, R. (1990, December 15). NASA aura dims as city fights rocket test. *The New York Times,* pp. 1, 22.

Tompkins, P.K. (1968). Organizational communication: A state-of-the-art review. In G. Richetto (Ed.), *Conference on organizational communication* (pp. 4-26). Huntsville, AL: MSFC/NASA.

Tompkins, P.K., & Anderson, E. (1971). *Communication crisis at Kent State: A case study.* New York: Gordon & Breach.

Tompkins, P.K., Fisher, J., Infante, D., & Tompkins, E. (1974). Conflict and communication within the university. In G.R. Miller & H. Simons (Eds.), *Perspectives on communication in social conflict* (pp. 153-171). Englewood Cliffs, NJ: Prentice-Hall.

Tompkins, P.K., Fisher, J., Infante, D., & Tompkins, E. (1975). Kenneth Burke and the inherent characteristics of formal organizations: A field study. *Speech Monographs, 42*, 135-142.

Tompkins, P.K. (1977). Management qua communication in rocket research and development. *Communication Monographs, 44*, 1-26.

Tompkins, P.K. (1978). Organizational metamorphosis in space research and development. *Communication Monographs, 45*, 110-118.

Tompkins, P.K. (1984). The functions of human communication in organization. In C. Arnold & J. Bowers (Eds.), *Handbook of rhetorical and communication theory* (pp. 659-713). Boston: Allyn & Bacon.

Tompkins, P.K., & Cheney, G. (1985). Communication and unobtrusive control in contemporary organizations. In R.McPhee & P.K. Tompkins (Eds.), *Organizational communication: Traditional themes and new directions* (pp. 179-210). Newbury Park, CA: Sage.

Tompkins, P. K., & Cheney, G. (1990, November). *Identification as a general theory of communication.* Paper presented at the University of Helsinki, Helsinki, Finland.

Tompkins, P.K., & Whalen, S. (1990, March). *On feminism and organizational communication.* Paper presented at Arizona State University, Tempe, AZ.

Tompkins, P.K., & Kiianmaa, A. (1991). Narrative, transfer(ence) and organizational identification: The story of Paula. Paper presented at the Conference on Narrative and Organizational Studies in Communication, Keystone, CO.

Trento, J. (1987). *Prescription for disaster: From the glory of Apollo to the betrayal of the shuttle.* New York: Crown Publishers.

Weick, K. (1979). *The social psychology of organizing* (2nd ed.). Reading, MA: Addison Wesley.

Wilford, J. N. (1969). *We reach the moon.* New York: Bantam Books.

Wolfe, T. (1986, February 10). Everyman vs. astropower [Editorial]. *Newsweek*, p. 40-41.

# COPYRIGHT ACKNOWLEDGEMENTS